Martin B. Hellriegel:

Pastoral Liturgist

by

Noel Hackmann Barrett

**Dedicated
to the memory of
my father,
Edward F. Hackmann
who first taught me
to appreciate the liturgy.**

CONTENTS

Foreword

It is my pleasure and privilege to write these few lines before Noel Hackmann Barrett's definitive biography of Monsignor Martin B. Hellriegel, P. A. I hope that in doing so I may be pardoned for dwelling on personal recollections of the Monsignor.

During my seminary years I was an avid reader of *Orate Fratres*, the liturgical monthly published at St. John's Abbey in Collegeville, Minnesota (one of the few periodicals permitted to seminarians in those days). In its pages one met the best scholars of the liturgical renewal, then taking its halting steps in the Church of the United States. There were Virgil Michel, OSB, Godfrey Diekmann, OSB, Gerald Ellard, SJ, Clifford Howell, SJ, Hans Reinhold, Reynold Hillenbrand, Frederick McManus, Martin Hellriegel and many more. But I noticed in my monthly reading that only Monsignor Hellriegel was putting all that liturgical theory into practice day by day as pastor of a typical American parish with its cosmopolitan congregation and parochial school. I determined to see it all in practice some day at Holy Cross Parish in Baden, a city neighborhood of Saint Louis.

Some years later as a recently ordained priest in Chicago I attended the convention in Easter week of the National Catholic Educational Association in Saint Louis. The second morning I played hookey from the agenda to drive out to Holy Cross for a weekday Mass celebrated by Monsignor Hellriegel with the school children and a considerable adult congregation. It was a beautiful paschal experience for me in the pew (before the days of concelebration) to see and hear the fatherly liturgical style, the simple and yet touching homily, the pastor par excellence in Martin Hellriegel.

Through the following years I saw and heard the Monsignor in his regular appearances at the National Liturgical Week and then they faded away after Vatican Council II which fulfilled their dreams for a new day in the solemn and public worship of the Church. Little by little I lost touch with Martin Hellriegel especially when his monthly articles no longer appeared in *Worship*, the retitled *Orate Fratres*.

The years rolled on and in 1980 I was serving as Bishop of Mobile when one day I was notified of my transfer to the Archdiocese of Saint Louis. A few days later the mail brought me an audio tape which was my companion in driving the back roads of south Alabama. It was a warm welcome to Saint Louis from Monsignor Hellriegel, now a blind nonagenarian, but still celebrating the liturgy with the people of Holy Cross where he resided as pastor emeritus. The tape rang with his sonorous Latin quotations interspersed with his encouraging and edifying words of welcome. I played both sides of that tape over and over during those weeks before going to Saint Louis in March of 1980.

After my installation one of my first parish visits was to Holy Cross where Monsignor Hellriegel and I concelebrated the liturgy and sat at his old dining room table afterwards reminiscing of those old days when I sat at his feet in the pages of *Orate Fratres* every month.

Just a year later in Holy Week, April 10, 1981, Martin Hellriegel went to the Lord whom he had served so long and so faithfully. It was my privilege to celebrate his funeral liturgy.

"Ecce sacerdos magnus, qui in diebus suis placuit Deo." May he rest in peace, and may this, his life's story, be a blessing to God's people everywhere.

+ John L. May
Archbishop of Saint Louis

Preface

This story of Martin Hellriegel is both engaging and scholarly. It is scholarly because the life and works of Hellriegel have been inquired into, recorded, and evaluated with great care and skill. It is engaging because it is the well written history of an authentic liturgical pioneer, one who carried out the pastoral office with deepest religious commitment combined with a distinctive style, warmth, and even flair. His impact in the American Catholic community — through writings, preaching, presence during two or three generations — was tremendous enough, and reason for this book. Even aside from this, however, the account of his pastoral ministry — leadership in the Christian community, proclamation of the Christian Gospel, presidency over the Christian eucharist — is worth recalling as ideal and model for others today. So keen a pastoral (and pedagogical) sense should be recalled and imitated.

In 1989, when praising another liturgical pioneer of Hellriegel's time, H.A. Reinhold, a commentator writing in *Commonweal* felt obliged to identity H.A.R. for the present generation as "anti-Nazi refugee and promoter of Mass in the vernacular." In a splendid biography of another pioneer, Archbishop Paul J. Hallinan of Atlanta, also published in 1989, Thomas J. Shelley began with a true but sad observation: "His [Hallinan's] reputation faded quickly after his death [in 1968], and few American Catholics today would recognize his name or be able to identify any contribution which he made to American Catholicism."

That tragic loss of continuity with the great figures of our immediate past, whether Reinhold or Hallinan or Hellriegel, is intolerable as well as unnecessary. And the present book can fill the void, where there is one, with its account of a lively personality whose impact enlightened and stirred others far, far beyond the communities where he carried out the pastoral ministry.

The writing of biography surely involves some element of *pietas*, of loyal devotion, esteem, and appreciation. It is good to move succeeding generations to that same appreciation and to gratitude to those who have gone before. But there is another dimension, particularly apt today in a biographical study of Hellriegel's life, namely, the contemporary lessons to be learned — about celebration of worship, proclamation of the word of God, and liturgical catechesis. This dimension is satisfied, and more than satisfied, by Noel Barrett's study.

In 1976, five years before Monsignor Hellriegel's death, I ventured a summary appraisal of his contributions — barely doing justice to the wealth of his influential bibliography or his central place in American liturgical renewal and reform:

> No listing of pioneers would be complete without reference to the very many parish priests and lay leaders who translated pastoral theories into practice. One who may stand for all the rest is Msgr. Martin Hellriegel of St. Louis, now pastor emeritus of Holy Cross parish in that city. A towering and impressive figure of great faith and enthusiasm, Hellriegel has been known less for his writings than for his pastoral sense and ingenuity. With strong folk piety from his native Germany, he approached every parish celebration with warmth. His influence spread through his major role at the Liturgical Weeks, his translation of German hymns, his example of parish liturgy — even in the unreformed Latin — at its best.

Looking back, as this book does, the extraordinary thing is that Martin Hellriegel could lead his assembly of the Christian people to such expressions of faith and devotion, to such proclamation and celebration, without the riches of the revised, postconciliar liturgy. This he did without the present wealth of euchological texts and readings from the scriptures in the official liturgy, without the reform of Church orders in a combination of insights from the patristic period of the Church with cultural demands of our times, without the restoration of the catechumenal process and the rites of Christian initiation.

The fact is that Hellriegel and his contemporaries in the

preconciliar liturgical apostolate — who were often following his example and his writings — has already achieved, within the limitations of the period, "that full, conscious, and active participation in liturgical celebrations called for by the very nature of the liturgy." These words of the 1963 constitution on the liturgy, *Sacrosanctum Concilium* 14, were welcome support and justification to Martin Hellriegel, as were the next assertions of the conciliar fathers. Such participation, the document continues, is for the Christian people "their right and duty by reason of their baptism" and, remembering Saint Pius X as Hellriegel himself so often did, "the primary and indispensable source from which the faithful are to derive the true Christian spirit . . . ."

My not very novel point is that as much and more can surely be done nowadays in a revised or reformed liturgy, with vastly larger opportunities for responsible creativity in song and ritual. If anything, the demands for liturgical catechesis are even greater — even though some of the obstacles of language and rigidity are now gone from the official orders of eucharistic and other celebrations. This is where Hellriegel is a model: to catechize and to proclaim and to bring to the liturgy a lively faith, a profound and authentic (and ecclesial) piety, and a warmth of song and sharing, also known as participation in the holy mysteries.

None of this is to downplay the need to move further, beyond the revised Roman rites of the 1960s and 1970s. It was the intention of the Second Vatican Council, in *Sacrosanctum Concilium* 37-40, that the Church should move beyond the immediate and universal reforms and refurbishings. Such development may be in the lesser matter of liturgical adaptation or the more profound inculturation of liturgy, illustrated in the Zaire Order of Mass of 1988. But the immediate and pervasive need, recognized by Hellriegel before and after the conciliar decision, is for the People of God, under the presidency of their pastors, to celebrate the holy mysteries with comprehension and faith, with vigor and enthusiasm, and with a zeal for Christian life and mission engendered by the liturgy.

If anything, the message or the lesson of Martin Hellriegel is just as timely for the 1990s as for the period of his pastoral leadership — in the communities he shepherded and in the wider Church to which he preached as well. This is the contribution of Noel Barrett's account, even beyond the interest in a worthy pioneer and giant.

If I may add a personal note, the influence of Martin Hellriegel upon this New Englander was first an indirect one, partly through his writings in the 1940s, in *Orate, Fratres* especially, mostly through the priests of the Church of Boston who were his disciples and colleagues in The Liturgical Conference. It was only in 1956 that I shared a platform at the University of Notre Dame with him, to help introduce the first major reform, the rites of Holy Week decreed by Pope Pius XII, and that same year to appreciate his company, wit, and guidance at the Assisi-Rome congress on the liturgy. And I still take a certain pride in having been asked to respond, in his behalf and in the last months of his life, when he received the Notre Dame award named for his own friend, Michael Mathis, in 1980.

This personal recollection, however, explains only in part the enthusiasm with which I offer a preface to this volume. Its own merits speak for themselves, and it gives a new generation of liturgical promoters of the 1990s a fresh motive for the works of catechesis, celebration, and indeed faith.

Frederick R. McManus
The Catholic University of America
Washington, D.C.

Introduction

In 1926 in the foreword of the first issue of *Orate Fratres*, the first liturgical periodical in the United States, Virgil Michel said that liturgical renewal was aimed not "at a cold scholastic interest" but at affecting "both the individual spiritual life of the Catholic and the corporate life of the natural social units of the Church, the parishes."[1] Sixty-five years later the challenge of liturgical renewal remains much the same. Great growth in understanding of the liturgy has taken place; far-reaching structural changes have been implemented; a genuinely liturgical spirit flourishes at many specialized centers such as monasteries and schools of theology; yet, a living spirit of liturgical prayer is found only rarely at the parish level.

There stood in the liturgical movement one man who for forty years led a parish in worship according to the vision of Virgil Michel and the drafters of the Vatican II document on the liturgy. The man was the Monsignor Martin Hellriegel and the parish was Holy Cross in St. Louis. This book will tell the story of that man and his parish and how, together, they became the practical embodiment and expression of much of the finest in the liturgical movement. Included also will be a discussion of Martin Hellriegel's contribution to the national liturgical movement. This movement, as an organized movement, began with the first pooling of liturgical efforts by Virgil Michel, Gerald Ellard and Martin Hellriegel in 1925. The accounts of the work of Virgil Michel and of Gerald Ellard have been written by Paul Marx and John Leo Klein respectively. This book will document the life and work of the third member of the original triumvirate.

* * * *

I would like to express my gratitude to Monsignor Alphonse Westhoff and the late Felix Tuger without whose help and encouragement this book would not have been published. I would also like to express my gratitude to Kay Schmitt and to my husband, George Barrett, for their help in proofreading.

CHAPTER ONE

Martin Hellriegel's Boyhood

Martin Hellriegel was both a pastoral liturgist and a liturgical pastor. His preparation for this dual role actually had its origin in the European liturgical renewal that had influenced Hellriegel's parish in Heppenheim, Germany, even before his birth 1890.

The person widely cited as the initiator of the nineteenth century liturgical movement is Dom Prosper Guéranger,[1] the first abbot of the Benedictine Abbey of Solesmes, France. His work dates back to 1833, the date of the founding of the Abbey of Solesmes. Guéranger emphasized the liturgy as the official prayer of the Church and the one to have priority over all forms of private prayer. He leveled a strong attack against the liturgical practices that were at variance with the prescribed rite and succeeded by 1860 in gaining widespread acceptance of the Roman Missal and the Roman Breviary purged of nonofficial accretions.[2] By 1840 Guéranger had begun work on his fifteen volume series *L'Année liturgique* in which he explained the Church Year as a basis for spirituality.

Guéranger also initiated the scholarly study of Gregorian chant, thus laying the foundation for its reintroduction into worship. Yet Guéranger's work constituted only a limited beginning for liturgical renewal. His work had both scholarly[3] and practical drawbacks. His efforts tended to reach more the specialized groups such as his monks at Solesmes rather than the ordinary Catholic. Yet, he did restore life to the liturgy and was able, through his *L'Annee liturgique*, to contribute indirectly to that lively involvement with the liturgy that characterized Martin Hellriegel's boyhood.

Germany received the influence of Guéranger's liturgical renewal through two Benedictines who were brothers, Dom Maur Wolter and Dom Placid Wolter. The Wolter brothers made their novitiate at Solesmes where they caught Guéranger's love for the liturgy and took it with them to the founding of the Benedictine Abbey of Beuron, Germany, in 1863.[4] The liturgical movement in Germany also drew inspiration from the theological work of Möhler and of Scheeben and their rediscoveries of the fathers of the Church and of ecclesiology.[5] Their work helped to provide a solid theological foundation for the growing interest in liturgy.

Dom Placid went on to become the first abbot of the Belgium Abbey of Maredsous in 1872. It was his abbey that published in 1882 the first complete missal translated into French for the use of the laity.[6] Another contribution of the Abbey of Maredsous to the liturgical movement was its foundation of the Abbey of Mont César in 1899. It was from this site that Dom Lambert Beauduin was to take the liturgical renewal beyond the framework given to it by Guéranger. However, this new movement was not launched until 1909; therefore, its story must await a future chapter.

Meanwhile, back at Beuron, one of brother Dom Maur's monks, Dom Anselm Schott, was preparing an edition of the text of the Mass in both Latin and German, along with the Vesper service and brief liturgical explanations. His work was published in 1884 and quickly became so popular that within a time span of fifty years it went through thirty-seven editions.[7] The Schott missal would have certainly been available to, and probably used by, the people of Germany by 1890, the year in which Martin Hellriegel was born. However, the exact translation of the canon was not printed until the sixth edition in 1900.

It can be seen that the renewal of the liturgy in Europe as a whole and in Germany in particular had barely begun during the years of Martin Hellriegel's childhood. Yet, this newly nascent movement did reach into the diocese of Mainz and into the town of Heppenheim which is located within that diocese.

During the years of Martin Hellriegel's boyhood, Mainz was emerging as one of the leading areas of liturgical reform in Germany. In the late 1800's Dr. John Baptist Heinrich was the rector of the Mainz seminary. Dr. Heinrich was a close friend of Prosper Guéranger and had all fifteen volumes of *L'Année liturgique* translated into German. Dr. Heinrich himself wrote the foreword to the German translation. In his foreword he notes that the liturgy is neither an outward doing nor a mental remembrance but rather in the liturgy what the Lord did during his mortal life is continued.

> The liturgical year is the divine story of our redemption symbolically and sacramentally reenacted in the sacred cult. It is the life of the God-man and His kingdom renewed mystically, but in all reality, and placed before us so that we may more profoundly understand it and more lovingly receive it.[8]

Thus the concept of Christ and the saving actions of His life as present in mystery in the liturgy was understood and written by Dr. Heinrich long before it became widely known through the writing of Dom Odo Casel. It was this dynamic concept of the liturgy and the liturgical year which permeated the teaching given to the seminarians of the Mainz diocese and it was this lively awareness that flourished in the town and the parish and the home of Martin Hellriegel's youth.

The town of Heppenheim was both scenic and historic. The Heppenheim of Martin Hellriegel's childhood had a population of about 800 nestled around a 900-foot hill called the Starkenburg, meaning "strong castle." The town is located about midway between Frankfurt and Heidelberg in the state of Hesse about two miles from the border of the state of Baden. The founding of Heppenheim dates back to 755 and traditionally served as the summer residence of the Archbishop of Mainz who was the chancellor of the Holy Roman Empire. The Hellriegel home itself dates back to 1603 and its residents of each generation have shared that sense of history so prevalent in the town.[9]

The parish itself, St. Peter's, also had a glorious history. The old church of the parish went back to the time of Charlemagne and was given by Charlemagne into the protection and charge of the Benedictines of Lorsch in 768. The Benedictines remained in charge of the parish until 1223. The door of the old church through which Charlemagne walked in procession in the year 802 when he paid a visit to the church was the same one through which the infant Martin was carried to the baptismal font.[10]

Thus the Christian life of Martin Hellriegel began in an atmosphere of deep historical as well as religious roots. The significance of this baptismal day was to be a quite conscious part of the life of Martin Hellriegel; for on each of his many visits back to Heppenheim he paid a visit to that font both upon arriving and again upon leaving.[11]

The boy Martin learned much from his early years at St. Peter's Parish and especially from the priest who became its pastor in 1900, Father Mischler. In 1900 Martin was ten years old and it was about this time that he became the faithful assistant to the sacristan of the parish for the task of decorating the altar for the feast days of the liturgical year. Father Mischler led his sacristan and the young Martin to a sense of the beautiful as well as a sense of the prayerful in the celebration of the liturgy. He emphasized such things as good music, insuring the presence of a good organist to lead the way, appropriate vestments, with a sense of the proper color for each liturgical feast and using the fuller vestments rather than the abbreviated ones used in most places, proper cassocks for the servers, again with special ones for special feasts. Father Mischler held to a principle which was to be later a key one in Monsignor Hellriegel's own thinking: nothing can go into the mind except through the senses.[12]

Another characteristic of Father Mischler which was to be carried on by his young helper was that of explaining all ceremonies thoroughly so that the congregation could participate with a sense of real meaning. Father Mischler's efforts were so successful that about 3,000 to 4,000 people from the 7,000 to 8,000 residents of the town would come to such events as the Corpus Christi and rogation day processions. Vespers, or evening prayers, were a regular Sunday night event.

The people of St. Peter's Parish, as well as the people of the Mainz diocese as a whole, were encouraged toward both interior and exterior participation in the liturgy. The people used as their Mass prayerbook the *Officium Divinum*, published by the Mainz diocese and containing the readings of the Sunday Masses, the text of the ordinary of the Mass including the Canon, and the text for vesper services. Congregational singing was a regular part of worship and the people of Mainz had a special permission to sing some parts of the Mass in German; Martin Hellriegel had fond memories of the congregation singing the *Gloria* of the Mass in their native tongue.[13]

Special blessings provided by the Roman ritual for special occasions were utilized. Wine was blessed on the feast of St. John; herbs, seeds, and new fruits were the object of special prayer on the Feast of the Assumption.

In spite of Father Mischler's great emphasis on the liturgy, a twelve year-old first communicant in 1903 seemed to have even bolder ideas. Martin Hellriegel, who was one of forty-three boys and forty-five girls to receive their first communion on Low Sunday of that year, decided that he would like to try to get together the boys of the first communion class to receive communion the following Sunday. Martin went to the assistant parish priest with his idea, but the permission of the pastor was needed and the pastor said, "No." The children were required to wait until Pentecost for their next communion.[14] Later that same year Pius X became pope and within two and one-half years encouraged everywhere the frequent communion for which the boy Martin had asked.[15]

Great as was the influence of the parish and its pastor on the youthful life of Martin Hellriegel, an even greater influence was his family. In later life whenever Monsignor Hellriegel was asked how he first came to be interested in the liturgy, he answered without hesitation that it was through his mother.

The sense of direction toward things liturgical from his mother began even before Martin was born. During the time of Eva Hellriegel's pregnancy with Martin, she made a pilgrimage form Heppenheim to Waldurn, a distance of forty-eight miles, on foot. She went with a group of about twenty-five persons and spent three days walking and two nights sleeping in barns; for food she had only bread and water. Her prayer during this pilgrimage was that if her child were a boy, he would be a priest.[16] Martin Hellriegel himself looks back at this event as the laying of the cornerstone of his liturgical life.

The Waldurn shrine itself originated out of a deep concern for the Eucharistic liturgy on the part of a priest named Henry Otto, who in 1330 found himself questioning the issue of whether the body of Christ was also the blood of Christ and vice versa. With this question still unresolved in his mind, the priest was celebrating the Eucharist in the Church of St. George at Waldurn. During the Eucharistic celebration, Father Otto accidentally spilled the chalice. On the corporal where the consecrated wine had been spilled there appeared to Father Otto the body of the crucified Christ, thus assuring him that the whole Christ was indeed present in the consecrated wine. Yet this assurance did not fully put his mind at rest; he was reticent to have anyone else know of the wonder he had experienced. He, therefore, hid the corporal with the image of the body of Christ under the altar stone and said nothing to anyone. Finally after 51 years, Father Otto told of his experience to a Benedictine monk, who eventually informed the bishop. The bishop had the corporal taken to Pope Eugene IV in 1445. Pope Eugene regarded the event as a miracle and had a basilica erected. It has been a place of pilgrimage since the fifteenth century. Thus it was that this shrine built on the concern of one priest for the Eucharist and on God's sign to him of the real presence of Christ became the site of the first prayer said for one who was to devote his life to renewal in Eucharistic prayer. The one for whom that prayer was said was to visit the shrine himself in 1952 and find the visit a quite moving experience.[17]

On November 9, 1890, at 4:00 p.m., the "if" part of the prayer of the mother at the shrine was granted. A boy was born to her, the first of four natural children and seven adopted children.

Martin's formal education began when he was six years old. He studied at the state school in Heppenheim. Religion classes were taught by the parish priest who visited the school three times a week. At the age of nine Martin undertook further study at the Lyceum at Heppenheim. It was here that he began his study of Greek, Latin, French, and English — all of which he was to put to much use in his future life.[18] Even in those days he had a decided preference for language, poetry and music over such subjects as mathematics. Thus those areas which contribute to the liturgy were already becoming dear to Martin.[19]

The formal religion classes taught to the young Martin by the parish priest were certainly not his only, or even his main, experience of religious education. The Hellriegel family lived a deep religious life and the parents stimulated a genuine faith in their children. Martin at the age of five was going with his parents to daily

Mass during Advent. The mature man looked back on these very early liturgical experiences with a sense of joy and even fondly remembered the blue knickerbocker suit and short overcoat he usually wore. Rorate Masses also saw the presence of the Hellriegel family, with the young Martin standing on the kneeler eager to see all that was going on.[20]

In addition to full participation in the liturgy of the parish the Hellriegels also had home celebrations of the various feasts and seasons of the liturgical year. The Advent wreath was a standard from Martin's earliest years. St. Nicholas came on December 6 accompanied by brother Rupprecht and bringing apples and nuts. The Christmas crib was carefully distinguished from the trains and other toys under the Christmas tree. In fact, the Hellriegels did not put their crib under the tree at all; rather the crib was a focus of attention in its own right. It was large and served as an altar around which the family gathered for prayer. The tree too bore religious symbolism; the candles on the tree were in memory of the departed in the family. Both tree and crib were kept until February 2. During the weeks between Christmas and February 2, the family would gather each evening for songs and stories around the tree. It was only on February 2, when the tree was being cut down, bough by bough, that the children ate the fruit that had been hanging on it. The goodies were greatly appreciated after waiting so long for them.[21]

Another feast day celebration of the Christmas season was the Epiphany. The chalking of the lintels of the door with the names of the three kings brought home to the children of the family the meaning of the day.

During the season of Lent, a bit of healthy competition was engendered among the children of the family. The contest was to see who could make the most Lenten sacrifices for the poor. The child who was judged by the parents to have put forth the greatest effort was rewarded by the privilege of being the one to bring home the jar of blessed Easter water on Holy Saturday.[22]

The familiar dyed eggs were a part of the Easter celebration at the Hellriegel home, but their eggs had a special note. Each one contained some reminder of what it was that was really being celebrated on this day. "Alleluia" or "He is risen" or some such indication of the resurrection appeared on each egg. The children were taught that the egg was symbol of the resurrection in that Christ had come forth from the tomb just as the chick comes forth from the egg. The eggs were taken along with bread and meat to church on Easter Sunday for the Paschal blessing.[23]

Pentecost was another special occasion for the Hellriegel family. As on each major feast day, the family dinner was served with the best linen and silverware. The centerpiece for this day was a large candle as a symbol of the Spirit with red streamers going to each place at the table. The streamer going to the place of the father was of double width, indicating his role as head of the family. Seven large rosebuds represented the seven gifts of the Spirit. All of the special celebrations were carried out without very much talking or preaching to the children. The liturgical year was lived and prayed; not much needed to be said.

The saints, and especially the Blessed Mother, were also venerated in the Hellriegel household. The family traditionally took part in the blessing of seeds and herbs and new fruits on the feast of the Assumption. All Saints' day was the day for a visit to the family grave plot. Some lesser known days were also special to the Hellriegels; for example, on December 4, the feast of St. Barbara, each child would plant a shoot or twig and see who could grow the largest blossom by Christmas.[24]

Family prayer was not confined to the special occasions of the Church Year. Table prayer and the Angelus were said in common every day. The ringing of the Angelus bell was a signal to the children that they were expected home promptly. The family gathering for the Angelus was considered a significant part of the day from which no one was lightly excused. The family also had evening prayer together; they would say a litany or a decade of the rosary (but never the whole rosary so as not to overburden the children), or some of the prayers from the Mainz diocesan prayerbook. That prayerbook was to remain important in the life of Martin; he was still using it in the final years of his life. Sundays were special days; preparation began on Saturday night with a reading of the gospel for the next day and an explanation.

The Hellriegel family not only fostered prayer and worship in the lives of its children but also a Christian attitude of sharing with others and concern for others. Martin Hellriegel especially recalled the outstanding example of his mother. Any time that the family butchered she would see to it that some of the meat went to the poor. On one occasion Eva Hellriegel had packed up so much for the poor that her husband was led to wonder whether he had butchered for his own family or for the poor. Eva Hellriegel's reply was, "It was slaughtered for the poor, I mean, for Christ."[25] There can be seen in this response of Martin Hellriegel's mother a living awareness of the concept of the Mystical Body of Christ, a concept which would remain a key one in the life and work of her son Martin.

In 1905 Martin received the sacrament of confirmation and was given the name Balthasar after the black Magi. He later looked back upon this event as the beginning of a sense of concern for the rights and liberties of the black race.[26]

Thus it can be seen that in regard to diocese, parish, and family, Martin Hellriegel did spend his boyhood in something of a liturgically favored atmosphere, even though, as was illustrated in the first communion anecdote, liturgical renewal was not yet full blown. Martin Hellriegel himself looked back to these years of his life as the beginning of his love for the liturgy. Yet, he left this spiritual oasis at the age of fifteen and did not find a parallel in the United States until he himself created one.

It was during his young years in Heppenheim that Martin Hellriegel experienced awareness of his vocation to the priesthood. For Martin the idea of becoming a priest was one that was with him virtually as long as he could remember. At the age of six the young boy Martin used to play priest. His father, a man who earned his living making furniture of the fine inlay and carved type, built for his son a small altar. Monsignor Hellriegel recalled his father's artistic sense and attributed to his father's influence something of his own sense of the beautiful. To go with the altar, a small tabernacle, too, was built by his father. And from religious goods stores, miniature cruets, chalice, etc., were purchased. Each Sunday the young boy would "say his own Mass", sometimes even two of them. Monsignor Hellriegel looked back upon these experiences of childhood play as occasions of great joy and as means of nurturing his interest in the priesthood. Through his own experience of playing priest, he also developed a great awareness of the details that went into liturgical celebration. Thus the seeds were sown for later sensitivity to the beautiful and the appropriate in such things as music, architecture, vestments.[27]

His interest in becoming a priest wavered only once when he was about twelve years old. He had the opportunity to attend a part of a convention of Catholic male teachers in Heppenheim and was greatly impressed by the idea of Catholic teachers participating in the teaching authority of the Lord. However, within three or four months the thought occurred to him that the priesthood also involved the teaching of the Word of God, and, therefore, the two were not mutually exclusive.[28] In his work in later years in the liturgical movement, Martin Hellriegel certainly did live out both of these ambitions; he was a master teacher of the liturgy, in both formal and informal situations, in addition to being a deep and reverent celebrant of the liturgy as a priest.

Influence toward the idea of living his priesthood in the United States came from two sources, his childhood reading of Indian stories and a priest who was an old friend of his family, Father George William Hoehn. By the time Martin was eleven or twelve years of age, he had read numerous stories about Indians written by Karl May. Although the author had never been to the United States, he described the Indians with great vividness. Martin, in reading these stories, pictured himself with cross in hand going through the primeval forest in search of Indians to convert. With this image of the natives in the vast forests of America imprinted in his imagination, the young boy nurtured a dream to go to America and teach Indians about Christ. However, this dream of boyhood adventure was probably a less strong influence than that of the inspiring family friend.

Father Hoehn himself was a native of Heppenheim and there was a close relationship between the Hoehn and the Hellriegel families. Father Hoehn's parents had died when he was only five or six years old. Martin Hellriegel's grandparents and older uncles had made a point to remain close to him. At the age of sixteen George Hoehn departed for America. This was between 1875 and 1880 when many immigrants were coming from Europe to the United States. He landed in St. Louis and worked as a baker for a while, and then started a religious goods store. It was during this time that there grew gradually in George Hoehn a desire for the priesthood. He approached one of the assistants of his parish, Sts. Peter and Paul at 1919 Seventh Street, and began to take lessons in Latin and Greek. His decisive step was the selling of his store and entering St.

Francis Seminary in Milwaukee, Wisconsin. He was awarded a scholarship from the St. Louis Diocese. His scholastic accomplishments were so impressive that the diocesan authorities sent him to the University of Louvain in Belgium to study theology. This well grounded education earned for him recognition as an intellectual and linguistic man as well as a deeply spiritual man. In 1886, George Hoehn was ordained priest and celebrated his first holy Mass in Heppenheim. After spending a short while in Germany, Father Hoehn received his first appointment as assistant to Father Wilmes at St. Peter's Parish in St. Charles. It was twenty-eight years later that Martin Hellriegel received the identical appointment, to the same parish and under the same pastor, as his first priestly assignment.[29]

Father Hoehn returned about every five years to visit his native Heppenheim. On these visits he would talk to the boys of Heppenheim of the priestly vocation and of life in America. His talks were heeded by his young listeners, and he was directly instrumental in leading a total of nine young men to the priesthood, five of the nine being Heppenheim boys. In fact his reputation for recruitment soon became so proverbial that when the folks of Heppenheim heard that Father Hoehn was expected for a visit, they were soon wondering who it would be that he would take with him on the return voyage to the United States.[30] One of these boys was a cousin of Martin's; he was ordained when Martin was twelve years old.

Martin himself was ready to be "one of those boys" by 1900 when he was ten years old. However, Father Hoehn told him that he was too young this time; perhaps he could go next time. Although the next time did not occur for five and one-half years, until the summer of 1906, Martin had not forgotten; he was ready to depart. Father Hoehn had arrived in Heppenheim on a Saturday evening; Martin saw him the next morning and reminded him that "next time" was here. Father Hoehn talked to Martin's parents and on August 15, 1906, they left on their long journey. Mr. Hellriegel's parting words to his eldest son were, "Become a good Christian man." Martin would treasure these words; they were the last he heard his father speak because his father died eighteen months before Martin made his first trip back to Germany.[31]

CHAPTER TWO

Liturgical Renewal in the U.S.

W hen the fifteen year-old Martin Hellriegel arrived on the shores of the United States, what could he expect to find in the area of liturgical vitality? The question would not have been formulated so explicitly in his mind, for he lacked any awareness that his childhood liturgical experience was unusual. Yet, he must have soon become aware that something of the liturgical vitality of his home was missing in this new land.

To appreciate the exact stage of liturgical piety in the United States in 1906, a brief look must be taken at the efforts toward liturgical vitalization that had been made in the United States up to that time. Although the story of zeal for the liturgy in the history of the nation is a sparse one, it is not non-existent. In fact, interest in the liturgy and the promotion of understanding and appreciation of that liturgy by the laity goes back to the founding of the nation.

The first known written expression of this concern for understanding of the liturgy comes from John Carroll in 1787. In a letter written to an English priest and controversial writer, Father Joseph Berington, John Carroll comes out strongly in favor of changing the liturgy from the Latin to English, for the English-speaking peoples. He saw this step as ". . . essential to the service of God and the benefit of man."[1] In a letter that is undated but probably written shortly after the previous one, Carroll tells Father Arthur O'Leary, O.F.M., the chaplain to the Spanish Embassy in London and an adversary of Carroll's ideas, that having the liturgy in the people's own language would both help to hold the attention of the poor people who cannot read and remove one of the major causes of popular prejudice against the Catholic Church.[2] Carroll seemed to have logic on his side. His argument in the first cited letter to Berington had stated:

> Can there be anything more preposterous than for a small district containing in extent no more than Mount Libanus and a trifling territory at the foot of it, to say nothing of the Greeks, Armenians, Coptics, etc., to have a "liturgy" in their proper idiom and on the other hand for an immense extent the Countries containing G. B., Ireland, also N. Am., and the W. Indies, etc., to be obliged to perform divine service in an unknown tongue; and in this country, either for want of books or inability to read, the great part of our congregations must be utterly ignorant of the meaning and sense of the publick offices of the Church.[3]

In the same letter, Carroll goes on to reflect his realization that there can, at times, be reasons of practicality or prudence in favor of refraining from change away from the Latin; however, he makes it clear that in his opinion no such justifying reason exists at this time.

> It may have been prudent, for aught I know, to refuse a compliance in this instance (the change to vernacular) with the insulting and reproachful demands of the first reformers; but to continue the practice of the Latin liturgy in the present state of things must be either due to chimerical fears of innovation or to indolence and inattention in the first pastors of the national Churches in not joining to solicit or indeed ordain this necessary alteration.[4]

Whatever the reason may have been, the pastors did not, at that time, follow Carroll's ideas and join together to solicit a change. In fact, Carroll was actually under no illusion that there was much likelihood that this step would be taken. For, in the letter to O'Leary previously cited, Carroll wrote: "I should find no cooperation from my clerical brethren in America, were I rash enough to attempt their (steps toward the vernacular) introduction upon my own authority."[5]

In fact when Carroll did assume a position of authority as the first American bishop, he was quite a bit more conservative in his actual steps than he had been in his earlier correspondence.

For example, the synod of November 7 to 10, 1791, in its recommendations concerning official Church prayer, specifies the use of the vernacular only for the reading of the gospel on Sundays and feast days; it does add that the prayers after Mass should be said in the vernacular and that it was desirable that some hymns or prayers be in English during afternoon vespers and benediction.[6]

However, some of the American clergy must have had stronger feelings favoring the vernacular in the liturgy than Carroll had anticipated, for by 1810 there seemed to be a need to crack down on unauthorized use of the vernacular. In that year the following statement was drawn up by Carroll along with his coadjutor bishop and three suffragans:

> It is being made known to the Archbishop and Bishops that there exists a difference of opinion and practice among some of the clergy of the United States concerning the use of the vernacular language in any part of the public service, and in the administration of the Sacraments. It is hereby enjoined on all Priests not only to celebrate the whole Mass in the Latin language, but likewise when they administer Baptism, the Holy Eucharist, Penance and Extreme Unction, to express the necessary and essential form of those Sacraments in the same tongue according to the Roman ritual: but it does not appear contrary to the injunctions of the Church to say in the vernacular language the prayers previous and subsequent to those Sacred forms, provided however, that no translation of those prayers shall be made use of except as authorized by the concurrent approbation of the Bishops of this ecclesiastical Province, which translation will be printed as soon as it can be prepared under their inspection. In the meantime the translation of the late venerable Bishop Challoner may be made use of.[7]

This statement, which starts out with a note of caution and conservatism, actually is quite liberal in that it assumes that the use of the vernacular in the ritual prayers of the sacraments, apart from the words of the essential form, were acceptable in the vernacular. Actually this use of the vernacular was given official Church approval only in 1956. Sometime considerably before this date — surely before 1906 — the practice had been discontinued in the United States.

The second outstanding leader of the American Catholic Church who showed evidence of concern for lay understanding of the liturgy was Bishop John England. Within his first year in episcopal office, Bishop England had completed an edition of an English missal. It was printed in 1822 and was the first to be printed in this country. The text of the Mass was largely printed from a British missal already in use. To this text, England added his "Explanation of the Mass," in which he explained the theology, ritual, prayers, vestments, etc., of the Mass. In the preface of the work, Bishop England states,

> The object of the present publication is to instruct the members of the Roman Catholic Church on the nature of the most solemn act of their religion. The Saviour who established that religion, charged His apostle, saying, "That which I speak to you in the dark, speak ye in the light; and that which ye hear in the ear, preach ye upon the housetops." And the council of Trent lays a solemn injunction upon pastors frequently to explain to the people the nature of the Holy Sacrifice of the Mass. To discharge his duty of obeying those distinct directions of Christ and His Church, in the best manner he could, was the intention of the editor of this work. He was also of the opinion that many well-disposed members of other communions might be greatly benefited by its perusal; as he generally found them not only uninformed of the Catholic doctrines, but having on their minds the most extraordinary and erroneous impressions as to the belief of Roman Catholics.[8]

From this statement it can be seen that England shared with Carroll the double purpose of making the liturgy more understandable to the Catholic laity as well as dispelling something of the misunderstanding and prejudice that existed toward Catholics by those outside the Catholic Church. Yet England does not see the solution to the problem of prejudice to be in the substitution of the vernacular for the Latin. On the contrary, England staunchly defends the use of Latin and enumerates its many advantages in his "explanation of the Mass."[9] In spite of his quite orthodox views, the publication of his missal did cause some suspicion to be aroused against him by authorities in Rome. The original impression of the Sacred Congregation of Rite was that England's missal was an original translation rather than a reprint of an already accepted British translation. Since new translations were forbidden, England's missal temporarily fell under a cloud of disapproval.[10]

Once the misunderstanding in Rome was clarified, the missal was released for sale in the United States. The entire first edition was sold and succeeding editions were published in 1843, 1865, and 1867. The missal was certainly a step forward in understanding of the liturgy for those who made use of it; yet, it makes no suggestion that lay participation in the liturgy should move beyond this intellectual understanding to active participation. Also, by the 1861 edition, the explanation of the theology of the Mass was being omitted, leaving only the explanation of the rubrics.[11]

Actually, even England's theological understanding of the Mass, although containing much of great value and certainly informative to the people of his time, also reflected the lack of theological development characteristic of his time. For instance, England's essay entitled "Ceremonies of the Mass," written in 1833 and containing ideas very similar to those in his "Explanation of the Mass" that was written with his missal, puts very little emphasis on the liturgy of the Word. England states, "The Mass of the Catechumens, properly speaking, is only a preparation for the sacrifice." He would seem to be implying here that the aspect of the Mass which he would be emphasizing would be the sacrificial aspect. Yet later in the same essay, he devotes only two pages to an explanation of the Mass as sacrifice, whereas he devotes six pages to an explanation of transubstantiation. England also defends the custom of reciting the canon in a voice too low to be heard by the people on the grounds that they are given to understand "that the change which is effected in the bread and wine is the effect of the invisible and imperceptible operation of the Holy Ghost...." England takes for granted that the faithful will usually not receive communion at High Masses and makes no mention of a need to change this custom.[12]

In spite of its limitations, the Catholic laity would have certainly been on more solid ground by sticking with Bishop England's instruction on the Mass and his missal in the praying of the Mass than they were by using most of the available popular prayerbooks designed for use at Mass. These, in spite of the success of England's missal, seemed to remain the more predominant form of Mass prayer for the laity. These prayerbooks were common enough and bad enough that the American hierarchy in the third Plenary Council of Baltimore in 1884 found it necessary to speak out against them.

> The criticism of the Council was quite strong. Prayer-books, the number of which is almost infinite, for the most part compiled by

incompetent writers, are found to be straying more and more day by day from the true and wholesome norm of prayer which the Church proposes in the sacred liturgy. (No. 220)...

...The prayers in common use among the faithful are often defective in literary quality, and sometimes stray from the path of sound doctrine. (No. 222) .... [13]

The Council went on to deplore the fact that many Catholics were totally unacquainted with the Church's official prayer and recommended as an antidote to this situation the preparation of a new prayerbook which would draw its material primarily from the Missal, the Breviary, and the Ritual. The Council fathers saw in this move an implementation of the directive of Trent to explain the sacred mysteries to the faithful. [14]

The bishops' decree was carried out by 1889 when the *Manual of Prayers for the Use of the Catholic Laity* was published. One of its early reviewers pointed out that of the seven hundred ninety-two pages that made up the new prayer book, only about twenty of them were taken from sources other than the Missal, the Breviary, and the Ritual. [15]

The Third Plenary Council of Baltimore sought to remedy not only the problems that flowed from poor quality prayer books but also the problems arising from poor and inappropriate music that was being used as a part of official Church worship. The Council points out that music can "elevate the aspirations of the heart toward God and ... render to the Divine Majesty a more splendid worship" (No. 114). However, music performs these functions only if it is "that kind of music which is the faithful servant of religion and which corresponds closely to the sanctity of that with which it is joined" (No 115). In the same paragraph, the Council document goes on to prohibit "worldly compositions and sensual song which distract the mind from the contemplation of things divine and greatly entice it to dwell upon the allurements of the world." [16]

Paragraph 117 makes explicit what kind of music it is that is being outlawed for Church use:

... we command the exclusion from the Mass of that kind of song which mutilates the words of the liturgy or which waxes excessive in repetitions or so transposes the text that its meaning is altered entirely or in any degree.

In paragraph 19 the document goes on to specify that it is

Gregorian chant that is regarded as the type of music considered most appropriate for liturgical use. The directives given in paragraph no. 380 of the decree of the Second Plenary Council of Baltimore of 1866 are quoted and reaffirmed: ". . . we consider it greatly to be desired that the rudiments of Gregorian chant be taught and practiced in parochial schools. . . ." The hope was expressed that this initiation into the singing of the chant at the elementary school level would eventually result in the majority of the faithful being able to sing along with the clergy and the choir.[17]

Efforts paralleling those of the Second and Third Plenary Councils were being made by a few farsighted individuals who had grasped the significance of congregational participation in appropriate Church music. One such individual was Father John Young, S.J., who held the position of Choirmaster at St. Francis Xavier Church in New York during the latter part of the nineteenth century. He had a keen desire to bring the liturgy to the people[18] and worked out a system whereby he could easily implement the Council's exhortation to teach the basics of Gregorian chant in the parochial schools. His system, whereby the children could read Gregorian notation through numbers, was later popularized by Mrs. Ward who had been Father Young's pupil.[19] By the 1920's this method, "the Ward Method," was commonly known; but in 1906, when Martin Hellriegel arrived in the United States, it was still quite an oddity.

There was another Father Young, Father Alfred Young, a member of the Paulist society and choir director of St. Paul's Church in New York, who was also a pioneer in supporting authentic liturgy and liturgical music. Father Young wrote a series of articles which appeared in the *Catholic World* during 1869 and 1870. Young provides ample evidence of the kinds of offensive music which were criticized by the Third Plenary Council of Baltimore. One example of the waxing "excessive in repetitions" is the Gloria from Mozart's Mass No. 12 in which there is repetition of almost every phrase, or sometimes only part of the phrase, or sometimes a single word taken out of all context; and, some of the repetitions occur as often as eight to ten times.[20]

The Council's warning against a mutilation of the words of the liturgy was also apparently quite necessary. For Young indicates that it was not at all unusual for the popular masses of the time to contain musical selections in which the words of a traditional hymn were sung to the music of well known arias of different operas. The result must have been highly questionable. Young describes the outcome as, ".... the words of some devout hymn are adapted in the most shockingly garbled manner, without regard to grammar or sense...."[21]

That the Council's warning against so transposing the text that its meaning was altered was not a hollow one can be seen by an example which Young quotes from a contemporary article in the *Dublin Review* regarding an Italian composition of the *Credo*. In the selection one voice would sing, "*Genitum non factum*," while the second voice responded, "*Factum non genitum*."[22] In this example the meaning of the text was altered not only in such a way that it became incomprehensible, but it actually became heretical. The reference to this example in both the *Dublin Review* and the *Catholic World* suggests that such musical aberrations were not the exclusive domain of the Italian musicians.

Young's concern extended not only to the outright abuses and errors that were common in the area of Church music but also to the spiritual benefit lacking to the faithful by certain omissions in liturgical music. He pointed to the fact that it was rare that a Catholic ever heard the Introit, Gradual, Offertory, or Communion antiphons of the Mass. In missing these prayers, the faithful misses the selections "... which give a distinctive color, tone, and meaning to the seasons and festivals...."[23] Young was thus showing evidence of an appreciation of the theological and spiritual dimensions of the Church year as well as a sensitivity to appropriateness of art forms for worship.

Young makes it clear that the remedy to the abuses in Church music is to be found in the reintroduction of the Gregorian chant and devotes a good portion of his articles to refuting the "practical" arguments presented against the Gregorian chant.[24] Young describes at length the role of the schola in the singing of the Gregorian and strongly emphasizes that it must be all male. However, he also has researched the liturgical celebrations of the early Church and found that there is indeed a place for congregational participation in responding to the prayers of the priest at the altar and in praying together the *Pater Noster*. Although Young sees the restoration of these congregational prayers as ideal, he is not too optimistic about prospects for this restoration actually taking place, "We do not think it at all probable that this old form of congregational accompaniment of the Mass ever can be universally revived."[25]

Given the general climate of the Church as a whole in 1870 and the Church in the United States in particular, Young's attitude was understandable. He was, in his own time, something of a voice crying in the wilderness. For, in 1906, when Martin Hellriegel arrived in the United States, he found conditions not greatly improved. In fact, Martin Hellriegel was himself to see a need to take up the work inaugurated by Bishop England in the making available of the text of the Mass for the prayer of the faithful, the work of the Third Plenary Council in bringing together from solid liturgical sources prayers for the laity for many special occasions, and finally the improving of the quality of Church music by the introduction of Gregorian chant into his parochial school to this parish congregation and also by doing himself extensive musical writing especially after the liturgy was translated into the vernacular and no longer had the same fitting together of text and music as was true with the Latin and the Gregorian chant.

Thus, the early efforts in American liturgical renewal that have been seen so far were all first steps which Martin Hellriegel would build upon in his mature life. In addition to bringing to completion these beginnings on the level of external participation, Martin Hellriegel had another and even more significant work to complete on the level of theological understanding. This level too saw a beginning in the United States before Martin Hellriegel's arrival.

While the decrees of the Third Plenary Council and the writings of Father Young were aimed primarily at correcting abuses in the paritice of the liturgy, there were also some developments in the area of theology of the liturgy. One such example can be seen in a paper entitled "Worship and Grace in Religion" delivered at the Parliament of Religions held in connection with the 1893 Chicago's World's Fair. The paper was written and presented by Dr. Thomas O'Gorman who, at the time, was a professor of Church History at Catholic University. He had previously been the rector of the seminary in St. Paul and was later to become bishop of Sioux Falls. In his paper, which takes up only eight pages in its reprinted form in *Orate Fratres*, O'Gorman presented with stringent logic a synthesized yet highly developed theology of the Mass as a sacrificial meal.[26] His explanation of the Mass was so outstanding for the time that Godfrey Diekmann, in a short comment regarding the article, called it ". . . A remarkable statement . . . of a point of view which the liturgical movement of the present is trying to foster."[27] O'Gorman emphasized the primacy of the Eucharist as sacrifice, the presence of Christ as Victim to be offered rather than only as divine majesty to be adored, and the importance of receiving communion to complete the sacrifice. Although these were all ideas clearly brought out by O'Gorman, they were largely ignored by most Catholics until the work of men like Martin Hellriegel brought them to the fore in the mid-20th century.

Other early liturgical endeavors of note were undertaken by two priests who were stimulated by their German heritages. The first of these was Father Herman Untraut of the diocese of La Crosse. Untraut had been educated in Germany and had become familiar with the liturgical scholarship that had been undertaken there. As early as the 1880's Untraut was contributing articles on different aspects of the liturgy to German papers and magazines, and in 1901 he published a book of prayers and hymns drawn from the liturgy and in keeping with its spirit.[28] However, Untraut's work was of limited value because it reached only German-speaking Catholics and had a rather limited circulation even among them.

The other predominant promoter of the liturgy was Father Bede Maler, a monk at St. Meinrad's Abbey in Indiana. Maler introduced this country into the Priests' Eucharistic League in 1891. He assumed a leading role in the foundation of *Emmanuel*, the official monthly periodical of the Eucharistic League and edited St. Meinrad's publication *Paradiesesfrüchte*. However, Father Maler apparently undertook more work than he was physically able to carry through and in 1903 suffered a physical breakdown which aborted his attempts to begin a liturgical movement centered at St. Meinrad's. In his later years, he was quite disappointed by the Eucharistic League for promoting a narrow emphasis on the adoration of the Blessed Sacrament to the point of neglect of any stress on the Eucharist as sacrifice. He also felt that the periodicals over which he had labored went downhill after his illness and saw little support for liturgical renewal even among the Benedictine abbeys. As late as 1926 Maler had no real hope for unanimous support for the liturgical movement from the Benedictine abbeys.[29]

If there were justifying causes for discouragement at the prospect of liturgical renewal in 1926, the justification was quite a bit stronger twenty years previous to this date. By 1903, when Pope Pius X issued his Pontifical Instruction on Sacred Music, abuses in Church music still abounded in the United States. The concert approach to the Mass had become complete by the practice of printing and distributing programs of the music and performers for various Church functions. Reviews were sometimes published after the performances. Sensitivity to the abuse was so slight that many suggested that the Pope's Instruction was meant to apply only to Italy and did not apply to the United States. Yet, few Catholics had even one experience in their life of having heard the Mass sung in Gregorian chant.[30] Stockley, writing in the 1904 volume of *The Ecclesiastical Review*, quotes an excerpt from *Encylopedia Britannica* as aptly describing the situation in the Catholic Churches of the United States:

> The music sung does not form an essential part of the service. In reciting the prescribed form of words with the prescribed ceremonies, the officiating priest fulfils unaided all the necessary conditions of the service, while the congregation looks on, and worships, and the choir endeavors to excite its emotion by singing appropriate music.[31]

Stockley, far from agreeing with those who would dismiss the papal instruction as not pertinent to the United States, saw in this country great scope for application and great difficulty on the part of American Catholics if they were willing to make the "troublesome journey" the pope was asking of them.[32] Yet the time of departure on the journey seemed to be yet some years away for the American Catholic Church.

In spite of the beginning made by such men as O'Gorman and Maler, the theological development so essential to any genuine liturgical renewal was largely lacking. For example, discussion of the doctrine of the Mystical Body of Christ, one of the foundation stones for a really deep liturgical spirituality, was almost completely absent from periodical literature of this time. If, as is often claimed, periodical literature reflects topics of current interest, then concern for the doctrine of the Mystical Body of Christ was almost nonexistent. During the period from 1890 to 1906 only one periodical article on the Mystical Body was published in the United States.[33]

With little or no appreciation of the Church as the Mystical Body of Christ united with Him to give praise and thanks to the Father, it is little wonder that Catholic congregations were content to be spectators at Mass. It was seen above how this spectator status related to the problems of Church music. The spoken prayer of the congregation also reflected similar problems. By the decade surrounding the turn of the century neither the earlier missal of Bishop England nor the Manual of Prayers of the Third Plenary Council were in widespread use. Most Catholics lacked both a solid doctrinal understanding of the liturgy and the opportunity to enter into liturgical prayer.

The national background of the immigrant Catholics also influenced their approach to liturgy. They brought with them the customs of the Church in their respective native lands. For the Irish Catholics, this meant bringing with them to their new land a tradition of silence at Mass. Because the Irish had suffered persecution at the hands of the English for so long and had lived in situations in which the practical thing to do was to celebrate the Mass in such a way that it was likely to attract the least possible amount of attention from outsiders, the Irish had become accustomed to a quite austere liturgy. Congregational participation in the form of praying together, of singing together, was unheard of. In fact, singing in Church was regarded by most Irish Catholics as a Protestant custom. The prayer of the faithful at Mass was seen as an individual thing. Missals were not common; each person used whatever form of private prayer he preferred.[34]

The German immigrants came with a much stronger tradition of both theological understanding and of liturgical participation than did the Irish. The immigrants had benefited from a more educated clergy at home and in general were better educated themselves. As seen in Chapter One, by the nineteenth century the work of theologians such as Möhler and Scheeben were having an impact in Germany and the liturgical renewal of Solemes was bearing fruit in parts of Germany. The use of the missal was more common in Germany and a solid tradition of good congregational singing existed in many areas.[35]

When Martin Hellriegel came to the United States in 1906, he settled in a German community in Starkenburg, Missouri. Thus, he came to an area which was probably one of the most liturgically vital areas of the country. Yet, the deficiencies in the liturgical life of the Church in the United States as a whole soon became obvious to him. He saw much that needed to be done and set out to do it.

CHAPTER THREE

Early Years of
Martin Hellriegel in the U.S.

T he journey from Heppenheim, Germany, to Starkenburg, Missouri, was a long one. Father Hoehn and his young companion, Martin Hellriegel, traveled by way of Paray-le-Monial, Lourdes, Paris, and Cherbourg and then took a steamer to the United States.[1] It was August 29, 1906, when they arrived in New York. Martin found his first view of the Statue of Liberty quite an experience, even though he was a bit surprised to find skyscrapers rather than Indians. After spending a few days in New York, Father Hoehn and Martin left for St. Louis, where they spent a few more days before finally going to Starkenburg, about one hundred miles from St. Louis.[2] Father Hoehn had named the area after the hill around which Heppenheim was built. Thus, Martin on coming to a strange new land did find something of home and familiarity.

Starkenburg, at this time, had already become a pilgrimage center. In May 1888, Father Hoehn was already the pastor of St. Martin's Church in Starkenburg and had brought his nephew, August Mitsch, to Starkenburg from Heppenheim. August, while staying with his uncle, discovered an old statue in storage. It was a statue which the original settlers of the area of Starkenburg had brought with them from a pilgrimage site in northern Germany near the border of Holland. The people of northern Germany used to treasure this statue and would decorate it and carry it in procession on special feasts of the Blessed Mother. The statue had since been replaced by wood statues of St. Joseph and the Blessed Mother which the Franciscan fathers had arranged to have carved. August was impressed by the old statue and its heritage and he took it out of storage, cleaned it up, put it in the Church yard under a dogwood tree, and invited the people of the area to May devotions. The people responded enthusiastically, and soon visitors were coming from neighboring towns such as Hermann and Washington as well. Interest grew and word spread, and Starkenburg became a noted pilgrimage site.[3]

The date of Martin's arrival at Starkenburg was September 5, 1906. The first visit upon arrival in town was to the Blessed Sacrament in St. Martin's Church and the second visit was to the shrine of Our Lady of Starkenburg. These steps were a clear indication of Father Hoehn's priorities.[4]

Martin plunged into work and study along with a companion, John Melcher. Father Hoehn instructed the two boys in Latin and English and they studied Greek under Father Denner, Martin's cousin who had come from Heppenheim with Father Hoehn somewhat earlier and had been ordained for about three years. Martin did his share of odd jobs, some involving good hard physical work such as taking care of the pastor's garden and helping with the building of roads. Other tasks drew out his knowledge and musical talent for Martin also found himself as teacher in the parish school and the parish organist.[5] The two latter proved to be his first of many experiences in teaching and in creating music for the worship of God.

The young Martin also found opportunity for liturgical participation at Starkenburg. Although he did not find the parishioners at St. Martin's praying the text of the Mass or singing the *Gloria* in their native tongue, he did find that Father Hoehn had led his flock toward something of an appreciation of liturgical prayer. Father Hoehn himself had received through his education at Louvain an understanding of the bourgeoning liturgical renewal. He also had a poetic sense and a good voice. With the combination of natural talents and a liturgical education that was unusual for the time, Father Hoehn was able to develop a spirit of liturgical prayer at his parish. The congregation had learned to sing solemn vespers for major feasts such as Christmas and Easter. Again, Martin was fortunate enough to be able to enjoy experiences on which he could draw when he himself would be a pastor.

Martin's life in the new world was busy and rich in many ways and for the most part he thoroughly enjoyed it. Yet, he did miss his family. The sense of adventure and challenge largely overcame any tendencies toward homesickness, yet, when the first Christmas in the the new country came, Martin had just turned sixteen and did find it hard to be away from his parents and brothers and sisters. He felt the homesickness the most during the morning and afternoon of Christmas eve. As the afternoon wore on, snow began to fall. The parish was scheduled to have a service at five o'clock. (There was no midnight Mass held.) Martin's friend John Melcher had some red lanterns which the two boys were to take up to the Church tower at four. As the boys accomplished their task, they were quite stunned by the beauty of the red light shining over the snow as the people approached the Church for the Christmas eve service. The beauty of the afternoon and the joy of the feast displaced the homesickness.[6] This ability to be so uplifted in spite of pain would stand Martin Hellriegel in good stead in years to come.

By 1909 Martin had completed his preparatory studies and was ready for the seminary. He had known of the Benedictines and their interest in the liturgy in Europe and had visited the ruins of the monastery of Lorsch as a boy. Even though there was no monastery at the site when Martin paid his visit, he reconstructed in his mind the splendid praise of God that must have once existed and was impressed. In the United States, Dom Bede Maler and his efforts at liturgical renewal had given St. Meinrad's Abbey something of a reputation as a liturgical center. Martin, then, chose to pursue his studies for the priesthood at St. Meinrad's; his intention was not to join the ranks of the Benedictine monks but to prepare himself for life as a St. Louis diocesan priest by living and studying in a place in which he could pray the liturgy.

At St. Meinrad's Martin did not find himself the only one preparing for the diocesan priesthood, for the seminary also trained men preparing to serve in the Indianapolis Diocese. Martin was happy with his choice and appreciated the opportunity to hear the Church's chant prayed beautifully and devoutly by the Benedictines.[7] Yet, as a student, Martin was not allowed actually to participate in the chanting. He and the couple of hundred other students were listeners only. In fact, they did not even receive communion at the high Mass chanted by the Benedictines but attended a low Mass two hours earlier each day as their communion Mass. In spite of this drawback, Martin appreciated the liturgical life at St. Meinrad's and wanted to complete the two-year course of study in philosophy. However, after the completion of one year of study at St. Meinrad's, the St. Louis Seminary Board decided that, if the young Hellriegel were to became a priest of the St. Louis diocese, he should study at Kenrick.[8]

So in 1910, Martin Hellriegel began his four-year course of study at Kenrick Seminary. During this time, his hunger for deeper knowledge of the liturgy continued but went unsatisfied. Even books that purported to be concerned with liturgy dealt only with rubrics. On several occasions the young seminarian was frustrated by spending some of the little money he had on a book that was supposed to be on the liturgy, only to find that he had purchased a directory of ceremonies.

The emphasis on rubrics never did sit right with Martin. Holding his hands "just right", meaning not one inch higher than his shoulder, made him feel like an Egyptian mummy. It always seemed an unnatural way to act when addressing the congregation. Even the seminary classes on liturgy dealt almost exclusively with rubrics. A regular assignment for the seminarians was to observe the servers at the Sunday high Mass and watch for their errors which would then be the subject of the discussion at the next meeting of the liturgy class. The actual observation could be performed quite easily, for there was no active participation in the liturgical action to distract one from that chore.[9]

Martin Hellriegel's final months at Kenrick were an especially difficult time for him. War broke out in mid-August of 1914 and cut off communication between Martin and his family. The small allowance Martin's father had sent each month was no longer getting through. Plans for Martin's First Solemn Mass in Heppenheim and a reunion with his family whom he had not seen in eight years had to be cancelled. Martin found himself with no chance of sharing the joy of the event with his loved ones in his family and without even having enough money for a new cassock or new shoes. Friends had given him a little money for invitations to the ordination and remembrance holy cards, but that was about all that he could purchase. Later in life Martin Hellriegel looked back on this time of loneliness and poverty and was grateful for the painful experience; for, he felt that it gave him even a deeper sensitivity to the poor.[10]

Yet, in spite of the pain he experienced, Martin Hellriegel on December 20, 1914, entered into the joy of becoming a priest of God. He was ordained by Archbishop John J. Glennon, a man especially admired by Martin Hellriegel and supportive of the latter's efforts in liturgical renewal. Glennon was celebrating the thirtieth anniversary of his own ordination.

For his first Mass, Martin Hellriegel went to Starkenburg to be with his good friend and spiritual father, Father Hoehn. The day was icy and the branches of the trees were bent by the burden of their icy coat. Father Hoehn saw in the trees a bow of reverence for the newly ordained and attributed to them the biblical words addressed to the young priest, "You are a priest forever according to the order of Melchisedech." Many years later Monsignor Hellriegel recalled this incident as an example of his friend's sensitivity to the symbolism of nature and to his supernatural outlook.[11]

Father Hoehn had ordered for the occasion a special vestment made in Europe and of a fuller and more flowing design than those usually worn in this country. The fuller style of the garment made its symbolic meaning more evident; "chasuble" means "house" or "house of charity." It was to engulf its wearer in a spirit of charity. Father Hoehn put the garment on his newly ordained friend and reminded him of the Lord's saying, "My yoke is sweet and my burden is light." Father Hoehn then told Martin to wear this vestment and every other vestment in the Spirit of the Lord.[12] This sensitivity to symbolism and sense of meaning and reverence toward even small gestures surrounding the liturgy was to become very much a part of Martin's own priestly life.

The young clergy were given their first appointments the day after ordination, December 21, 1914. Martin Hellriegel was assigned to St. Peter's Parish in St. Charles, following in the footsteps of Father Hoehn. The chaplaincy to St. Joseph's Hospital was also a part of the assignment.

In both the parish and in the hospital chapel, the new young assistant began, cautiously, to introduce more participation in the liturgy. He formed a boy's choir in the parish and taught them to sing the high Mass. By Sunday, July 4, 1915, the boys' choir was able to sing its first Latin high Mass in the parish. In 1917 the solemn introit procession was begun. Father Hellriegel learned from his twenty-eight young choristers as well as instructing them. The experience of the choir added to his conviction of the necessity of congregational singing if the liturgy were to be celebrated in a fresh and alive manner. He also saw in the music of the Church a transforming and unifying power, a great benefit for the personal spiritual life of the congregation and for the sense of community between the members.[13]

The liturgical life of the sisters at the hospital also received some impetus from the new young chaplain. He encouraged the sisters to make the responses at their Masses and helped them to center their holy hours on a more scriptural piety.

Father Hellriegel's two fellow priests in the parish were of great help and inspiration to him. Monsignor Francis X. Wilmes, the pastor, impressed his new assistant with his preaching ability; he was able to explain the truths of the faith with both solid theology and simplicity. Concrete examples were also used to aid understanding. This ability which Father Hellriegel so admired in his early days in the priesthood was to be one for which he himself would become widely known and respected.

The other assistant in the parish was Father Christian Winkelmann, a man who impressed his new cohort as a man of God and an example of the pastoral approach to the ministry.

It was during the years at St. Charles that Martin Hellriegel's childhood dream of seeing the Indians was finally realized. Three visitors had traveled into the area from the Catholic mission in North Dakota. One of the party asked Father Hellriegel if he had ever seen a real American. The reply was, "I am happy to say that you are the first one."[14] Martin Hellriegel, even then, had an awareness that the dignity of the Indian Americans had been little respected by the immigrants to this country.

That same awareness of the dignity of minority groups was shown in another incident during these same years.[15] Father Hellriegel had read that the Ukrainian rite Catholics who had come to the area of St. Louis around the turn of the century were dedicating a new Church. The Ukrainians had lived for a number of years without an actual church building but were now taking over a former Episcopalian Church and laying a new cornerstone. Father Hellriegel knew that the Ukrainian Catholics had a rich cultural and liturgical tradition, and therefore he decided to attend the dedication of the Church. He was very favorably impressed by the ceremony, especially by the participation of the people. The congregation exemplified Father Hellriegel's hope for his own people — to become active doers rather than dumb spectators.

However, not all Roman Catholics were responding in the same way to their fellow Catholics of this Eastern rite. Father Hellriegel was, in fact, hearing from Roman Catholics derogatory remarks about the Ukrainian Catholics. They were regarded as "foreigners" and second-rate Catholics. Father Hellriegel sensed their need for moral support and appreciated the beauty and depth of their liturgical prayer. He therefore, decided to give his personal support to their Church and began a lifelong custom of going to the Church of the Assumption two or three times each year to pray with the Ukrainian Catholics and encourage them in the preservation of their rite.

The qualities which Father Hellriegel so admired in the Ukrainian Catholics are ones which he himself would exemplify and encourage among his own congregations: an appreciation of culture, a sense of refinement, congregational prayer through appropriate song, a sense of solidarity in action. Along with these qualities which are imitable by Roman Catholics, Father Hellriegel also saw and valued the uniqueness of the Ukrainian Catholics. He disliked the image of America as a melting pot, for anything can be thrown into a melting pot and blended into the sameness. He preferred the image of a mosaic in which each piece is precious and must retain its uniqueness to make its contribution to the whole. This insight was another one which would contribute to his ability to assume leadership in the liturgical movement and which would become widely recognized only later in this nation.

Father Hellriegel, then, even during his first few years as an ordained priest, was already demonstrating those attitudes and abilities for which he would soon become famous. The years of parish ministry at St. Charles were brought to an end in July of 1918 when Father Hellriegel received a new assignment. He was to become the chaplain for the motherhouse of the Sisters of the Most Precious Blood at O'Fallon, Missouri. At this time Father Hellriegel was only twenty-seven years old and was quite surprised and somewhat fearful of assuming the task of the spiritual direction of the nuns. Father Hellriegel had already been introduced to the O'Fallon Community, for his boys' choir had sung a high Mass at O'Fallon the year before. Monsignor Wilmes encouraged his young assistant and Father Hellriegel took up the post which was to be his for the next twenty-two years.[16]

Father Hellriegel felt a great responsibility for the sisters under his direction. The weight of the assignment was much heavier than that of the St. Charles assignment because it was now he who would make final decisions, and the training he would give to the young sisters would greatly influence their work in parishes and schools.

One of the important daily tasks of the new chaplain was the offering of the Mass with the sisters. When Father Hellriegel took up his position, he more or less expected to follow the established traditions of the sisters. One of these traditions was that the chaplain would vest in surplice and stole before mass and come out to the altar and distribute holy communion. After communion, he would go back to the sacristy, vest for Mass, and come to the altar to offer the Mass. At this time all the lights in the chapel other than the light over the altar would be extinguished. One of the first steps of the new chaplain was to help the sisters see that holy communion was a part of the Mass and belonged within the Mass. Yet, Father Hellriegel did not want to upset the community by abruptly demanding that things be done differently. As he put it, he wanted to oil the wheel rather than put a clog into it. Within a year, the sisters were happily receiving communion at the appropriate time.[17]

Another early step in regard to participation in the Mass was the encouraging of the use of the missal.[18] There was some opposition to this step on the part of some of the sisters. One sister, who had held a prestigious rank in the community, pointed out to Father Hellriegel that their community had been saying the Precious Blood Rosary and the seven offerings during Mass "from day immemorial". The young chaplain had a witty response: "But Mother, your community was started only in the last century!" He went on to present a more challenging thought. Pius X had said that active participation in the liturgy is the primary and indispensable source of the true Christian spirit. This presents a dilemma. Who should be followed — the pope or your tradition? The sister came away convinced that Father Hellriegel had a point. The missal finally became the accepted thing and the lights had to be on during Mass.[19]

The Precious Blood Sisters had already learned something of Gregorian chant before Father Hellriegel had become their chaplain. Some of the sisters had received instruction from the Benedictine monks at Conception Abbey. However, the sisters regarded the chant as something of a second-rate form of music and did not think it appropriate for big feasts. On the first Easter of his chaplaincy, Easter of 1919, Father Hellriegel had not yet been able to do anything to change this attitude and the sisters sang their usual feast day selections. After this, Father Hellriegel began a weekly music appreciation class. By Easter of 1920, the sisters sang the chant Mass. In the years following, some polyphonic motets were also sung, but with the instruction and encouragement of their new chaplain they were moving away from "sweetness to a bit of power."[20]

The gentle nudges of Father Hellriegel were felt in regard to extraliturgical community prayer also. One Sunday a month the sisters had a day of recollection and Father Hellriegel had the task of exposing the Blessed Sacrament at the beginning of the day right after the Mass. The sisters would say some of their prayers before the Blessed Sacrament aloud in groups. One day, after hearing one of these communal prayers, Father Hellriegel went to the Reverend Mother and said, a bit tongue-in-cheek, "I feel so sorry for your sisters; they have no faith, no hope, no charity." The Reverend Mother was, of course, shocked and surprised. Father Hellriegel went on to tell her that he had just heard the sisters say this in their prayers before the Blessed Sacrament. The prayer read, "Thou art the highest truth and we believe not in thee; thou art mankind's hope and we trust not in thee; thou art the supreme good and we love thee not." Father Hellriegel asked to see a copy of the German text from which the prayer had been translated into English. He found that the original text had read, "Many there art who do not . . . ." in place of "we do not". He asked that the erroneous form be corrected.[21] For the young chaplain to bring a change in the sisters' mental attitude from one that would accept unquestioningly a prayer in which they said that they did not believe or trust or love to one in which there was a lively awareness of having a share in the redemptive power of Christ was quite an undertaking.

During these early years at O'Fallon, Father Hellriegel himself was constantly studying and trying to improve his own knowledge of theology and his understanding of the liturgy. He kept up with current books and periodicals published in both Germany and France and spent much time in the study of the Fathers of the Church. A companion in his study was Father Anthony Jasper who himself was known for his efforts to develop a liturgical spirit among his fellow priests.[22] The two of them would spend several nights a week discussing the reading that they were both doing.[23] One key work that they read and discussed in these early years was Romano Guardini's, "The Spirit of the Liturgy," which was published in 1918 as the first volume of the *Ecclesia Orans* put out by Maria Laach. The discussion and sharing between them was of great help in clarification of understanding and in mutual support. They became great friends and worked together well. They started a flower garden together in order to have appropriate flowers for the altar. They encouraged the sisters in the vestment department to make a fuller style vestment adorned with appropriate liturgical symbols.[24]

By 1920, Father Hellriegel was beginning to make contact with others who would be, along with himself, national leaders in the American liturgical movement. At this time his attention had been drawn to Father William Busch of Minneapolis and his interest in the liturgy. Father Hellriegel promptly wrote to Father Busch: "So you have discovered that (the liturgical movement) too. ...Won't you come down and visit me and we'll talk it over?[25] Here also can be seen a glimpse of the hospitality and the willingness to take initiative which contributed to the making of the Precious Blood Motherhouse at O'Fallon, and later Holy Cross, a center for visitors interested in liturgical renewal.

Thus, during the first six years of Father Hellriegel's chaplaincy at O'Fallon, definite progress toward liturgical prayer and understanding and participation had been made. In 1922, Father Hellriegel had the opportunity to visit Europe for the first time since he had left as a boy of fifteen in 1906. While in Europe, he had the chance to spend a week at Maria Laach and to converse with Abbot

Ildephonse Herwegen and a number of his monks. He himself looked back on this event as a major step toward a deepening of his own understanding, especially in regard to the Mystical Body of Christ and the importance of the Church year. After this time, liturgical renewal at O'Fallon became even more outstanding and its leader became a national figure.

However, before subsequent developments at O'Fallon can be discussed, it will be helpful to shift back to the European scene to see what liturgical growth had taken place there since Martin Hellriegel had departed.

CHAPTER FOUR

Liturgical Developments in Europe

W hen Father Martin Hellriegel paid his first visit back to Europe after being away for fourteen years, he found that much progress had been made in liturgical areas. The Church was feeling the impact of Pope Pius X's statements on Church music and on frequent communion much more fully than it had been able to in the very brief period between the issuing of these statements and Martin Hellriegel's departure. Therefore, to appreciate the liturgical renewal taking place in Europe it is to these documents that one must first look.

On November 22, 1903, Pope Pius X issued his *Motu proprio* on the restoration of church music.[1] The document dealt mainly with the subject which its title suggests emphasizing that liturgical music was to be an expression of the liturgical text (rather than vice versa) and that it was the Gregorian chant which was the type of music ideally suited to carry out this norm. He critized abuses in Church music and made recommendations for the enhancement of the sacredness and the liturgical appropriateness of music to be used in worship. However, the *Motu proprio* was also more than an instruction regarding sacred music. It also enunciated the principle which came to be the cornerstone of the liturgical movement. In his introduction to the *Motu proprio*, in which he explained the reason for his concern for Church music, Pius X clearly indicated that his basic concern was for an intelligent and active participation in the liturgy on the part of the faithful. His often quoted statement reads:

> It being our ardent desire to see *the true Christian spirit* restored in every respect and to be preserved by all the faithful, we deem it necessary to provide before everything else for the sanctity and dignity of the temple, in which the faithful assemble for the object of acquiring this spirit from *its foremost and indispensable fount*, which *is the active participation in the holy mysteries and in the public and solemn prayer of the Church.*[2]
> (Italics added for emphasis.)

It was this exhortation to active participation in the liturgy which spurred on the leaders of the liturgical movement.

The second statement which was an encouragement to liturgical renewal was the document entitled "The Daily Reception of Holy Communion." This decree was issued by the Sacred Congregation of the Council and ratified by Pope Pius X on December 17, 1905, and made public on December 22, 1905. In this decree a firm stand was taken against those who laid down excessively rigid conditions for the frequent reception of holy communion. The document pointed out that frequent communion was desired by Christ himself and should be open to all who are in the state of grace and have the proper intention, that is, the desire to please God, to be more united with Him, to receive help in overcoming weaknesses.[3] Thus, this statement laid the basis for the understanding that the reception of communion is of primary significance for participation in the Mass. This understanding was yet to be developed and publicized by the leaders of the liturgical movement.

Lest the outlook on the leadership of the official Church be presented too optimistically, it should be noted that there also were a few instances in which official statements from Rome were more detrimental to liturgical renewal than encouraging of it. For example, on January 14, 1921, the Sacred Congregation of Rites decreed that the *Benedictus* at a high Mass should not be sung until after the Consecration. This decision seems to be at variance with the concept of adapting the music to the text, for it ensures that the music being sung will not be the text that is simultaneously being prayed by the celebrant of the Mass. Furthermore, it creates an obstacle to intelligent participation in the Mass by the faithful for they are faced with the dilemma of either trying to ignore the music so as to add to the prayer of the Mass or of giving their attention to the sung prayer of the *Benedictus* and ignoring the prayer of the celebrant.[4]

In spite of drawbacks, such as the one just cited, the official leadership of Rome was mainly stimulating to liturgical renewal. The most significant document was certainly Pope Pius X's *Motu proprio* which called for active participation on the part of the faithful. Liturgical renewal which had taken place previous to this 1903 statement had influenced mainly specialized centers such as monasteries. Even when the liturgical influence had spread to the parish priest as in the case of the priests of the Mainz diocese, participation on the part of the congregation really did not center on the text of the Mass itself. Although missals were known before 1903, they were not widely used. Separation still existed between the prayer of the priest at the altar and the prayer or song of the congregation.

The first outstanding individual to initiate a widespread response to Pope Pius X's call for active participation in the liturgy was Dom Lambert Beauduin, a monk of the Abbey of Mt. César.[5] His great desire was to foster a lay liturgical spirituality. It was at the Catholic Conference held at Malines, Belgium, that Dom Beaudiun had his first opportunity to make public his program for bringing the liturgy to the people. He advocated new translations of the Roman missal and the promotion of its use among the faithful as their prayer book for use during Mass. He recommended the necessary instruction and encouragement to the people so that they could come to see their participation in the prayers of the Mass as best means both of preparing for the reception of holy communion and of making a thanksgiving after communion. Dom Beauduin pointed to the attendance at Mass and Vespers in the parish as well as to the restoration of paraliturgical traditions in Christian homes as means of putting the piety of the faithful on a more solid and liturgical basis. In order to foster a living and deep understanding of the liturgy on the part of those most actively involved in it, he encouraged choir members in parishes to make annual retreats at a place, such as a Benedictine Abbey, where liturgical life flourished. The fostering of Gregorian chant was also recommended in this initial speech.[6]

The concepts of retreats at liturgical centers was quickly expanded to include the parish priests, for Dom Beaudiun soon saw that it was the priests who must first of all both be convinced of the necessity of liturgical participation and, even more importantly, be living a deeply spiritual life centered in the realities of the liturgy. The program was soon enlarged to include liturgical weeks which came to be held at the rate of two a year from 1911 and a liturgical review entitled *Questiones liturgiques et paroissiales*.[7] The new missals, accompanied by sound explanations, became circulated rapidly and themselves helped greatly to spread the movement. Beauduin concentrated on making the liturgy as it existed in the present the prayer of the people. He did not concern himself, as had Guéranger, with the restoration of the pure form of the liturgy. Nor was he interested in innovation and experimentation with changes not yet approved by the official Church. His efforts were pastoral; he combined concern for the spiritual life of the people with a deep personal spirituality and sound theological understanding. It was Dom Beauduin who would have a great influence on Virgil Michel during his stay in Europe in 1924 and 1925.

In Germany, too, progress in liturgical renewal was taking place. The initial impetus came from the abbey of Beuron but before long the main center for theological development in the liturgy was the abbey of Maria Laach, a daughter-house of the abbey of Beuron. The development at Maria Laach exerted a more direct influence on Martin Hellriegel than Dom Beauduin did because it was Maria Laach that Father Hellriegel visited in his 1922 trip to Europe. The influence of Dom Beauduin was more indirect, but nonetheless present, for his work had promoted an atmosphere of liturgical prayer among the laity which was spreading to Germany and which Maria Laach also was beginning to foster even though its primary contribution was of a more theological nature.

The story of Maria Laach's leadership in liturgical renewal dates back to 1913. Four or five young men paid a visit to the eight-hundred-year-old monastery in the Rhineland.[8] They were professional people; there were among them a university professor, a doctor, and a young priest. These men spoke to a learned young monk by the name of Dom Ildefonse Herwegen of the gap they experienced between their personal prayer and the official worship at the altar. They wanted real participation in the holy sacrifice of the Mass. They were not content to pursue "devotions" of the laity while the priest prayed in a different vein. Some of them had used missals, but it was very difficult to "keep up with the priest" even if one could

decipher through the low mumbling which of the texts he was praying at any given time. Shortly after this meeting Dom Herwegen was
made abbot of Maria Laach and invited these men and their friends
to come to the abbey for Holy Week of 1914.[9] During this week the
dialog Mass was initiated as a means of providing an opportunity
for participation by these laymen in the actual prayers of the
Mass.[10] This week became known as the first "Liturgical Week" and
developed into a permanent and fruitful institution in the German
liturgical movement.

World War I interrupted the movement but it resumed as soon
as the war ended. Romano Guardini's booklet *The Spirit of the Liturgy* was the first significant post-War publication. Dom Herwegen,
from the time of his appointment as abbot, had been directing his
monks into liturgical study. He himself was already recognized as
an authority in liturgy before assuming the role of abbot. He advocated the scholarly, scientific method of the German universities,
and he encouraged such study for his monks, even permitting them
to reside outside their monastery temporarily in order to further
their education. The result was that about twenty of the fifty monks
at Maria Laach obtained higher degrees in theology, philosophy,
history, music, and canon law. The monastery had no responsibility
for a specific group such as a parish or school; therefore, the monks
could devote their time to research and creative work as well as
reach a variety of people through lectures, retreats, and hospitality.[11]

The already cited *Spirit of the Liturgy* was the beginning of a
scholarly series entitled *Ecclesia Orans*. The series continued with
significant contributions by both Dom Hammenstede and Dom
Casel.[12] It was edited by Dom Herwegen himself and translated into
many languages. It was in this series, as well as in *Jahrbuch für Litur-
giewissenschaft*, that Dom Casel developed his "mysterion" theory
emphasizing the reality of the presence of the mystery celebrated in
the Mass. The latter series was an annual which provided a valuable
and comprehensive survey of the liturgical studies of each year.[13]

The monks of Maria Laach also carried on and developed the
tradition of liturgical art begun at Beuron. Again it was Abbot
Herwegen and his own expertise in liturgical art which gave stim-
ulus to this endeavor. The liturgical art of Maria Laach reflects
influence of Egyptian, early Christian, and Byzantine art but
is not a mere duplication of any of these. Rather it gives outward

expression to the present and living realities of Christian faith and prayer.[14]

The message of Maria Laach was spread mainly through lectures, retreats, conferences, visitors to the monastery. Abbot Herwegen traveled throughout Germany and spoke to groups of all kinds. The first to be reached were the intelligentsia, the youth, and the priests. From them the movement gradually spread to the laity. Visitors were welcome at the abbey, and a stay at the abbey often constituted the best way to imbibe its spirit. Father Hans Anscar Reinhold gives an account of his visit to Maria Laach in 1920 when he was still a layman. His account is similar to what Martin Hellriegel experienced two years later, only from the priestly side. Father Reinhold's account is as follows:

> ... One of the novices showed me the crypt of the glorious old Romanesque abbey church and pointed out that the lay brothers and novices had their community Mass there every morning at which they recited the *Gloria* and *Credo* in common with the celebrant, replied in unison to his acclamations, and took part in an Offertory procession, bringing their own altar bread to the altar rail....
>
> Since I was on my way back from Rome, I was not shocked at the fact that the altar was facing the people, because I had seen this in all the major churches in Rome....
>
> ... The next morning at Mass I discovered that this was really the form that enabled me as a layman to share in the Church's sacrifice. This form flowed quite naturally from the real meaning of the Mass; it was almost suggested by its ceremonies and texts. The amazing thing was only this — why on earth had it not been thought of before? The atmosphere was normal and manly and the gray-bearded old lay brothers were just as happy and at home in "their" Mass as the fervent young students fresh from the universities.[15]

In spite of the fact that Maria Laach was reaching a significant number of German leaders, it was still impossible for one monastery to single-handedly achieve a nationwide popularization of a movement. This feat was left to a number of other organizations. Among these groups were the youth organizations which numbered millions of members. Romano Guardini was a great influence in these groups. (He also served as an assistant in Martin Hellriegel's home parish in Heppenheim in 1912 and 1913.)[16] Associations of

Catholic university graduates were another significant force. It was among these two groups that the dialogue Mass first enjoyed popularity. The use of the missal quite naturally led to this next step. For if silent reading along with the priest was preferable to pursuing some devotion that did not deal directly with the Mass text, then it follows that it would be still more preferable to participate through some external expression of this internal and silent reading. This conclusion was especially easy to come upon because the rubrics of the missal itself in several places seemed to call for some audible response from the congregation. Thus the groups of university graduates and youth, who were interested in and desirous of active participation in the liturgy soon followed the precedent of Maria Laach and began having dialogue Masses. The custom gradually spread to the parochial level also.[17]

But probably the most effective agency for the popularizing of the liturgical movement was the school of the Augustinian canons under the leadership of Dr. Pius Parsch at Klosterneuberg. Dr. Parsch's concerns were more directly parallel to those of Dom Beauduin, namely, to bring the liturgy to the person-in-the-pew. The Klosterneuberg movement emphasized an understanding of the Mass as a sacrifice to be offered by the community and a sacrificial meal. The sermon was seen as an integral part of the liturgy and its function was to explain the liturgy of the day.[18] Another significant contribution of Parsch and his school was the promotion of the study of scripture in conjunction with the liturgical movement. This step constituted, not only a widening of the liturgical movement to include a new impetus for greater understanding of the Word of God, but also a deepening of the liturgical movement to reach to the source from which the liturgy flows.[19] This emphasis on the role of scripture was given concrete form both in the direction of the homily of the Mass and in the encouragement of evening services based on Bible readings and the singing of psalms at the parish level.[20] By 1923 the ideas of Parsch were coming out in print in the form of his *Das Jahr des Heiles* in which he explained the Mass and the breviary on a popular level and showed how a better knowledge of the Bible contributed to an enhanced appreciation of an intelligent participation in the liturgy.[21]

Influential as Parsch was in Austria and Germany by the mid-1920's, he apparently was not known to Martin Hellriegel during his first visit to Europe in 1922. Father Hellriegel met Pius Parsch only in 1928 and began corresponding with him only in 1925. Therefore, Father Hellriegel did not have the advantage of Parsch's example of a pastoral liturgical orientation to guide him in bringing the theological understanding derived from Maria Laach to the practical level. As will be seen in the next chapter, Hellriegel did not seem to need this model. Even though Father Hellriegel did look to Pius Parsch as a help and source of guidance to him, his early work was achieved without that help, and what Father Hellriegel was able to achieve was on such a par with the achievements of Parsch that, many years later on another visit to Europe, Hellriegel was greeted by Father Joseph Jungmann with, "the Pius Parsch of America."[22]

CHAPTER FIVE

A Full Liturgical Life at O'Fallon

Father Martin Hellriegel departed in 1922 for his first visit to Europe since he had left at the age of fifteen in 1906. During the stay of about six months he spent much time visiting his family and was able to get a good view of how the liturgical movement had taken hold in Germany. His European travel also included the opportunity to study the liturgy at Maria Laach.[1] At Maria Laach there was also ample occasion for discussion with such renowned liturgists as Abbot Ildephonse Herwegen, Dom Odo Casel, Dom Albert Hammenstede, and Dom John Vollmar. Father Hellriegel came away from this first of ten visits to Maria Laach with two significant concepts in mind: the reality of the Mystical Body and the importance of the Church year.[2] Neither of these ideas were new for Father Hellriegel but both became more fully developed in his own understanding as a result of his Maria Laach experience.

In regard to the Mystical Body, Father Hellriegel explained his new insight in the following way:

> Of course, I had a certain inkling concerning the reality of the Mystical body of Christ, all the more, since I had read a statement by the Fathers of the *First* Vatican Council that "this is the outstanding nature of the Church...." But it took this contact with Maria Laach to make it clear to me that the Mystical Body is as

real as the *physical* and *eucharistic* Body of Christ, only a different mode of reality and certainly not "just a metaphor."[3]

Hellriegel's insights into the reality of the liturgical year also deepened through the contact he had with Maria Laach. He explained his fuller understanding as follows:

> In the course of the liturgical year the work of redemption wrought by our Savior 1900 years ago is rendered present *before* us, so that, qualified, we may as God's holy sons and daughters render with Christ a fitting worship to His and our heavenly Father.[4]

Along with the advance in theological understanding came the opportunity to celebrate the liturgy with the monks at Maria Laach. It was here that Father Hellriegel had his own first experience with the dialogue Mass and with Mass celebrated with the altar facing the people. Thus the stay at the abbey combined for Father Hellriegel growth in intellectual and spiritual understanding with the opportunity to express these new realizations communally and visibly in liturgical prayer. Father Hellriegel later described this experience as "A door was opened and I marched in."[5] He also referred to his first visit to Maria Laach as a "turning point in my life."[6]

The deepened insights derived both from growth in theological understanding and from the experience of liturgical prayer were to have a lasting effect on the pastoral work of Father Hellriegel. The developments in the area of liturgical art undertaken at Maria Laach also had their impact on Father Hellriegel. The more symbolic, less sentimental style of art came to be one which Father Hellriegel favored in such things as the design of vestments and the interior decoration of a chapel.

Upon returning to O'Fallon, Father Hellriegel intensified the efforts he had already begun in bringing greater understanding of the liturgy and greater active participation in the liturgy to the sisters under his charge. He also continued his own study and discussion with Father Jasper. Together they grew in their own knowledge and appreciation of the liturgy and began to take steps toward more congregational participation in the liturgy in both the convent chapel of Father Hellriegel and the parish church of Father Jasper.

In the convent Father Hellriegel began to hold evening sessions to study the Mass text and prepare for the Mass of the next morning.

In Advent of 1922 the sisters began having the *Missa Recitata*, and homilies became a standard part of the Mass.[7] The responses, which at that time were usually made by servers alone were made by the whole congregation. By this time all the sisters were using the missal, so the responses were easy to make. Also, all joined the celebrant in the praying of the *Kyrie, Gloria*, Gradual, *Credo, Sanctus, Pater Noster, Agnus Dei*, and *Domine non sum dignus*.

Special emphasis was placed on the festive observance of Sundays and feast days. High Masses became the norm on these days, and the proper as well as the ordinary was usually chanted by the whole congregation. On these days as well as during Advent and Lent, Father Hellriegel began preaching his homily before the Mass so that the readings would be heard with even greater understanding. Feast day liturgical celebrations were also enhanced by the use of larger altar breads and by the sharing in a cup of wine. The cup was given by the altar boys after the Mass. It was a symbolic sharing and perhaps a forerunner to communion under both species. The chanting of solemn Compline also became a regular part of feast day celebrations.

Holy Week of 1923 saw further movement in the direction of the prayer of the Church. The sisters for the first time included Tenebrae as a part of their liturgy. It was also that year on Holy Thursday that the offertory procession was begun. This rite was carried out with dignity and solemnity. As the celebrant unveiled the chalice, the servers went to the back of the chapel and processed down the center aisle carrying, on a small white cloth covering the palms of their hands, their hosts for communion. They were followed by four postulants, four novices, and four professed sisters, each representing their respective groups. They also carried altar breads on white cloths. The entire procession went to the communion table where the celebrant received the breads and put them into the ciborium.[8]

In 1924 Father Hellriegel put together a booklet entitled *The Holy Sacrifice of the Mass*. It was an arrangement of the texts of the Mass for congregational participation in a dialog Mass. The booklet was used in the parish church, The Assumption, in O'Fallon. Here the congregation said the Mass texts in the vernacular. By 1925 there were 12,000 of these booklets in use in the United States. By 1939, when the booklet went out of print, it had sold 250,000 copies.[9] Thus,

Father Hellriegel's leadership toward greater participation of the congregation in liturgy was actually being felt at the parish level, at least to a degree, long before he himself came to be the pastor of a parish.

Special seasons of the year became times of special liturgical prayer at O'Fallon. The prayer of the community was nourished by the use of special liturgical symbols. For instance, during Advent the spirit of the season was communicated through the furnishings of the main and side altars of the chapel. The main altar was adorned with its somber purple, but the altar of the Blessed Mother suggested joy and hope. On the altar was a large candle, rich in the symbolism of the season. The candle, with its meaning, is explained by a member of the O'Fallon novitiate of 1925.

> The candle holder, draped in blue and white and arranged with small buds, represents her (Mary), in whose chaste bosom the Savior rested before His nativity. The Candle signifies Christ, the Light of the world, the Flower from the Root of Jesse. It typifies also the Church in whose bosom there lies concealed the Redeemer of the world, so soon to be born anew.

During Advent Masses were chanted without organ accompaniment and solemn Compline was a part of the prayer of the Sunday. The Christmas novena, chanted in common each of the last days before Christmas, completed the Advent prayer.[10]

The celebration of the feast of Christmas began with the last day of the novena chanted just before midnight. All would realize that the "little while" of the prophet Isaias was just a very little while. At twelve midnight the celebrant began the joyful announcement, "In the forty-second year of the Empire of Octavianus Augustus, while the earth was at peace. . . ." The congregation then walked in procession to a temporary shrine within the convent from which they joined the celebrant in a solemn entrance procession in which all carried palm branches and lighted tapers. The chapel, which had been in symbolic darkness just a few minutes before, was transformed into brilliance and light for the Eucharistic celebration in which the coming King is made present. The liturgical prayer was resumed throughout the day with the morning *Missa Recitata*, Terce, a morning high Mass and finally evening Vespers. The day was described by a member of the 1925 novitiate as one "full of supernatural joy and peace."[11]

Lent was another special time for the sisters at O'Fallon. Their fundamental motto as set down by their chaplain was "Interior transformation and transmutation through the Lenten Eucharist, under the leadership of our stational saint in holy fellowship."[12] Emphasis was placed on the idea that spiritual renovation was not the work of man but of God. Special Lenten practices of prayer, fasting, and almsgiving, while good in themselves, were still the work of man rather than the work of God. These practices were an asset in preparing and disposing one to receive spiritual renovation from God but could not, of themselves, effect an inner conversion. Therefore, Lenten efforts should not remain focused only on these secondary activities but should concentrate the greatest attention on "the primary source of the true Christian spirit," as Pius X called the Eucharist in his famous *Motu proprio* of 1903. Lenten practices at O'Fallon, therefore, were rooted in the Eucharist.[13]

In carrying out its deepened focus on the Eucharistic liturgy during Lent, the O'Fallon community followed the example of the early Church. The Christians of the early days would prepare themselves to enter the church at which the Eucharist of the day would be celebrated by the Supreme Pontiff by gathering together in a nearby church, which came to be called the "collective Church". The congregation would then go in procession to the Church in which Holy Mass was to be offered. This latter church came to be called the "stational church". This practice allowed more time for the significance of the action that would take place in the stational church to sink into the consciousness of the faithful.

To achieve a similar goal, Father Hellriegel would, at 7:00 P.M. each evening during Lent, assemble with the sisters in the auditorium, which became transformed into a "collective church." The stage was furnished with an altar on which were placed a cross and two candles. To the one side of the altar was a large map of the stational churches; on the other side of the altar was a lectern and a blackboard which would be handy for illustrations during the lectures. The program each evening would begin with a prayer; the major portion would consist of an explanation of the Roman station and the mass text for the next day. The presentation was a preparation both for the next morning's meditations and the Eucharistic celebration. The sisters were encouraged, as a fruit of their meditation, to choose some practical point for their own daily living on which they would then focus their particular examen. At the conclusion of the presentation there was a procession into the chapel during which the short form of the litany of the saints was chanted. In the sanctuary of the chapel between the high altar and the communion table was small altar with the relic of the stational saint. The sisters were given a blessing with the relic and an opportunity to venerate the relic on the way out of the chapel. A Lenten hymn was sung during the procession from the chapel. The stational relic remained on the small altar during the whole of the next day. Two continually burning oil lamps would remind any visitor to the chapel of its presence. The celebration of the Mass of the day, a high Mass without organ, at 6:00 a.m., was the culmination of the Lenten liturgical prayer.[14]

Holy Week climaxed the Lenten efforts of interior renewal through Eucharistic and liturgical prayer. It has already been pointed out that Holy Thursday was the day selected for the introduction of the offertory procession. The liturgies of Good Friday and Holy Saturday also were looked upon by Father Hellriegel as opportunities for bringing the sisters more deeply into the prayer of the Church. For the liturgical celebration of the day of the Lord's death, Father Hellriegel put together a small pamphlet called simply *Good Friday*. It was an arrangement of the Mass of the Presanctified for congregational participation. It also allowed for the possibility of celebrating the liturgical service of Good Friday during the afternoon time from 12:00 noon to 3:00 p.m. The community at O'Fallon entered completely into the liturgy with active participation on the part of all the sisters and conducted their liturgy at the most appropriate time. Both this practice and the use of the pamphlet spread, partly because of the publicity given to it in *Orate Fratres*.[15]

Holy Saturday furnished another opportunity for the chaplain at O'Fallon to lead his flock in to the genuine spirit of the liturgy. The Mass of Holy Saturday was originally an Easter vigil Mass and was textually constructed in such a way that the then current practice of celebrating the liturgy on Easter Saturday morning effectively clouded many of the sentiments of the liturgical prayer and symbolism. Father Hellriegel was one of the first in this country to see this problem clearly and to attempt a solution to the problem. Father Hellriegel's solution was to restore the liturgical celebration to its proper time, at least during some of the years of this chaplaincy at O'Fallon. On a number of occasions the sisters with their chaplain began the celebration of the Easter Vigil at twelve midnight on Easter morning. They would conclude the vigil celebration with lauds and then join together for joyous agape.

During the years when the Easter Vigil was not celebrated at midnight on Easter morning the creative chaplain would look for some other way to help the sisters to enter more fully into the mystery of the resurrection of Christ. One experience which stimulated a greater understanding of the feast was the holding of a paraliturgical service in the form of a mystery play at 5:00 a.m. on Easter Sunday. For this event the sisters would use their "mortuary chapel," the place in which deceased sisters were waked. A statue of the risen Christ was in the chapel. Several postulants would dress as the holy women and would act out the scenario recorded in the gospel as the events of the first Easter morning. After this short drama, the sisters would go in procession to the chapel for the chanting of Matins. The Mass of the resurrection would be celebrated with great festivity, complete with the sounding of the bugle at appropriate times. The bugle was also used to wake the sisters at the early hour for the mystery play.[16]

Dramatizations such as the one for Easter morning were also frequently used for a part of the preparation program the evening before a feast. This would be the case especially on the ember days on which the gospel gave the account of the Annunciation of the angel Gabriel to Mary or the visitation of Mary to Elizabeth. On such an evening the sisters would devote themselves entirely to the preparation for the Mass of the next morning, foregoing even their recreation period. Similar sacredness was maintained on Saturday evening and afternoons; these times were devoted to preparation for the Sunday. Even the typical convent house cleaning had to be over by Saturday afternoon so that a spirit of prayer and meditation could prevail throughout the convent.[17]

Special feast days such as All Saints' Day were often enhanced by special ceremonies within the liturgy which helped the congregation to enter more fully into the spirit and grace of the day. The *Asperges* and a sermon usually preceded the high Mass. The celebrant would enter the chapel in solemn procession with servers bearing palm branches, candles and incense. The incense was used at the consecration of the Mass as a symbol of the completeness of the sacrifice.[18]

The Kiss of Peace also was more than the skeletal ritual usually found at that time. The exchange of the Pax at O'Fallon began with the head server uncovering an ikon that had been placed on the altar near the altar card on the epistle side. The ikon was a majestic figure of Christ on a small brass plate. The boy presented the ikon to the celebrant who kissed it and gave the salutation. "*Pax tecum.*" The boy then presented the ikon to one of each pair of servers. The boy to whom it was presented kissed the ikon and then embraced his partner, as do the ministers at a solemn high Mass.[19]

Holy Communion also was frequently distributed with a special sign of reverence. Acolytes bearing candles would accompany the celebrant.

The end of Mass, at times, brought a special ceremony honoring Christ as the crucified king. For this ceremony was used a "triumphant" crucifix which Fathers Hellriegel and Jasper had designed.[20] It was a tall wooden cross on which hung the figure of Christ clothed as priest in alb and stole and cope. For the feast of All Saints' Day the servers would wear relics of the saints around their necks and would hold palms in their hands. They would form a semicircle around the one boy holding the crucifix and the two on either side of him with lighted candles. The congregation, then, led by the celebrant would sing the triple acclamation to Christ as king, "*Christus vincit, Christus regnat, Christus imperat.*" Prayers for the Church, the pope, and the bishop would alternate with the repetitions of the triple acclamation. The whole ceremony was an example of reverent and enthusiastic worship of the Lord.[21]

In all such ceremonies great attention was given to each detail so that the liturgical prayer could be rendered with all devotion and fittingness. The adornments of the sanctuary and the dress of both servers and celebrant were regarded with care and were designed with unusual fullness and grace. Tabernacle veil, antependia, and vestments were designed in keeping with liturgical symbolism. The great care and attention to detail was to become an ongoing characteristic of liturgical celebrations conducted by Father Hellriegel.

Father Hellriegel also made full use of the many blessings provided by the Roman Ritual. He used to say, "The priests are loaded with blessings; why don't they give them to the people?"[22] Father Hellriegel did use them and used them with great beauty and impressiveness. The blessings would always include a prayer for all whom the object of the blessing would touch. For example, Father Hellriegel blessed the sisters' chickens and prayed not only that the chickens would thrive but that all who would partake of them would receive the love of God.[23] The blessing of bread and meat and eggs at Easter was another ancient custom which Father Hellriegel revived.

Father Hellriegel gradually led his community toward a greater appreciation of liturgical prayer and toward the opportunity to engage in more liturgical prayer. When he took over the chaplaincy at O'Fallon, the sisters had the office of the Blessed Mother as a part of their prescribed prayers. However, those who had duties to perform were excused from the common recitation of the office. There were times when so many sisters had duties that of the hundred or more sisters in the community only six or seven were present for the office. After several years of preparation and explanation the sisters finally switched their prescribed prayer to the day hours of the divine office. The experience of meaningful prayer of the office of the feast brought such joy to the community that it became rare for anyone to have duties so pressing that she had to be excused from the office.[24]

The liturgical life which Father Hellriegel inspired among the sisters at O'Fallon was one that began with inner understanding and devotion, flowed into a visible manifestation in the beauty of the rendering of liturgical prayer and continued flowing into a spirit of joy and charity within the convent. One great theme that Father Hellriegel stressed in terms of the actual living of the liturgy was the importance of reconciliation. If ever there were any hurt feelings of misunderstanding between sisters, Father Hellriegel would strongly encourage the sisters involved to become reconciled before the next Eucharistic celebration. That he himself practiced what he preached can be seen from one minor incident. One evening at vespers the singing had turned out rather poorly and the celebration of the prayer seemed to be less than what Father Hellriegel felt it should have been. He was provoked and "let off steam" to the sister, who was in charge of the sacristy. The next morning he sought her out, before the Eucharist, and apologized, even though his only opportunity to offer an apology was in the presence of a priest guest.[25]

Father Hellriegel lived and spoke the message of the liturgy as the heart of Christian living. He inspired the sisters to a love for the liturgy because it so obviously flowed from his own inner depths. The sisters he instructed, especially the younger members of the community such as the novices, were filled with a spirit of awe at his teachings. They lived with the awareness of being caught up into something of real spiritual depth and beauty. The older sisters in the community, too, were responsive to the liturgical life Father Hellriegel fostered. Some of the sisters in their middle years had some reservations because they rightly anticipated some suspicion and adverse reaction from pastors of the diocese, a point to be taken up in greater detail later in the chapter.

Father Hellriegel was careful that any new forms of liturgical prayer to which he introduced the sisters would be preceded by thorough instruction. To this end he gave classes on the liturgical year, its overall meaning as well as its specific feasts; the psalms, especially the psalms of the office and their special pertinence to those in religious life, the spiritual and corporal works of mercy so that the union with Christ brought about in liturgical prayer might be lived in practical day by day decisions. The Mass was the subject of a lecture series with slide illustrations.

Special emphasis was given to explanation of the psalms of the divine office in order that the sisters could intelligently enter into their community prayer. Through daily lectures Father Hellriegel explained in detail each verse of each psalm, reflecting the spirit of the author of the prayer and helping the sisters to assimilate the prayer as their own.[26]

Father Hellriegel spent his time not only instructing the sisters at O'Fallon but also continued his own study with Father Jasper. In 1925 one of the fruits of their common labor was published in the July-August edition of the *Central Blatt*; it was an article entitled "Der Schilüssel zur Lösung der sozial Frage."[27] The article is very significant because it provides a good indication of the advanced theological understanding possessed by Father Hellriegel at this early stage of liturgical development in the United States.

The article begins by noting that it is the excessive emphasis on individualism and the corresponding lack of any appreciation of man's solidarity with his fellow man which is at the core of the social problems of modern times. The logical conclusion is then that if a sense of solidarity could be built up in the consciousness of mankind, a gigantic step would be taken toward the solution to modern social problems. But the Christian is fortunate in that he does not need to create this human solidarity out of nothing; rather it has been created for him by Christ who came into this world to found a kingdom and then made the relationship between himself and his kingdom to be one of mystical and organic unity.[28]

In explaining this relationship the authors draw upon two biblical examples, St. John's image of the vine and the branches and St. Paul's image of the head and members of the one body. The first image suggests that even as branches cannot live unless they are joined organically to the rest of the vine, trunk and other branches, so too man cannot live unless he is joined with Christ and his fellow man. As the individual branches retain their uniqueness, so do the individual persons; yet as each branch has a relationship to the whole and therefore to each of the other branches, so too does each man have a relationship with the whole of mankind-united-with-Christ as well as with each of his fellow men.

In the second image Christ is identified as the head of the body and the Church, that is, all the faithful, are identified as the members of the body. The authors are aware that the understanding they have of the Church is not likely to coincide with the concept triggered by the term in the minds of their readers. They, therefore, take pains to point out that the word "Church" does not refer to a building in which people pray, nor to an insurance company which guarantees security in the life to come, nor to a system of law and authority. Here Father Hellriegel is showing one of his typical strengths in addressing an audience of any kind. He senses where his readers or listeners are in their own understanding and addresses himself to the concerns and ideas that are in their minds, thus achieving communication.

Continuing with the same image, the Church is further explained as an organism rather than an organization. "The Church is Christ Himself in a peculiar manner of His abiding presence in the world." The Church's deepest essence is seen to be its identity as the body of Christ. The authors demonstrate that this concept is not one unheard of since Biblical times. Even though it was used rarely in the 1920's, it was taught by the Fathers of the Church, the medieval scholars, Vatican I, and Pope Leo XIII.

Again the problems of the readers are anticipated and an explanation is given of the term "mystical". The point is made that the word is not being used to refer to anything that is fanciful or unreal or unsubstantial. Rather the term is derived from the word "mystery" and is used to refer to the Church as the "mystery of God's bounty and wisdom and omnipotence".

Lest misunderstanding still prevail, it is further pointed out that the term "mystery" is not here referring to a supernatural truth which lies beyond the grasp of the mind of man but to "those sacred things and actions which communicate divine life to man and by which man is made partaker of the divine nature". Again can be seen a characteristic trait of the writing and preaching of Father Hellriegel. He explained his message in detail and made sure his readers and/or listeners could understand every term or phrase he used.

The concept of the Church as the mystical body was further elaborated by drawing upon the writings of Dr. Karl Adam and of St. Augustine. Dr. Adam expresses the reality of this truth by saying, Christ the Lord is the actual ego of the Church, her animating principle, her life-giving spirit. In his *Treatise on John*, St. Augustine exclaims, "Let us congratulate ourselves, let us break forth into thanksgiving, we are become not only Christians but Christ". The repetition of the words of these great Christian teachers not only enhances the understanding of the reader but also provides some indication of the breadth of reading and study accomplished by the authors.

The article goes on to point out that if the Church is really a living organism, it must show forth in some active way the content of its inner life. And the natural activity by which the Church shows its nature as a divine organism and as the Mystical Body of Christ is through its liturgy. As in the cases of the terms "church", and "mystical", so too the term "liturgy" must be cleared of possible misconceptions before it can adequately be discussed. The misconceptions consist in the notions that liturgy is to be identified with visible ceremonies or with certain kinds of vestments or music. The problem with these ideas is that they confuse the gem with its setting. The proper setting is significant but it is only the beginning; the significance of the liturgy is much greater:

> The liturgy is the reenactment of the life of Christ; it is the re-pres-
> entation (making present) of the work of redemption.... The lit-
> urgy is that divine worship which the mystic Christ, that is, the
> Church as a body joined with Christ as its head renders to the
> heavenly Father; it consists in the a) celebration and b) applica-
> tion of the mysteries of redemption, executed in mystery-drama
> by the particular priesthood made up of those specially endowed
> by Holy Orders, and by the universal priesthood, made up of
> those baptized and confirmed.

From these selections it can be seen that the authors possessed
clear understandings of the mystery-reality dimension of the liturgy
and of the concept of the priesthood of the believers, two subjects
that would remain in the center of focus in the liturgical movement
for many years to come.

From the understanding of liturgy presented above it can be
seen that liturgy intrinsically involves the role of the human person
as a member of the body of Christ, that is, in his union with Christ
and with others Christians. Therefore, liturgy is primarily social and
must have a community character. Those participating in liturgy are
not mere aggregates of individuals but are united together into a
oneness rooted in Christ. Yet, liturgy does not stifle the individual;
rather, it lifts him to spiritual heights beyond the grasp of the
particular ego. The liturgy takes the piety of the individual beyond
the petty formulas of, "Grant me this, O Lord," into the song of universal praise and thanks and joy. The individual who participates in
liturgy and experiences this widening of his horizon will be the individual who is also sensitive to modern social problems.

However, what is experienced by most of the faithful when they
attend Mass is *not* solidarity in worship with Christ and with one
anther. On the contrary, most are caught up in their favorite private
devotions which have little or nothing to do with the liturgy. It is
only if active participation in the liturgy by the faithful is restored
that a sense of solidarity and social consciousness can be restored.
As Pope Pius X said in the November 1903 *Motu proprio*, "the active
participation of the faithful in the holy mysteries... is the primary
and indispensable source of the true Christian spirit." These words
are to be taken literally. This true Christian spirit, which is characterized by love for one's fellow man, flows from active participation
in the liturgy. However, it must be emphasized that what is intended

here is not the mere performance of exterior rites but the interior entering into the divine reality. It is only if a real "renewal and intensification of the religious life through the Christian mysteries" takes place that the renewed social consciousness will result. If this active participation in the liturgy does take place in the depths of the people who constitute the Church, then a renewal of society will follow. This inevitability exists because of the very nature of liturgical action.

The awareness of the intrinsic connection between participation in the liturgy and concern for social problems has been pointed to as the most distinguishing characteristic of the American liturgical movement. The concern that the social implication of the liturgy be a part of American Catholic social thought and life was a significant one in the mind of Virgil Michel.[29] It has also been demonstrated that this concern revealed itself regularly in the annual liturgical weeks which began in 1940.[30] However, in this work by Fathers Jasper and Hellriegel one can see this theme of American liturgical revival surfacing some fifteen years before the liturgical weeks began and several months before Virgil Michel even returned from his European studies to begin his plans for launching a liturgical periodical.

The development of the relationship between liturgical renewal and social involvement displayed a healthy balance. Although the authors clearly portrayed the intrinsic relationship between the two factors, they did not confuse the issue of where one stops and the other begins. The primary focus of liturgy as the worship of God was kept in the foreground; liturgy was not the same as a social action planning session. By their clarity of distinction here they avoided a pitfall not always avoided by the liturgical movement of the late 1960's.

Father Hellriegel's thesis that participation in the saving mysteries of Christ through liturgical prayer would result in the kind of solidarity that would manifest itself in concern for the needs of one's fellow man was one of the principles by which he worked at O'Fallon and later at Holy Cross. It was borne out by the active concern of the sisters for one another and for the needs of the poor, and much later, by an active program of social service in the parish which he would lead.

"Der Schlüssel zur Lösung der sozial frage" was also outstanding for its lucid exposition of the doctrine of the Mystical Body of Christ and the relationship of this doctrine to liturgy and to the whole life of society. A comparison of this article with the encyclical of Pius XII of 1943 on the same topic reveals many similarities.

Although the great farsightedness of this article can easily be seen in retrospect, its value was not apparent to all in the years immediately after its publication. In 1928 the Central Bureau of the Central Verein, St. Louis, wanted to reprint the article in booklet form. They submitted the article to appropriate diocesan offices for a "*Nihil obstat*" and an "Imprimatur." These were granted, but along with the "*Nihil obstat*" came a letter from the diocesan censor, Father John Rothensteiner, who offered a few reservations. His position was that "the exposition does not prove the thesis that the solution of the social question is to be found in a larger participation of the laity in the liturgy of the Church." He characterized Father Hellriegel's statements as "an exaggeration". Although Father Rothensteiner acknowledged that "religious regeneration is, indeed, a prerequisite for genuine social reform," he did not think that "the simple recitation of the Mass prayers during Mass" would "necessarily mean religious reform."[31] Father Rothensteiner seems to have missed the main point of inner participation being the most significant factor.

However, Mr. Kenkel of the Central Bureau took Father Rothensteiner's objections seriously enough that he wrote to Virgil Michel at St. John's Abbey for advice on the matter.[32] Virgil Michel apparently favored the idea of publishing the article; it did get printed in booklet form even though Father Rothensteiner's ideas were also taken into account.

The results of his criticisms were some changes in the article, some "toning down", and a change in the title from "The Key to the Solution of the Social Question," the translation of the original German title, to *The True Basis of Christian Solidarity*, with subtitle of *The Liturgy an Aid to the Solution of the Social Question*. In spite of the less forceful title, the booklet sold thousands of copies in both German and English and was still enough in demand by 1947 to warrant a reprinting. Virgil Michel quotes from it in two different places in his 1938 book *The Liturgy of the Church*. In one instance he refers to it as a "notable pamphlet".[33]

Both through his writing and through personal contact, Father Hellriegel and his "strange" liturgical ideas and practices came to be known by various members of the clergy of the St. Louis Archdiocese. Many priest visitors would come to O'Fallon to the vestment department to view the sisters' embroidery work to select a pattern for a vestment they would like to order. Father Hellriegel's large bell vestment invariably caught the eye, and sometimes provoked a raised eyebrow of the priest visitor. Also priests would come to visit sisters in the convent as relatives or friends of theirs and would often take part in the liturgy during their visit. Some of these priests were quite unaware both of the point behind the liturgical rites and of the origin of the rites. Some of them went so far as to tell the sisters that they were being heretical and would soon be excommunicated from the Church, or at least would never get the papal approbation they were seeking. Such comments were difficult for both the sisters and for their very convinced and dedicated chaplain.

A time of particular difficulty for Father Hellriegel was the period immediately after the death of Father Jasper on June 26, 1925. In a letter written about two months later, Father Hellriegel refers to Father Jasper as "my best friend".[34] Losing one's best friend is trial enough. Yet for Father Hellriegel, this was only part of the cross he bore. He found himself with a double responsibility for the convent and for the parish Church and school during the interim until a new pastor would be assigned. This heavy burden of responsibility had to be borne at a time when his joint liturgical efforts with Father Jasper were coming under heavy criticism from clergy. Father Hellriegel now had to bear the brunt of the unkind remarks pretty much alone.

At the time of his most deeply felt discouragement Archbishop Glennon sent to Father Hellriegel a most welcome letter. It was dated October 14, 1925, and read:

My dear Father Hellriegel:

I am very much impressed with the effort you are making, and making successfully, of bringing our priests and people to a truer knowledge of the spirit, meaning and form of the great liturgy of the Church.

Your work is not an innovation. It is a restoration, and especially am I pleased to see your endeavor to more closely associate — indeed incorporate — the Catholic laity in this liturgy.

I feel that the Blessed Savior, whom you are bringing nearer and nearer through His love and the Sacraments to the people, will continue to bless your work; and I need not add you have my commendation and benediction.

Sincerely yours,

(signed) John J. Glennon[35]

Father Hellriegel hailed the day of the arrival of the Archbishop's letter as "red letter" day.[36] It did much to soothe the feelings of both the chaplain and the sisters.

Even though the reception of the written support of the Archbishop did not end the battle for respectability for those promoting liturgical renewal, things in the immediate future did seem to look up. For it was near this same time that Father Hellriegel made his first contacts with Dom Virgil Michel, O.S.B., of St. John's Abbey, Collegeville, and with Mr. Gerald Ellard, S.J., a seminarian who was currently studying at St. Louis University and who would be ordained the following June. It was through these contacts that an organized liturgical movement in the United States actually came to birth.

CHAPTER SIX

The Liturgical Movement in the United States

Virgil Michel returned to St. John's Abbey on September 12, 1925, after spending a year and a half studying in Europe.[1] While there Virgil Michel was especially influenced by Dom Lambert Beauduin and the liturgical renewal that he had begun in Belguim. He returned to the States filled with the conviction of the necessity of doing something to bring about a similar liturgical revitalization in his own country. His correspondence with his Abbot, Alcuin Deutsch, had been filled with hopes for the founding of a liturgical periodical and a liturgical press at St. John's Abbey. Michel lost no time in trying to make contact with others in the United States who were sympathetic to his ideas. One attempt at contact was a letter addressed to Father Jasper of whose death Michel had not heard, Father Hellriegel opened the letter and sent a reply to Virgil Michel on September 23, 1925. Father Hellriegel had already been in contact with Abbot Alcuin and knew of Virgil Michel and the impending plans for a review. Father Hellriegel described for Father Michel the work he and Father Jasper had been carrying on, offered his help and support for the review, and invited Michel to O'Fallon.[2] Michel accepted the invitation at Christmas time of the same year, but in the meantime there was an ongoing exchange of ideas by mail.

Michel solicited suggestions for the planned liturgical review and Hellriegel accomodated him. Hellriegel's approach was thoroughly realistic and practical. He saw clearly that the mentality of the reader must be kept in mind if the review were to be able to communicate. Therefore, Hellriegel recommended beginning with the task of dispelling ignorance and misunderstanding and focusing on the purpose of the liturgical apostolate. He advised the concrete spelling out of the purpose as the glorification of God and the renovation of the Christian life. He stressed that appreciation and understanding of the liturgical texts and active participation were means of achieving the purpose; they were the starting point, not the final goal.[3]

Hellriegel and Michel also discussed proposals for a title for the new review. Originally Hellriegel had intended to put together a prayer book which he was planning to entitle *Orate Fratres*. This was the title adopted for the review.

The first meeting between Martin Hellriegel and Gerald Ellard took place on November 1, 1925.[4] Ellard had written a letter to the editor of *America* the previous April. In his letter he cited a questionnaire which had been answered by the young men in Jesuit universities. In this questionnaire the men had expressed a desire for sermons dealing with liturgical instruction. Ellard pointed out in his letter that in spite of progress that had been made in the use of the missal and in the sacred chant, the liturgy for the layman is still "all but sealed." He advocated "opening up the liturgy" and laying bare the significance and the symbolism behind the various liturgical rites and instruments.[5]

By fall of the same year Ellard had become aware of one place fairly close to St. Louis University where the liturgy had already been "opened up." As Father Hellriegel later said, "Those were really days of much pain for those of us active in liturgical reform; when we heard of another bird of the same feather, it didn't take long to get us together."[6]

Ellard arrived at O'Fallon for his first visit on All Saint's Day early in the morning and assisted at the Mass in the sanctuary. The experience was quite an eye-opener for Ellard, for his enthusiasm for the liturgy up to this time had been based on what he had learned in the classroom rather than on personal experience.[7] Ellard was so favorably impressed by this first liturgical experience at O'Fallon that he returned for several other occasions, taking with him for the December 8th services several other Jesuit friends. Mr. Ellard then wrote a description of his experiences and reactions for *America's* December 12, 1925, issue. He speaks of the liturgical life at O'Fallon as fulfilling the objective proposed by Pope Pius X, "To bring all things to a head in Christ." He sees the active participation in the liturgy as it is carried out at O'Fallon to be providing the means by which those who are already incorporated into Christ are brought to the realization of their membership in Christ's body. He also appreciated the aesthetic dimension of liturgical celebration at O'Fallon. He says, "...it is a liturgy enriched with much of the external beauty of the Ages of Faith. Everything unfamiliar at O'Fallon represents a bringing back of old customs."[8] Apparently Mr. Ellard and his Jesuit friends were not the only ones going to O'Fallon for liturgical inspiration, for he comments in the same article that O'Fallon is becoming "a place of pilgrimage."[9]

Ellard's article was filled with praise and enthusiasm for the liturgical spirit and prayer he had found at O'Fallon. However, some who read his description of liturgical ceremonies at O'Fallon found areas to criticize. The letters to the editor in the next issue of *America* carried complaints about such things as the offertory and the corpus on the crucifix being "robed in alb, stole and cope."[10] These criticisms did not seem to keep away the prospective "pilgrims," for by 1931 another report indicated that over 300 priests had visited O'Fallon just within that year.[11]

At this time the liturgical efforts that were going on in the United States were still individual strands rather than an organized movement. Finally, at Christmas, 1925, Michel, Ellard, and Hellriegel met together for the first time. The historic meeting of the three took place at O'Fallon. They spent Christmas eve discussing plans for the liturgical journal and spoke the final word of decision just before the celebration of midnight Mass.[12] This was the moment of the birth of the journal and the moment of its christening as *Orate Fratres*. It was an occasion of great rejoicing for all three of them and the birth of the liturgical movement as an organized movement in the United States. They gave thanks together at a midnight Mass in which, the celebrant was Father Hellriegel, the deacon was Father Michel, and the subdeacon was Mr. Ellard.[13] The coming together of these three represented the three different streams of interest and talent flowing together into one corporate effort. Michel brought to their joint effort great skills in organizational ability; Hellriegel brought a great depth of pastoral insight; Ellard came to be the one who translated the work of liturgical scholars into widely read books and articles on the theology of the liturgy.[14]

Once the plan for the journal was solidified, there was still much spade work to be done before its first issue would appear. one major task was the contacting of other interested and knowledgeable individuals to form a board of editors. Hellriegel and Ellard were, of course, to be members. The other members were solicited mostly by Michel through correspondence.

A second major task was the publicity necessary to create a market for the magazine. To meet this need, Michel had printed a folder which gave information regarding the purpose and contents of the coming journal. Hellriegel was a great help to Michel in distributing these folders. During the summer of 1926, some 250 visitors came to O'Fallon; each departed with a folder and a bit of knowledge regarding the newly formed liturgical apostolate. Hellriegel himself gave out six or seven hundred folders. Also, he was instrumental in getting Frederick Kenkel of the Central Bureau to distributed several hundred folders. Another several hundred persons learned of the coming review through their correspondence with Father Hellriegel.[15] Michel was so impressed with Hellriegel's efforts that he wrote in the margin of letter received from Hellriegel, "Hellriegel, great propagandist!"[16] The same energetic desire to share permeates all of Hellriegel's work in the liturgical apostolate.

Father Hellriegel encouraged the sisters at O'Fallon to get involved in making contributions to the new review. One sister who was artistically talented submitted several designs for *Orate Fratres*. The second issue expresses "its indebtedness to the Sisters of the Most Precious Blood, O'Fallon, Missouri," for a set of tailpiece designs for *Orate Fratres*.[17] The sisters in the novitiate submitted articles on Advent and Christmas at O'Fallon for the first and second issues repectively.[18] Father Hellriegel corrected and approved the articles and sent them on to Virgil Michel.[19] Two more articles in this series, "Quadragesima in a Convent" and "Palm Sunday in a Convent" appeared in the second volume of *Orate Fratres*.[20]

During the months of preparation for the first issue of *Orate Fratres*, Michel and his newly formed liturgical press were also busy working on other publications. One of these was a new booklet for participation in a dialog Mass called *Offeramus*. Advice was asked of Hellriegel concerning this booklet too. Hellriegel again showed his great practical and pastoral approach. He recommended more simplified directions and the putting of all of the explanatory sections either in the front or in the back of the booklet so as not to be confusing during actual use. His criticism was of a supportive nature, mixed with praise and followed by an order for fifty copies.[21]

Father Hellriegel's own first article in *Orate Fratres* appeared only near the end of its first year of publication. It was the first of a series of articles on the liturgical year written in conjunction with his friends and protege, Alphonse Westhoff. A closer look at this article and some of the subsequent ones written by Father Hellriegel during his O'Fallon years will provide insight into the development of the ideas on which his pastoral work of both present and future were based. Some indication of the influence he was exerting on *Orate Fratres* readers through the ideas he was stimulating in them can also be discerned.

In his writing as well as in his preaching and lecturing, Hellriegel was always the master teacher. He explained each of his points simply and thoroughly. He took nothing for granted and always kept a realistic perspective on the amount of previous knowledge he could expect on the part of his reader or listerner. For the American Catholic of the late 1920's and 1930's previous knowledge of the liturgy was quite meager. However, Hellriegel did manage to draw on concepts familiar to most through the catechism or through personal experience to lead them to the new understanding he wished to communicate.

The introduction to the first of the articles on the liturgical year begins with a clarification of the meaning of the term "liturgy." After giving etymological and historical background on the term, the basic ideas are synthesized into a short definition: "Liturgy is the public official divine service which the Church offers to God."[22]

The major section of the article begins by asking the reader to recall what he learned in the days of his youth about the Lord's institution of the Eucharist on the night before he died. From this starting point the authors move to a discussion of the Eucharist as remembrance, first of the death of Jesus, then of His death and resurrection, and finally of His death, resurrection, and total life of redemption. Having gradually built up the idea of Eucharist as remembrance of the saving actions of Christ, the authors then forcefully make the point that the Eucharist was not "the mere recollection of those past events" but a new making present of those events. The final thought is that it is the new making present of the saving events of Christ that is the source of the liturgical year.[23]

Subsequent articles written for *Orate Fratres* during Father Hellriegel's O'Fallon years deal with the liturgical year, both in general and in regard to specific feasts and seasons, with the sacraments, with liturgical retreats, and with practical suggestions which parish priests could follow in leading their congregation to a full liturgical life.[24] Hellriegel's writings during this period exemplify that combination of profundity on the level of the truths presented with simplicity on the level of style for which he came to be known and appreciated and which proved to be such an asset in bringing his people to lives of deep and active involvement in liturgical prayer.

The articles dealing with practical suggestions are especially important because they outline the approach which contributed so much to Hellriegel's pastoral success. Two of the articles which appeared in *Orate Fratres* advise priests on how to make the sacraments more of a living reality for the people of their parishes. The first of these is devoted to the sacraments of Baptism, Confirmation, and Eucharist. He gives a brief theology of each sacrament and then follows with a more lengthy section giving suggestions for ways in which the parish can help its people come to a living awareness of the significance of the sacrament.[25]

To enhance the appreciation of the sacrament of baptism, Hellriegel suggests the placing of the baptismal font in a prominent place in the Church when designing new churches and remodeling older ones. He rules out sacristies and church corners. In the actual administration of the sacrament the restoration of the full baptismal garment (instead of a symbolic "finger towel") and of a special candle would speak something of the meaning of the sacrament. The newly baptized could also be presented with a specially designed baptismal certificate which would serve as a reminder to him of this great day; further remembrance of the day could be encouraged by family celebrations of baptismal anniversaries. The whole parish, too, ought to be involved in the welcoming of its new member. At least the names of those baptized the previous week should be announced at the Mass of the next Sunday. But a deeper involvement of the parish could be brought about by having at least some of the baptisms in the presence of the whole parish accompanied by a short explanation. Or the grade school class of the older sister or brother could be invited to the baptism, again accompanied by brief commentary.[26]

Confirmation is another all but forgotten sacrament by most adult Catholics. Its significance in their lives could be kept alive by occasional (at least) preaching on the various aspects of the sacrament. The occasion of a bishop's anniversary or consecration could be used to talk about the bishop as the ordinary minister of this sacrament, an indication of its special role in the Christian life. The function of the holy oils and the prayers said at their blessing should be explained also. During the time immediately before the bishop comes to a parish for confirmation, the prayers for the novena for Pentecost could be said. During this time, as well as during the time of Pentecost, sermons could be given on such topics as "Confirmation and Catholic Action" and "Confirmation and the Apostolate." Through these sermons Christians can come to see that their living out of their Confirmation involves their becoming "fishermen and apostles."[27]

Hellriegel's recommendation for parish enhancement of the Eucharist must have sounded quite far-reaching to his priest readers of 1936. He recommends intelligent use of the missal which presupposes missal study and missal meditation, first of all on the part of the priest so that he can communicate an understanding of the missal to his people. This missal study should concentrate on the black print (the text of the Mass) rather than on the red print (the rubrics which were still the sole focus of most liturgical study). The priests should then proceed to introduce into their parishes the *Missa recitata* and the congregational singing of the Sunday high Mass. Holy Communion should be given at communion time, not before Mass nor beginning at the offertory of the Mass. Hosts consecrated at the Mass which the congregation is offering should be used for their communion, especially on Sundays and major feasts. Greater prudence should be used in electing to say a "black" Mass.[28] Many undoubtedly wrote off Hellriegel's ideas as unrealistic and thought he could speak in this vein only because he worked in an ivory tower existence in a convent; however, within five years he was to be in a parish, successfully carrying out his own ideas.

The manner of celebrating the sacrament of matrimony is discussed in an article entitled "St. Evaristus Decreed."[29] In addition to the importance of the explicit context, this article is also significant for two other reasons. It illustrates Hellriegel's ability to use the liturgy of even an obscure saint to bring to the attention of his readers and listeners aspects of Christianity with which they had to deal in their daily lives. This article also shows Hellriegel's caution against taking something away, even if it were of questionable value or appropriateness, without putting something better in its place.

Hellriegel's point of departure for the major ideas of this article is the third lesson in the Matins of the feast. St. Evaristus was a pope of the second century. The lesson of the Matins lists some of his pontifical decrees, including one that "matrimony should be celebrated publicly and by a priest."[30] The term "publicly" is pondered in the light of the wedding customs of the time. These included " 'wedding goosestep' performed by flower girls, bridesmaids and bride as they approached God's altar to the strains of the pagan Wagner's 'Lohengrin's Bridal March.' " To counteract or replace the theatrical approach to the altar, Father Hellriegal suggested that the celebrant could "proceed from the sanctuary towards the middle of the church at the same time as couple and witnesses are walking towards the altar... (the priest... should... lead to the holy altar the two who are about to enter into 'the great mysterium')."[31] This suggestion was tried by a confrere and found to be a change welcomed by the people of his parish.

Hellriegel's contribution to *Orate Fratres* consisted not only in regular contribution of articles but an ongoing evaluation of various aspects of the overall format with Virgil Michel. For example, after several issues of volume one had come out Michel and Hellriegel began discussing plans for volume two. Hellriegel suggested retaining the cover design and though the print currently being used was good, also suggested arranging the text in a double column. He thought more of the articles should be short and simple, reminding Michel that many of the readers were "liturgical orphans." He suggested a revision of the section "Liturgy of the Season" simply because in the time after Pentecost there actually was not a seasonal liturgy. A final suggestion was the merging of the Editor's Corner with the section called "The Apostolate." Many of these changes appeared in volume two. However, the double column was not adopted and the cover design was changed.[32] The plea for simplicity was one that Hellriegel was to repeat many times, but most of the writers of the *Orate Fratres* articles were just not able to express themselves as simply as he could.

In spite of Hellriegel's many contributions to *Orate Fratres*, Michel would have liked to see even more entries by Hellriegel. The latter was not always able to do all the articles he intended because of other pressing duties. Also, Hellriegel's work was always a mixture of head and heart. He drew on his vast knowledge of the liturgy but he also counted on the inspired moment and found it hard to plan far ahead of time somthing he would write at a distant date.[33]

During the time he was working on *Orate Fratres*, Hellriegel was continuing the intense liturgical program at O'Fallon as well as continuing classes for the novices and sisters and giving lectures and retreats in many places both within and outside the St. Louis Archdiocese. He was also writing occasional articles for other periodicals and putting together several booklets oriented to liturgical and paraliturgical prayer. It is to these activities that the next chapter will be directed.

CHAPTER SEVEN

Promotion of the Liturgical Apostolate

During the years of Father Hellriegel's chaplaincy at O'Fallon, he continued to promote the liturgical apostolate in a great diversity of ways. One of his chief means was through personal contact. O'Fallon continued to grow in its reputation as a liturgical center and to attract visitors from all parts of the United States as well as from Europe and Mexico. One of the early visitiors to O'Fallon was Gerald Ellard. After the famous meeting with Michel and Hellriegel at Christmas of 1925, Ellard continued coming to O'Fallon for the next couple of years for almost every major feast day, usually bringing with him some associates from St. Louis University. When Ellard was ordained he said his first mass at O'Fallon. The Mass was celebrated with full congregational participation and with the celebrant facing the people.[1] It was here at O'Fallon in the context of living worship that Ellard came to grasp the full force of liturgical experience. The next year, when Ellard was making plans to study in Europe, it was Hellriegel who advised about which centers and persons to contact.[2]

One of the many Jesuits who learned of Hellriegel's work at O'Fallon through Ellard was Father Daniel Lord. He visited O'Fallon for the first time on New Year's Day, 1929, and left " with great enthusiasm and the resolution 'to push the Liturgical Apostolate.' "[3] That Father Lord kept his resolution is evident from the strong encouragement which he gave to the dialog Mass in the Sodality movement. Father Lord's publishing company, Queen's Work, published at least one of Father Hellriegel's booklets. Father Hellriegel was also invited to give a lecture to the Sodality's Summer School of Catholic Action in 1931.[4]

A stream of visitors came to O'Fallon on July 22, 1926, for the dedication of the new chapel and the celebration of the golden jubilee of the sisters in the United States. In the presence of all the prominent visitors, Archbishop Glennon spoke of the great power and splendor of the liturgy and said that he welcomed with all his heart the liturgical movement.[5] Among the guests for the day were a number who were interested in promoting the liturgical movement, including Dom Bede Maler. The interested parties had a sort of miniliturgical conference and drew up a few suggestions for discussion of the liturgy at the National Eucharistic Congress to be held at Cleveland the following year. However, this effort, the fond desire of Dom Bede Maler for many years, really did not get off the ground.[6]

During these busy years of the chaplaincy at O'Fallon, Father Hellriegel kept up the contact he had made as a very young priest with the Catholic people of the Ukrainian rite. Hellriegel regarded their rite as a source of inspiration and a valuable form of prayer from which Catholics of the western rite could learn much. Consequently, on a number of occasions Father Merenkow, the pastor of the Ukrainain rite Church, would come to O'Fallon with his choir to sing a high Mass.[7] Thus Father Hellriegel not only taught his visitors but, at times, learned from them also.

This exchange of teaching and learning also went on between Father Hellriegel and the liturgical leaders of Europe. Hellriegel kept in close contact with the European centers for liturgical renewal both through his many trips abroad and through an extensive correspondence.

Hellriegel's second opportunity to breathe in some of the liturgical beauty and depth of the European centers came in 1928. At this time the Precious Blood order was seeking to change its status from that of a diocesan community to that of a papal community. Two of the sisters, the mother general and the mistress of novices, were planning a trip to Rome to carry out the necessary negotiations for the change in status. However, neither of them had ever been to Europe and they were fearful of making the trip alone. Therefore, Father Hellriegel agreed to accompany them.[8]

The intent of Father Hellriegel in departing on the trip was to "devote as much time as possible to the interests of the liturgical apostolate." His schedule indicates that he achieved this end; March was spent in Rome, Holy Week at Maria Laach; at least a week was spent at Klosterneuberg with Dr. Pius Parsch, and a visit was paid to San Anselmo where Dom Beauduin had been teaching.[9] It is no wonder the mother general, who was already a strong supporter of the liturgical apostolate, came back filled with even greater enthusiasm.

March coincided with the Lenten season and offered Father Hellriegel an opportunity to participate daily in the Eucharist in the stational churches, thereby giving an even deeper knowledge of and appreciation for the role of the stational church in the Lenten liturgy.

The visit to Dr. Pius Parsch was the first of four meetings between the two. Hellriegel regarded Parsch as his pastoral guide and Maria Laach as his theological guide. One very delicate issue discussed by Parsch and Hellriegel was that of liturgical experimentation. Such things as celebrating the Easter Vigil at midnight rather than on Holy Saturday morning really had not yet been officially sanctioned by the Church. Parsch, cautiously, saw a possibility for going ahead with such liturgical celebrations. He told Hellriegel, "...there are such things in the Church as charisms. And if one feels the spirit, one has to be true to the Spirit." Thus the Easter Vigil was celebrated at its proper time on some five occasions during Father Hellriegel's chaplaincy at O'Fallon.[10]

However, the exchange of the liturgical understanding was not completely onesided. Monks and priests at such centers as Maria Laach, Klosterneuberg, and San Anselmo were appreciatively reading *Orate Fratres*.[11]

Besides personal contact with those interested in the liturgy, Hellriegel also carried on a vast correspondence. He regularly exchanged letters with the men he had visited in Europe and also answered many requests for help in starting liturgical renewal in parishes, convents, seminaries, etc. The magnitude of the number of letters received and the kinds of questions asked at times almost overwhelmed Hellriegel. He commented to Virgil Michel, "The many questions that I am asked as though I were an authority! And it takes time, much time, to answer them satisfactorily."[12] On his return from his 1928 European trip Hellriegel found 250 letters awaiting him.[13]

Some of the requests coming to Hellriegel were asking him not to answer questions or give information by mail but to come in person to address various groups. Here again he gave generously of his time and complied with as many requests as he could.

One of Hellriegel's early lecture series was given for about one hundred fifty Jesuits at St. Louis University. In this presentation Hellriegel developed four major points: the first concerned itself with the question of what is liturgy; the second dealt with the object of liturgy; the third explored the foundation of liturgy, namely, the Mystical Body of Christ, and then took up the liturgical apostolate and its aim.[14] Hellriegel was following his usual philosophy of beginning with the basics and taking nothing for granted. This proved to be a necessary approach, for by his second lecture he discovered that even though his audience was appreciative and enthusiastic, they still showed a "profound helplessness in things liturgical." The remaining talks covered such topics as the liturgy in the ecclesiastical year with special sessions on Advent and Christmas, Lent, and Holy Week.[15]

Soon after the lecture series the schools of philosophy and theology had adopted a practice which supplemented Hellriegel's lectures and undoubtedly had been encouraged by them. Several bulletin boards displayed posters showing the location of the stational churches in Rome. An explanation of the daily stational church was posted and changed each day.[16] Interest in the liturgy among the theology students caught on to the point that they began meeting once a week to read papers on such subjects of the liturgical movement and its reasons and motives, the Mass and its prayers and historical development, the teaching of St. Paul on the Mystical Body, comparisons between Oriental and Latin rites. Discussion would follow the reading of the paper.[17] It was Hellriegel who was somewhat responsible for triggering this interest in the liturgy among the Jesuits. Virgil Michel writes in an editorial for *Orate Fratres*, "From O'Fallon — in part at least, unless we are mistaken — came the spark that grew to a live flame among some of the Jesuit Fathers of St. Louis, at whose University lectures on aspects of the liturgy have been given for some years. . . ."[18]

By 1940 that spark was reaching not only such specialized groups as Jesuit priests and seminarians and sodalists but also the Catholic public. During Lent of that year a daily noon *Missa Recitata* was offered at the Jesuit operated St. Joseph's Church in downtown St. Louis. During the Mass the altar and the celebrant faced the people. On Easter the people were invited to participate in the solemn procession carrying altar breads to the altar. During the octave after Easter a daily solemn high Mass replaced the *Missa Recitata*.[19]

Lay groups in and near St. Louis were also beginning to learn of the liturgical apostolate through Hellriegel's lectues. During 1927 and 1928 he spoke to such diverse groups as the St. Charles Knights of Columbus, the Jefferson City Catholic Women's Union, and high school girls of St. Elizabeth's Academy, St. Louis, and the Catholic men's and women's organizations associated with the Central Bureau in St. Louis. Hellriegel never had one pat talk which he could whip out for any occasion. He was always conscious of his listeners, their needs and interests, and their level of understanding. To the Knights of Columbus group he spoke of the liturgical apostolate and the Liturgical Press. When addressing the Women's Union, an audience numbering over three hundred, he followed up his preliminary exposition of the liturgy and the liturgical apostolate with a discussion of what the apostolate does for women and what women can do for the apostolate. The lecture series at St. Elizabeth's Academy was oriented toward the deeper involvement of the students in participation in the liturgy. The lectures were accompanied by the introduction of the use of the missal and by the *Missa recitata*.[20]

Father Hellriegel's reputation both as one quite knowledgeable on liturgical matters and quite able to communicate with an audience was gradually spreading. When Virgil Michel organized the first National Liturgical Day at St. John's Abbey in Collegeville,

Minnesota, on July 25, 1929, Hellriegel was given a prominent place on the roster of speakers. His talk was scheduled immediately after the opening address of the host of the conference, Abbot Alcuin Deutsch of St. John's.[21] The address Hellriegel gave on this occasion represented a survey of the liturgical movement. It was reprinted in the September 8, 1929, issue of *Orate Fratres* and mentioned previously in chapter six.

Work with diocesan organizations and diocesan priests of St. Louis was also a part of Father Hellriegel's endeavors. Archbishop Glennon remained supportive of the liturgical apostolate. He was among the first of the hierarchy to send a letter of approval and encouragement to *Orate Fratres*.[22] In December of 1932, Archbishop Glennon organized *The Diocesan Commission for Promoting Correct Church Music* and appointed Father Hellriegel as the vice-chairman of the commission. Among the restoration in Church music which the Archbishop hoped the commission would hasten was the congregational participation in the singing of the Mass.[23] The commission lost no time in getting to work. At its first meeting in the early part of 1933 it inaugurated plans for a diocesan hymnal for an organists' guild; it also encouraged the singing of the whole high Mass.[24] Once the organists' guild was set up, the liturgical commission worked with the organists to explain to them the importance of congregational participation in the sung Mass and to encourage them to move in this direction in their parishes.[25]

The liturgical education of the priests of the diocese was also being furthered. During 1934 lectures and discussions were conducted for priests on such subjects as Pope Pius X's *Motu Proprio*, the divine office, and liturgical law.[26] Hellriegel gave a number of illustrated lectures on the Holy Sacrifice of the Mass in various centers in the St. Louis Archdiocese.[27] In that same year Hellriegel was appointed by Archbishop Glennon to give examinations to the junior clergy of the diocese on the subject of liturgy. He found among them an interest in the liturgy.[28] Hellriegel was conducting monthly liturgical seminars for the priests of the diocese.[29]

Hellriegel's former associate at St. Peter's Parish in St. Charles, who became Bishop Winkelmann, also proved to be a friend of the liturgical apostolate. In the summer of 1934 he organized a summer school for liturgical music which drew a good number of priests, nuns, and lay choir directors of the diocese.[30]

Bishop Schlarman of the Peoria Diocese was another member of the hierarchy who actively sought to further the liturgical apostolate, and to do this, he called upon Hellriegel on a number of occasions. On October 19, 1932, at the Academy of Our Lady in Peoria, he sponsored an institute for the teachers of the diocese around the theme of the liturgy of the Church. Hellriegel was chosen as one of the principal speakers of the day. This day can be regarded as especially significant in that it was the first diocesan day sponsored by a member of the hierarchy which was dedicated to a study of the liturgy.[31] Bishop Schlarman also looked after the spiritual and liturgical nourishment of the German-speaking members of his diocese. For these too he called upon Hellriegel and arranged for a retreat from February 10 to 17, 1935.

From September 27 to October 2 of that same year, Peoria was also the scene of the National Conference of Catholic Charities. The program, hosted by Bishop Schlarman, was thoroughly permeated with the spirit of the liturgy. Gregorian chant and the *Missa Recitata* were important elements in the prayer of the meeting. Hellriegel was called upon to give an address on "Catholic Institutional Life as Shaped by the Liturgy of the Church." He developed his topic by starting with an explanation of what the liturgy is and then moving to a discussion of the liturgical movement. Once his listeners had this general but indispensable background he then turned to the more specific issues of the requirements necessary for the one who is to be appointed as chaplain of a Christian institution and finally to the duties of a chaplain.[32] In discussing the requirements for the individuals who is to be appointed as chaplain, Hellriegel raised a point which the four or five bishops in the audience found especially challenging. He asked why it was that the convents were so frequently the places to which the priests who were aged or disabled or somehow unable to function in a parish were sent. He questioned whether it was really appropriate to place those with lesser capabilities in a position in which so much responsibility must be assumed for the spiritual direction of the sisters and the indirect influence on those with whom the sisters would be working.[33] It is no wonder that Hellriegel's talk "evoked much interest and comment and gave rise to many questions."[34]

The two subsequent years also brought requests from educational conferences to Martin Hellriegel asking him to speak. In March of 1936 he addressed the Missouri Catholic Educational Conference. Hellriegel explained to the assembled teachers that liturgy was not to be identified with the externals of chant or flowing vestments. Rather the liturgy was first and foremost the celebration of the Eucharist and the other sacraments by which man renders fitting worship to God and receives the fruits of Christ's redemptive work. The externals are significant only insofar as they can help to express and to enhance the understanding and prayer of the liturgy. Hellriegel went on to explain that the liturgical movement was an international effort to bring priests and people back to a vital and wholehearted participation in the life of Christ through a celebration of the mysteries of faith in the liturgy. Two dimensions were involved, the deepening of prayer and the taking of this deepened spiritual life back to the life and work of the Christian. The teachers were urged, as Catholic educators, to be extensions of Christ the Teacher. It was pointed out to them that the major means of nourishing this oneness with Christ is by themselves living a life filled with liturgical prayer. This was necessary if the teacher was to be able to communicate the full Christ life to his students. The final section of the talk consisted of a number of practical suggestions which the teachers could follow in working with their students. The first requirement was the imparting of a basic understanding by instruction on the doctrine of the Mystical Body, the Holy Sacrifice of the Mass and the Liturgical Year. The next level would be that of experience. When possible, the teacher should try to arrange for the students to participate in the dialogue Mass, the sung high Mass, Vespers or Compline. Teachers should also provide suggestions for their students regarding paraliturgical practices that could be carried out in the home. The communal spirit begun in prayer should be fostered in the daily life and activities of the students.[35]

In March of 1937 Father Hellriegel was invited to address the minor seminary section of the National Catholic Educational

Association in Louisville, Kentucky. His talk, entitled "Liturgy and the Minor Seminaries," made a number of very pertinent suggestions on the question of what needed to be done if the seminarians were to receive a genuine beginning in their training as minister of Christ. Hellriegel sets down as the first requirement liturgically formed teachers, more specifically, men who are filled with a living awareness of the sacramental character of their own priesthood and who sustain their priestly Christian lives by daily meditation on the missal, breviary and ritual. The seminarians should be given a solid intellectual foundation through a study of scripture and the Mass. Attention should be given to liturgical correctness in the construction of chapels. The altar should dominate the interior of the chapel and not simply be the platform for displaying devotional objects. Another necessity was a living of the liturgical year. Charismatic celebrations of the mysteries celebrated on various feast days should be preceded by preparation through study of the meaning of the feast, mystery plays or dramatizations of the scripture readings, use of film when appropriate. Attention should be given to the Sunday as the Lord's Day and the eve of Sundays and feast days should be devoted to their preparation. Opportunity should be provided for full congregational participation in the Mass and the various blessings of the Roman ritual should be used at the prescribed times.[36] The preface to the outline of the address in the *National Catholic Educational Association Bulletin* referred to it as "brillant" and described Father Hellriegel as an "internationally known figure in the Liturgical Movement."[37]

In addition to reaching people through the spoken word of his many lectures and through the written word of his vast correspondence and his several contributions to *Orate Fratres*, Hellriegel also penned occasional articles for such publications as the *Midweek Herald*, the *Fortnightly Review* and *Acolyte*. One of these articles appeared anonymously in the August 10, 1929, issue of *Acolyte*, a magazine addressed chiefly to priests. After an introduction insuring that the readers were aware of the real meaning of liturgy, the unknown author (Father Hellriegel) pointed out to his fellow priests the incongruity between the words they were addressing to the faithful during their Eucharistic Sacrifice and what was taking place in the pew and choir loft.

> Reverend Fathers, allow me to exaggerate a little, in order to bring out my point. (a) After the Offertory we turn to the people and ask them: "Orate fratres, ut meum ac vestrum sacrificium, etc." (Pray, Brethren, that my sacrifice and yours may be acceptable to God.) But the "brethren" without looking up, continue in their May devotion. (b) After Consecration we say: "Unde... nos servi tui sed et plebs tua sancta offerimus" (Wherefore, O Lord, we Thy servants, and likewise Thy holy people... offer).
>
> But the "holy people" is busily engaged in another Novena to the Little Flower. At the same time the choir in the loft is trying to sing "Mother dear, O pray for me." Three distinct things during *one great Sacrifice*, the *common Sacrifice* of all, the sun and center of our Catholic life! — The attitude and conduct of many of the faithful at Mass has little relation to the action that goes on before their eyes.[38]

Hellriegel went on to make explicit the point he had illustrated above. The faithful were missing something of the redeeming presence of Christ if they were not opening their minds and hearts to his action in their midst. He further strengthened his position by citing the teachings of Popes Pius X, Benedict XV, and Pius XI. He points out that the liturgical movement was concerned with a renewal of the whole of Christian life by bringing Christian people to the "primary and indispensable source of the true Christian spirit" (Pope Pius X). The priest, as the one ordained to be a minister of Christ and a dispenser of the divine mysteries, is one who is by virtue of that ordination already centered in the "liturgoi of God." The priest must strive to bring his own spiritual life into line with his own inner reality and then to lead the faithful, who share in priestly consecration, to the same realization.[39]

The article was a strong one. The illustration of the inappropriateness of May devotions and Marian hymns during the Mass must have struck home to readers who would be just a few weeks away from the beginning of the month of May and probably planning May devotions for their parishes. Virgil Michel wrote to Hellriegel that his article had made "an immense hit.... [It] was in the right place."[40] Michel was so impressed with the article that he wrote to Father Michael Chapman, the editor of *Acolyte* for permission to reprint it, again anonymously. It was published by Liturgical Press as the first chapter in a small booklet entitled simply *The Liturgical Movement*. Chapters two and three were also reprints: Chapter two from an article written by Michel for the National Catholic Welfare Conference and dealing with the significance of the liturgical movement and chapter three another reprint of Hellriegel's talk at the first Liturgical Day at St. John's giving survey of the movement.[41]

Not all of Hellriegel's writings were of an explanatory or exhortative nature. He not only enlightened and encouraged his readers and listeners; he also provided them with the necessary tools to carry out his recommendations. He continued his earlier practice of putting together booklets that would aid a congregation in liturgical prayer. By 1929, Hellriegel's pamphlet giving a guide for a liturgical holy hour, *Vigilate et Orate*, had gone through two editions and was in its third.[42] The booklet *Good Friday*, providing for congregational participation on that day, was also becoming widely used.[43] To aid the faithful in a preparation for the great feasts of Christmas and Pentecost, Hellriegel put together booklets of liturgical prayer. These combined appropriate readings and prayers and hymns from scripture, the missal and the breviary in a manner that would foster sound piety and be suitable for use in a parish. Both the Christmas novena booklet, *Maranatha Jesu*, and novena for Pentecost, *Veni Creator Spiritus*, proved to be of great help to those who were attempting to encourage liturgical prayer.

As a complement to his earlier booklet, *The Holy Sacrifice of the Mass*, a dialogue Mass booklet, Hellriegel in 1930 put out a booklet designed for congregational participation in the high Mass. It was entitled simply *Our High Mass* and was published by the Queen's Work. Gregorian chant melodies or simple syllabic melodies are presented in modern musical notation so as to be more understandable to the congregation not familiar with the more esoteric square shaped notes. English translation was provided under the Latin text so that the song of the congregation could be for them an intelligent prayer. The prayers of the ordinary of the Mass were printed in English so that the congregation could pray along with the priest throughout the whole Mass.

A musical experiment of a few years before *Our High Mass* was a sung Mass composed in English in honor of Pope Pius X in 1926. At the time Hellriegel wrote the Mass he had little hope of seeing the day when it could be actually used at a sung Mass but did feel confident that the time would come sooner or later and wanted to see how a sung Mass in English might sound. In 1965 the Mass was given an "imprimatur" by Cardinal Ritter and was published and distributed by Pio Decimo Press. Father Hellriegel's dreams had been surpassed.

Art, as well as music, that would be fitting for the worship of God was also the focus of Hellriegel's efforts. He gave a "good bit of (his) time" to Gottfried Schiller, the artist from Germany who was commissioned to do the frescoing in the new chapel at the Precious Blood Motherhouse.[44] Father Hellriegel and Mr. Schiller worked together again in 1935 to do illustrations for Virgil Michel's new catechetical series, the Christ-Life. An even more momentous task in which Hellriegel was involved was the designing of the windows for the Junior Seminary in Kansas City. The windows dealt with the themes of vocation, seminary life, ordination, and finally the life, work and death of the priest.[45] In this project, Father Hellriegel worked in conjunction with Mr. Emil Frei, a specialist in stained glass work.

In addition to his contributions to liturgical art and music and literature, Hellriegel assumed the extra responsibility of parish administration on four different occasions between 1925 and 1935. Three times he had charge of Assumption Parish in O'Fallon just across the street from the motherhouse and once his duties extended to the neighboring parish, St. Paul's. The various lengths of his administrations lasted from two weeks to five months and together totalled nearly a year. Hellriegel was also a frequent guest speaker at parishes throughout the St. Louis Archdiocese for such occasions as the closing of Forty Hours' Devotion.

In spite of the many demands on Father Hellriegel's time and attention, his first concern was always the sisters under his care at O'Fallon and his duties as their chaplain. Priority was given not only to the formal classes he held with the sisters and the scheduled liturgical events but also the meeting of the needs of individual sisters. Father Hellriegel always tried to find some means to bring his message to the sisters no matter what personal inconvenience might be involved. For example, some of the older sisters did not understand English very well. In order that they not miss the message of the homily of the Mass, he would meet with them in the evening and give them in German the homily which he intended to give to the other sisters in English on the next morning.[46]

It was during Father Hellriegel's chaplaincy at O'Fallon that the status of the Precious Blood order was changed from diocesan to papal. To achieve this change, Father Hellriegel made several trips to Rome on behalf of the sisters. Hellriegel reworked the rites of investiture and profession to bring them to a less emotional and more solidly liturgical basis.[47] He also helped the sisters to see that the most solemn and elaborate ceremony should accompany the taking of final vows and not the reception of the habit and the beginning of the novitiate as had been the case when he first came to O'Fallon.[48]

For the sister's first profession he restored the Rite of Consecration of Virgins from the Pontifical, but, with the help of Maria Laach, reworked it into an abbreviated and simplified form. The text was approved by Archbishop Glennon in 1936 and consititutes one of the oldest adaptations of the rite. The rite emphasizes the action of Christ drawing the sister more deeply into the life of His Church.[49] Christ, through His Church, issues the call. The candidate for profession gives the response. The oblation of the religious takes place as a part of the great oblation of the Mass.[50] Through the revised rite for the consecration of virgins, the sisters were expressing in their taking of their religious vows the orientation of their lives toward living at the center of the Church and toward a full participation in the prayer of the Church. The perfecting of this ceremony involved for Father Hellriegel two years of research and writing and corresponding with Maria Laach and resulted in the Sisters of the Precious Blood gearing their profession ceremony in a direction toward which most other communities would come only after another twenty-five years.

Father Hellriegel was also available for private interviews, not only for the sisters stationed at the motherhouse at a given time but also for the sisters stationed at any of the thirty-two convents in the area. Many did come to consult him on both spiritual and pedagogical matters, or, if they could not come in person, would ask for advice by mail.[51]

Father Hellriegel's spirit of generosity was contagious, and the liturgical prayer into which he had immersed the sisters was bearing the fruit he had predicted it would bear in his *True Basis of Christian Solidarity*. At the beginning of January in 1938, Father Hellriegel wrote to his good friend at St. John's Abbey:

> We had a very fine Christmas. I have never seen the liturgy so fruitful and active in souls as in this Advent and Christmas. The spirit of charity and mutual respect, the cheerfulness in work and corporate cooperation, the thought that was given to the poor and negroes were outstanding.[52]

Father Hellriegel was himself in the forefront of efforts to aid those in need. It was during these years at O'Fallon that Hellriegel first made the acquaintance of Peter Maurin and Dorothy Day of the Catholic Worker movement. He had exchanged visits and ideas with both of them and had come to see the intrinsic relationship between his work and theirs. He gave them support, both moral and financial. When the Catholic Worker first opened its doors in St. Louis in the late 1930's, it was Hellriegel who paid their first month's rent.[53]

In June of 1940 came the end of Father Hellriegel's twenty-two years as chaplain at the Precious Blood Motherhouse in O'Fallon, Missouri. In his farewell speech Father Hellriegel urged the sisters to treasure the gifts they had been given by God, namely, "a deep Eucharistic Life, the Divine Office, and the Spirit of Holy Fellowship."[54]

In announcing his change from O'Fallon, the editor of *Orate Fratres* comments, "What Klosterneuberg has been to Austria and German-speaking countries, that O'Fallon, Missouri, has to a large extent come to be in America."[55] Yet, at his new assignment as pastor of Holy Cross in St. Louis, Father Hellriegel would come to demonstrate the truth of those words in a stronger way than he had at O'Fallon. For many, who saw the great liturgical spirit and life which he had brought about among the sisters, still doubted the practically of his program at the parish level. Those doubts were soon to be dispelled.

CHAPTER EIGHT

Liturgical Life at Holy Cross

I n June of 1940, Martin Hellriegel was installed as the pastor of Holy Cross Parish in St. Louis. Along with his new pastorate came his elevation to the rank of monsignor. He was to hold this position for an even longer time than he had been chaplain at O'Fallon. It was here at Holy Cross that he proved to the world that liturgical vibrance at the parish level was more than a fantasy. It was here that the critics who saw his liturgical program as impractical for parish participation were proven wrong.

By 1940 the liturgical movement was flourishing in many centers in both the United States and Europe. In absolute numbers, those who were interested in applying the teaching of Pope Pius X were increasing rapidly. Yet in terms of percentage only a very few in the Church had any knowledge of or contact with the liturgical movement. There had been encouragement from the institutional Church; Pope Pius XI had issued a statement calling for renewal of liturgical prayer and of the Gregorian chant in 1928. Yet even on the level of official church leadership, much still remained to be done. Pope Pius XII had not yet written his two encyclicals, *Mystici Corporis* and *Mediator Dei*, that were to have great positive influence on the liturgical apostolate. The encouragement of more frequent participation in the Mass and communion through the permission of evening Masses and less rigid fasting requirements were more than a decade off, as was the reformed Holy Week liturgy. And, a final statement against public recitation of the rosary during Mass did not come until 1960.[1]

In the United States, the request for Gregorian chant by the Council of Baltimore was mostly unheeded. No follow-up at all had been made on John Carroll's ideas on the vernacular. Bishop England's initiative on the missal had been carried on by such new translations as the St. Andrew's missal, but usuage was not yet extensive. *Orate Fratres* was a big help but had a limited circulation. The liturgical weeks had not yet begun.

At the local level, Archbishop Glennon remained supportive of the liturgical apostolate and had aided its progress by initiating such things as the Diocesan Commission on Sacred Music, the Liturgical Seminar for priests, and various lectures for the priests of the diocese. The election of Hellriegel to the rank of Monsignor was a sign of personal support. Yet, among the local priests many were suspicious of the liturgical apostolate and had little regard for it.

Holy Cross Parish was really no exception to the general atmosphere that existed in the Church as a whole and in the archdiocese of St. Louis. Holy Cross was a predominantly German parish located at the northern edge of the city in an area called Baden, named after an area in southern Germany near Monsignor Hellriegel's native home. The parish began in 1864 with thirty-five families — three French, fifteen Irish, and seventeen German. By 1872 there were one hundred twenty families in the parish — eighty Irish and forty German. The priests appointed to the parish were German; tensions arose and the Irish families withdrew to begin a new parish, Mount Carmel. Holy Cross became a German national parish and still retained that status at the time Monsignor Hellriegel became its pastor. It was made a territorial parish only in 1947.

The people of Holy Cross were not well to do and the parish had a tremendous financial struggle, but the people persisted and the parish did grow. By 1908 a new Church was needed. The one that was built at that time is the one in which Monsignor Hellriegel celebrated the liturgy during his many years of service as pastor of the parish. It is a modest church with a seating capacity of about 600. It is a Gothic church in thirteenth century motif. The design is simple; it is devoid of useless ornamentation. Its most outstanding feature is the very high tower which can be seen throughout the surrounding territory. It often had the effect of attracting those who were in need of some free food to the rectory door; all such persons were welcomed by Monsignor Hellriegel.[2]

By 1940 Holy Cross parish had about four hundred forty families, about two-thirds of whom lived in the city and about one-third of whom lived in the outlying rural areas.[3] The parish had been blessed with zealous priests and devoted people. Archbishop Glennon had told Monsignor Hellriegel at the time of his appointment, "You will find there a good soil for your liturgical endeavors."[4] Yet a good soil is not the same thing as the beginning of a crop or even a sown seed. There was really not even a beginning of liturgical renewal at Holy Cross when Monsignor Hellriegel went there. One parishioner told him shortly after his arrival, ". . . you will not find six Daily Missals in use in our parish." As another indicator, the choir was completely unfamiliar with Gregorian chant, and there was no congregational singing during Mass.[5]

The parish setting into which Monsignor Hellriegel came in 1940 was, then, a fairly typical one. Yet he came with a very atypical background, one that had been formed by an unusual home and parish experience as a child, fortunate early experiences with Father Hoehn and as an assistant at St. Peter's Parish in St. Charles, and an extraordinary amount of theological and liturgical study and practice and leadership during his years of chaplaincy at O'Fallon.

On June 30, 1940, this man of unusual talent and competence in theological and liturgical understanding and practice, of highly developed sensitivty to people, of proven generosity in giving to others, of uncanny ability in communicating with others was installed as pastor in a very ordinary parish of German working class people. No longer was he in a setting in which all who were present were dedicating their lives to the service of the Church. Here at Holy Cross many other concerns crowded the minds of his people. The nation was just pulling itself out of its greatest depression. The working class people did not have great resources on which to draw, either intellectual or financial. Most of the people of the parish had not finished high school; making ends meet on a laborer's salary was a daily concern. Would a life centered around the liturgy of the Church have any appeal for the members of Holy Cross parish? Would they have time to give to a full liturgical life, even if they had the good will? Would this new pastor, who had been working in such a different setting and who was known throughout the world for his liturgical leadership really be able to carry out his own ideas in this setting?

Monsignor Hellriegel came to Holy Cross Parish with an explicit philosophy of what the parish should be and how he hoped to approach his new ministry. Fundamental to his philosophy of the parish is the concept of the parish as the Mystical Body of Christ, in miniature but none the less real. As the Mystical Body, the parish has for its center and greatest concern the celebration of Eucharist.[6] The Eucharist was seen by Monsignor Hellriegel according to the vision of Pope Pius X as the primacy and indispensable source of the true Christian spirit; therefore, foremost among his pastoral goals would have to be promotion of that active participation in the liturgy which would enable his parish to live out its real inner identity as the Mystical Body of Christ and thereby experience the true spirit of Christ. Through this active participation in the Eucharist each member of the parish could come to experience his own inner being as a member of the body of Christ.

This active participation, as a participation in something sacred, must be carried out with great reverence. As Monsignor Hellriegel put it, "Do holy things in a holy way." Or again, "God's things must be done in God's way."[7] This sacred approach must extend to all the details of the liturgical celebration: gesture and diction, church and altar, minister and server. All the externals that are connected with each of these must be approached with care and reverence. The setting of the proper atmosphere is important in the spirit with which worship is carried out.[8]

The parish itself should, in the philosophy with which Monsignor Hellriegel approached Holy Cross, be the primary society or organization, taking precedence over any societies or organizations within the parish. The Eucharist should be the primary parish activity, having priority over any other parish function. Next in significance as a center of parish activities should be the family; the life of the parish should strengthen family ties rather than put demands on the members of the family that pull them away from one another. It is only after the greater significance of the parish as a whole and the family are given proper recognition, that the role of organization within the parish can be discerned. These organizations do have a part to play in the parish, but their role is not primarily as a social outlet or as a fund-rasising agency; rather parish organizations are to contribute to the central purpose of the parish, the living out of who it is, the concretizing of the Mystical Body of Christ. Parish organizations can contribute to this task of making the parish be more perfectly what it is by assuming a role of leadership in the worship and Christian work of the people of the parish. It is to this end that parish organizations ought to be oriented primarily according to the viewpoint of Monsignor Hellriegel.[9] The function of providing reasonable recreation together is also appropriate but secondary.

The pastor, of course, would have the key responsibility in the setting of the direction in which parish efforts and activities would be directed. In order that the pastor may be effective in leading his parish to live out its identity as the Mystical Body of Christ, the pastor needs to be aware that he is called upon to be as Christ was, a shepherd to his flock, a head towards his members, a man consecrated to the service of the people of his parish. The pastor carries out his task by instructing his flock; by praying with them and for them, especially in and through the Eucharist; by visiting their homes and fostering unity among their families; by ministering to those who are suffering from spiritual or physical sickness; all this brings to them the many blessings God has in store for them. The pastor also has the ultimate responsibility for the parish school and for the education of its children. Monsignor Hellriegel saw in the parish school a valuable opportunity to develop within the children a sense of thinking and living as members of the Church. He felt that religion lessons should be structured around the Church year and that the missal and the Bible should be used along with the catechism for the instruction of the school children.[10] These then were the basic ideas in regard to parish life that the new pastor brought with him to Holy Cross Parish that summer of 1940.

He also brought with him a realistic understanding of human nature and a good measure of prudence. His first six weeks were spent getting acquainted with the people of the parish, their neighborhood, their parish customs. Monsignor Hellriegel had the wisdom to know that he could not sow his seed without first tilling the soil. Parish life was left pretty much unchanged in the period immediately after his installation as pastor.

However, he did proceed to introduce one new custom the Sunday after his installation. It had been the custom to omit the Sunday sermon during the summer months. The new pastor felt that this deprivation of an explanation for the people of the Word of God was not justifiable; therefore, he began immediately to preach ten-minute homilies to the people during Sunday Mass.[11] This move also allowed the people to get some idea of what their new pastor was like. They quickly saw him as some one who could unfold for them the riches of the message of the scripture.

The short Sunday homily also provided an opportunity for Monsignor Hellriegel to do a little "cultivating of the soil" in which he soon hoped to plant the seeds of liturgical renewal. He spoke to his congregation of the message of the readings of the Sunday and related that message to key concepts of their unity as members of the Mystical Body of Christ, the holy Eucharist as their main source of holiness and unity with Christ, the Mass as the sacrifice which they offered together with one another and with Christ as members of the family of God. He began to prepare the people for an intelligent use of the missal and encouraged them in the frequent reception of holy communion.[12]

The people of Holy Cross were soon impressed by their new pastor, both as a person and as a spiritual leader. One parishioner reminisced many years later,

> I remember my first reaction was that here was a real priest —he was tall, and sort of stately, and he did things around the altar like they were the most important things in the world.[13]

The impression was not short lived, for after many years that same parishoner could still say,

> Even today, if you listen to him celebrating the Mass, you'll get the sensation that when he says "*Gloria in excelsis Deo*"

he's saying it with all the enthusiasm and wonderment of a person proclaiming the words for the very first time.[14]

Monsignor Hellriegel's obvious deep conviction and his joyous enthusiasm would be key factors in contributing to the contagion of his love for the liturgy.

After six weeks in his new post, Monsignor Hellriegel made his first attempt to lead his parishioners further into involvement with the official prayer and ritual of the Church. On the Sunday before the feast of the Assumption, he explained to his people that he would like to have for them on that feast the thousand year-old blessing for herbs and seeds and new fruits, the one he himself had experienced in his boyhood home parish. He further explained that the use of this sacramental and of the many sacramentals of the Church were means by which the blessings of the liturgical celebrations would be brought to touch the home and the fields, the ordinary things of daily life. Most of the parishioners who lived in the rural areas and even many of the city parishioners brought boxes of herbs and fruits for the blessing. The prayer of blessing asked that the herbs and fruits may have, in addition to their natural power, an endowment of a special grace from God.[15] A few of the parishioners were confused by the ceremony and told their pastor that this blessing was Polish. Monsignor Hellriegel helped them overcome their confusion by pointing that the blessing was a Catholic one which had reached "the Poles, the Italians, the Germans, and the French, but it hasn't reached us yet!"[16]

With the beginning of the school year in September of 1940, Monsignor Hellriegel began an all-out effort to introduce liturgical participation into his parish. He started with working with the children in the parish school. He himself went into the school and spoke to the children of their membership in the body of Christ and of the Eucharistic sacrifice as their praise of the Father and their way of living their unity with Christ. He spoke to them of the meaning of the Church year, of the reality of the presence of the saving events of the life, death and resurrection of Christ in their midst as these deeds are celebrated in the liturgy and of their opportunity to take part in these deeds of salvation and praise by their interior and exterior participation. He helped the teachers work out lesson plans for the days he could not be with a specific class.

He soon initiated the dialog Mass for the school children. The children were attending daily Mass at 8:00 a.m. Monsignor Hellriegel gave a daily homily of about eight minutes, usually before Mass and as a follow-up to the religious lesson of the previous day which had been used, at least in part, to prepare the children for the Mass of the next day. For use in the dialog Mass the parish had purchased the booklet, *Missa Recitata*, edited by Father William Puetter, one of the Jesuits, who as a young man used to accompany Gerald Ellard on visits to O'Fallon. The children learned to pray in Latin the prayers at the foot of the altar, the *Kyrie, Gloria, Sanctus, Agnus Dei*, and responses. The children were taught to pray in a natural tone and to avoid sing-song and monotone manners. During the first week the third through the eighth grades received instruction on the prayers and practiced the correct Latin pronunciation as a class. During the second week of school the children practiced together. After ten school days, the children were ready to pray their first dialog Mass. By October they had also learned the *Credo*. By November the first and second grades could join in just from listening to the older children. The daily homily continued to call to the children's minds the significance of their communal prayer. Ninety-six percent of the children in the school were present and on time for the 8:00 a.m. Mass each morning during that 1940-41 school year.[17]

As soon as the work on the dialog Mass was completed, plans were begun for the training of lectors. Boys were trained to read in English the proper of the Mass, including the scripture readings, the prayers, and the antiphons. They read these from the front of the Church over a loud speaker while the celebrant prayed them in Latin. The next addition to congregational participation was the recitation in English of prayers of the offertory of the Mass.

Also in October, plans were begun to introduce participation in the sung Mass to the children. A boys' schola was formed of about twenty participants. They concentrated on learning to sing the propers of the Mass. Simultaneously, an effort was made to teach all the children to sing the ordinary of the Mass. "Our High Mass" was begun in October; by Advent the children were learning the "Ferial Mass" and in Lent they learned the *Lux et*

Origo, the Mass for Paschal time. The children learned the latter from the record put out by the monks of Solesmes. The children would first listen, then hum along, then sing along, and finally to be able to sing without the record.[18]

Not all the efforts toward liturgical participation were directed toward the children. The adults too were encouraged to become more actively involved in liturgical prayer. In work with the adults, the choir was the first group to receive encouragement and new ideas from the new pastor. They first learned to sing a single high Mass in Gregorian chant. Then Monsignor Hellriegel introduced the Solesmes record of the *Lux et Origo* to the grown-up choristers also. On Easter Sunday morning his efforts bore their first fruits. The twenty members of the adult choir alternated with the children in singing the *Lux et Origo* and *Credo I.*[19] All was not perfect, but a start had been made. The choir also found itself in a new location. Monsignor Hellriegel saw the function of the choir to be that of leading the rest of the congregation in participation in the Eucharistic prayer; they were to be a link between congregation and altar. Therefore, their appropriate place was not removed from the congregation in a loft, but at the front of the church. For this first Easter Mass, the choir sat in the front pews; later, choir stalls were put in the sanctuary.

The people who were present for the sung Eucharistic prayer were impressed by its joyous spirit. Many of the adults of the congregation began to show interest in being a part of the singing also. Monsignor Hellriegel, therefore, took the Solesmes record to the meetings of the various organizations and by Pentecost had taught the Mass to enough of the adults of the parish that the congregation was able to join with the children in alternating with the choir of adults in the singing of the *Lux et Origo.*[20] This was characteristic of a method which Hellriegel frequently used in the introduction of some new form of prayer to his people. He would thoroughly explain the why and what and how to the school children either personally or through the teachers in the school; he would then work with the parish organizations, assuring that they were well-informed and ready to assume leadership, and finally would talk to the whole parish for one or two Sundays before the introduction of the new rite or ceremony.

This thorough preparation was undertaken to be sure that there would be no empty ritual or theatrical observance but that all would be understood and entered into as a part of rendering worship to God. Also the thorough preparation assured a spirit of great reverence in the carrying out of each liturgical function. Nothing was to be last minute or unforeseen. All was well planned and prepared so that the experience of worship could be free from worrying about externals that may go wrong and could be an occasion of beauty and prayer for all.

The adults of the parish also learned the dialog Mass as well as the sung parts for several high Masses. The typical Sunday came to be two dialog Masses and two sung Masses with congregational participation in each. The sung Masses were given the greater emphasis and were celebrated a bit earlier than usual — 7:30 a.m. and 10:15 a.m. — so that it would be easier for people to receive communion at the high Mass. A large number of people came to these Masses.[21] To facilitate understanding of and participation in the Mass, Monsignor Hellriegel also encouraged his parishioners in the use of the missal. At his suggestion many were given as Christmas gifts, and by the end of his first year as pastor some three hundred daily missals were being used and a missal study club was in operation.[22] Leaflet missals were provided for those who did not have their own missals. By 1943 all the school children from grades three to eight had their own St. Andrew's daily missals.[23]

Besides the weekly and daily participation in the Eucharist, Monsignor Hellriegel led both the children and the adults of his parish into many special liturgical celebrations and paraliturgical or sacramental prayers in keeping with the spirit of special times of the year and special seasons.

One of the first of these special ceremonies, after the blessing for the feast of the Assumption, was a special Halloween party which Monsignor Hellriegel planned for his parishioners. His intent was to move his congregation away from the rather pagan "trick or treat" mentality to a real observance of the eve of All Saint's Day. In his approach to the celebration of Halloween, one of his fundamental principles, can be seen: "Step on the unworthy thing, but put something worthy in its stead!"[24]

In preparing for his new kind of Halloween celebration, Hellriegel again began with the school children. He explained to them the history and ancient meaning of the once sacred eve.

They were called upon to build and decorate in the parish hall a shrine on which relics of the saints would be placed on Halloween. They also decorated boxes with red and gold to serve as reliquaries. On the Sunday before the feast an announcement was made at the Masses inviting all the parishioners to a "true Halloween party." At 7:30 on the designated eve, about 400 people assembled in the parish hall. The singing of a hymn opened the service; this was followed by an explanation of the original meaning of halloween and the ceremony that was to follow. All present then received a burning candle. The relics that had been in the reliquaries on the shrine in the hall were now distributed to presidents of parish organizations and representatives of the sisters and classes in the school, all of whom had been prepared ahead of time. Each relic bearer was accompanied by two palm bearers. As the procession of relics and candles and palms and 400 people walked the two blocks from the parish hall to the parish church, the choir chanted the litany of the saints and all joined in the responses. In the Church some of the relics were placed on the main altar and some on special repositories that had been erected and decorated just for the event. The ceremony closed with the chanting of the Magnificat and a blessing with the relics.[25] The Halloween party became an annual event in the parish for both children and adults. Acclamations to Christ the King were added to the closing. The ceremony was joyful and festive as well as inspiring. Parishioners many years later told Monsignor Hellriegel that their children enjoyed their parish Halloween party and had no desire to go to any other kind.[26] The overwhelming success of Hellriegel's Halloween party seems to have sprung from his own deep conviction of the importance of leading his people closer to the source and wellspring of the Christian life, the altar of God, as well as from his ability to bring together his theological and historical knowledge with his great power of imagination and creativity to plan an event that would both root out the traditional Halloween parties and lead his people to a deeper spirituality. Getting everyone involved and active enhanced the interest and meaning that were experienced. Having special roles for parish leaders was also an asset.

Advent was a time during which Monsignor Hellriegel made special efforts to lead his flock closer to the spirit of the liturgical season. In talking with his people during this time, he tried to help them to go beyond the current tendency to focus exclusively on the historical coming of Christ and to enlarge their vision to an expectation of the final coming. To center the devotion of his people on the mysteries of the season, Hellriegel introduced during his first Advent at Holy Cross the Advent wreath into both the Church and the classrooms of the schools. He also encouraged parishioners to put Advent wreaths in their homes as a daily reminder to prepare themselves for that final coming of the Lord. About twenty-five homes had Advent wreaths the first year Monsignor Hellriegel introduced them.[27] Symbols such as the advent wreath were regarded by Hellriegel as important, not in themselves, but as devices to draw the faithful into the mind and spirit of the Church and into the sacred mysteries being reenacted in its liturgical year. The custom of the Advent wreath caught on and spread. Boys in the eighth grade, and later in high school youth groups, began making stands for the Advent wreaths (wooden bases on which could be placed the circle of greens and containing four holes for the candles). They would sell these after Mass on the Sunday before Advent and use the proceeds for Christmas baskets for the poor.

Monsignor Hellriegel also composed a ceremony to be held on the eve of the first Sunday of Advent in connection with the lighting of the first of the candles of the Advent wreath. It consisted of a short introduction explaining the meaning of the Church year and of the Advent wreath, prayer giving thanks for the graces of the last Church year, asking pardon for the offenses of the past year, and officially opening the new year of redemption with hymns and prayers and finally a lighting of the candle of the Advent wreath by one of the parish trustees. The prayers were all gathered from the missal and the breviary.

Ember Wednesday was another occasion of special prayer in the spirit of Advent. Monsignor Hellriegel prepared his people for its celebration by explaining in both church and school the significance of the day. The gospel of the Mass for that day told of the announcement of the Incarnation by the Angel to Mary. The Mass had traditionally been called the golden Mass in honor of the mystery it celebrated. The priest wore golden vestments in honor of God's golden gift to the human race. On his first Advent Ember Wednesday, Hellriegel introduced, after thorough explanation, a solemn celebration for the people of Holy Cross. Abundant candles were used to create the glimmer of the golden gift. In honor of God's gift to them, the people of the parish, children and adults, were each asked to bring some type of food gift, wrapped in paper and ribbon. These gifts were then given to the poor. This first Advent Ember Wednesday the people of Holy Cross brought "more than twelve baskets" of gifts.[28] This was another custom that grew and became a yearly event. In future years, the Little Sisters of the Poor were invited to join in the parish liturgical celebration and take the gifts to distribute as they saw fit. On one occasion, the parishioners gave them twenty-three bushel baskets filled with food, clothing, and money.[29] Hellriegel had again managed to bring to his people a solid form of liturgical tradition with a sense of active involvement and practical life application. This event tied together liturgical prayer with that sense of responsibility for one's neighbor, especially the neighbor in need.

Monsignor Hellriegel's major efforts in leading his congregation in prayer consisted in events like the one just described in which he added no new prayers for his people but merely brought out fully the prayers already prescribed for the feast of the day. However, as was seen in connection with the Halloween party and the Advent wreath prayer, he also saw a place for prayer related to the liturgy of the day or season and drawn from the official prayer books of the Church and from her scriptures. A prayer to which he led his congregation for a final preparation for the feast of Christmas was of this latter type. He encouraged them to pray the Christmas novena, following the booklet he had composed earlier while at O'Fallon, *Maranatha, Jesu*, a collection of hymns and readings and prayers drawn from the Old Testament prophecies and from the prayers of the breviary and missal.

The novena was held during the nine evenings before Christmas of 1940. Priests and people gathered to chant the O antiphons and the other prayers of the novena. The church was carefully adorned to reflect and instill the proper spirit in those who entered for the novena prayer. Advent violet dominated altar and lectern. Pine branches and holly sprigs formed part of the decoration. The celebrant walked in procession from the Blessed

Mother altar to the sanctuary accompanied by servers bearing torches. This was the beginning of the ceremony. Hellriegel regarded these details as having a role to play in focusing the attention of the congregation. He followed one of his favorite axioms, "Nothing is in our mind which previously has not been in our senses."[30] For nine evenings during that Advent of 1940, the church was filled. Another Holy Cross tradition had been established. Again the creative pastor had fed his people solid spiritual food in tasteful form and surroundings.

The feast of the Epiphany presented another opportunity for Monsignor Hellriegel to enrich the prayer life of his followers by introducing them to the prayer of the Roman Ritual designated for that day. Since the feast of the Epiphany usually occurred on a day when most people worked and found it difficult to attend a morning Mass, the pastor planned an evening service for his parish. He built the service around the blessings found in the Roman Ritual of gold, incense, and myrrh and the blessing for homes. The school children were asked to solicit old gold in the form of jewelry, etc. This gold was to be acculumated for several years until the parish had enough for a chalice. The chalice would then be sent to the Rural Life Conference for the benefit of a poor mission. The officers of the Orphan Society were asked to provide the myrrh as a symbol of the suffering of those for whom they were working.[31]

The evening service began with a hymn to Christ the King followed by an explanation on the meaning of the blessings that were about to take place. The gold, incense, and myrrh were blessed and carried in procession to the Crib. Benediction of the Blessed Sacrament and a blessing of the homes of the parish by the pastor from the opened front entrance of the Church concluded the ceremony. The people were left with the symbolic statement that what they had just experienced in the Church went out from there into their homes and everyday lives. This truth was brought home even more forcefully in future years when a blessing of chalk, also from the Roman Ritual, was added to the Epiphany ceremony. The people then took the blessed chalk home and inscribed over the door to their house the names of the Magi and the year with the prayer that "their intercession may obtain health of body and protection for the soul."[32]

For his first Lent in Holy Cross Parish, Monsignor Hellriegel concentrated on a renewed understanding of the meaning of Lent for his people. He explained to them, through Sunday homilies, through talks with his choirs and other parish groups, through classes in school that the main thing to be accomplished during Lent was not perseverance with extra prayers or mortifications, though these have a place, but rather a conversion of heart. This inner change would not be accomplished primarily through the efforts of man but through the work of Christ. This principal work Christ accomplishes primarily through his uniting man to Himself in the Lenten Mass.

Therefore, Monsignor Hellriegel tried, within the limits of the Church law of 1941, to schedule Masses when the people of the parish could come to them. He also used the propers for the Lenten Masses rather than the propers of feastdays that happened to occur during Lent. In this way he was exposing his congregation to the special message and grace proper to the season, thereby facilitating that meeting with Christ through which hearts could be changed.

To help his congregation understand and receive more fully the message of the daily Lenten Mass, Monsignor Hellriegel explained to them something of the history of the stational churches and their influence on the propers of the Lenten Masses. Each classroom was furnished with a map of the stational Churches and one was provided for the vestibule of the Church. The whole parish adopted for its Lenten goal growth in Christ through the leadership and prayers of the respective stational saints in a spirit of fellowship with one another.

The children's daily Mass was a high Mass preceded by a stational procession carrying the relic of the stational saint, a banner card announcing the station, and lighted candles. The litany of the saints was chanted during the procession. Different children took part each day. A daily homily was a part of the liturgical celebration. The children were active, through the singing of the Mass, participation in its prayers and in the procession when their time came. They were made knowledgeable regarding what they were doing and why they were doing it through daily religion lessons and homilies. There was much to stimulate their sense of sight and hearing and thereby to keep their attention focused on the prayer of the liturgy and its inner meaning. Monsignor Hellriegel combined his skill as a teacher with his knowledge and experience of the Lenten liturgy to successfully lead his congregation deeper into the Lenten prayer of the Church and into the real meaning of Lent.[33]

Those who found attendance at daily Mass during Lent impossible or too difficult were not forgotten. Lenten evening services were also planned for the parish. In planning these services, Monsignor Hellriegel reserved the stations of the cross for the last two weeks of Lent, the time of passiontide which was specifically dedicated to meditation on the passion of Christ. During the first four weeks Monsignor Hellriegel constructed his evening services to lead those who attended them to a renewal of their Christian lives. He combined appropriate hymns with scriptural readings from the Lenten Masses, instruction on the sacraments through which one is initiated into Christian life, baptism and confirmation, as well as instruction leading his people to a deeper understanding of the Eucharist and of the sacrament of Penance. The penitential psalms provided the basis for the common prayer of the group.[34] After six years of use of his program in his parish, Monsignor Hellriegel put the program into a booklet entitled *Parce Domine*.[35] It was an evening Lenten service designed to lead those who could not attend daily Lenten Mass into contact with the liturgy of the season so that they too could open themselves to the message and grace which would bring about an inner renewal and conversion.[36]

In succeeding years a number of pre-Lenten activities were included as a part of the parish program to bring more vividly to the minds of the people the uniqueness of the season of Lent in the Church year.

The first of these was aimed at helping the people of the parish to be aware that Lent was a season of repentance rather than of festivity, and, therefore, the Church did not use the joyful term "Alleluia" during Lent or pre-Lent. To make this realization more concrete, the "Alleluia" was "buried" on the Saturday before Septuagesima Sunday. After the Mass on that day, a large red and gold Alleluia sign was carried in procession to the accompaniment of a sung "Alleluia" and the "Laudate" to the Blessed Mother altar. Here it would remain until the people would recover it with purified minds and hearts in the Easter Vigil ceremony.[37]

Another custom, which was not a liturgical one but which did aim at the realization of the liturgical season about to begin, was the Austrian folk tradition called "Fasching Sonntage." It consisted of a dramatization and a feast held on Quinquagesima Sunday.

The "Fasching Sontag," literally feasting Sunday, was a day of family fun. Schnitzelbank, a sausage, and sauerkraut formed the main course of the dinner served in the parish hall. Good German beer was the accompanying beverage. A schnitzelbank board with pictures of the pig from which the sausage was made and various people in German folk costumes was hung in the hall in a place visible to all. Various members of the parish would take the roles of the characters on the schnitzelbank board. Everyone would join in the singing and in dancing the polka. It was a good time for all and was a final feast before the Lenten fast of forty days. The celebration, by way of contrast, made the realization of what was involved in Lenten fasting more vivid.[38]

The practical significance of Lent for the children was made more concrete by encouraging them to write down their Lenten resolution or resolutions, but no more than three, on the Tuesday before Ash Wednesday. The resolutions would be read by no one but were put in a box, covered with violet, and placed on the altar during the offertory of the Mass on Ash Wednesday when representatives of each class brought their class resolutions to the communion table and handed them to the server. The resolutions were kept tied in the boxes all during Lent and on Easter Saturday were burned in the new fire. Periodically during Lent they were asked to examine themselves on how well they were doing and to renew their resolutions so that they were fulfilled promises given at the Easter vigil.

On the afternoon of the Tuesday before Ash Wednesday the children of the school gathered in the school yard to burn the palms of the previous year and thereby make the ashes to be used the next day. This was a simple step but one that was effective in getting the children involved in the spirit of Lent. After the burning, each child was given a candy bar; the suggestion was made that it could be their last until Easter.[39]

Each of these activities was a small way of leading the people to a closer contact with the real meaning of the liturgy; they were imaginative ways of moving from the concrete experience to the spiritual meaning, keeping in mind the principle of nothing getting through to the understanding without going through the senses.

When Holy Week of 1941 came, Monsignor Hellriegel was determined that the rich as well as beautiful liturgy of that week should not be occasions to which a handful of faithful but bewildered parishioners came to pursue their private prayer. Father Hellriegel made use of some of his Lenten sermons to explain the meaning of the final days of Holy Week and the significance of the liturgy for those days. Beginning with Palm Sunday, he made every effort to lead his parishioners into a real living of the realities that would be mystically reenacted during the week to come.

On Palm Sunday he helped his people to enter into the triumphant spirit of the day by decorating the outside of the main door of the church with a purple drape and palms. Over the door he painted a large sign with gold letters on a red background indicating that Christ was being hailed as the triumphant king. The specialness of the day was immediately evident; an atmosphere of expectancy had seen set. A group of boys from the schola learned the *Pueri Hebraeorum* and the whole congregation joined in singing the responses and the processional songs.[40] The procession with blessed palms and the reading of the passion account in the vernacular with the celebrant, readers, and the congregation all taking various parts were further steps toward greater participation by the people in the prayer of the Church.

On Wednesday, Thursday, and Friday evenings of Holy Week, the entire parish was invited to join in a shortened form of Tenebrae. An explanation preceded each nocturn. The congregation, along with the choir, chanted the psalms and lamentations in English; between seven and nine hundred people took part in the hour-long service.[41] By the following year the pastor had published a booklet, *Deo Volente*, for a condensed Tenebrae service, modeled on the one his parishioners had experienced the previous year.[42]

Holy Thursday Mass had to be held in the morning, but Monsignor Hellriegel still tried to make the prayer of the Church on this important day available to as many of the people of his parish as possible. For his first two years at Holy Cross he celebrated the High Mass at 8:00 a.m. Since this hour proved to be too late for working people, he moved the High Mass to 5:50 a.m. in 1943. The result was an eight-fold increase in the number of participants.[43] This reenactment of the Lord's Supper was celebrated with full congregational participation and with the celebrant facing the people.[44] Thus on the day on which Christ's giving of his Eucharistic gift to his people was being celebrated and relived, the people had the unusual opportunity to see more clearly the symbolic actions through which they were taken into the prayer of Christ. Thus, Monsignor Hellriegel had not only creativity and deep personal understanding of the liturgy and love for the liturgy; he also had the courage to try new modes of liturgical celebrations when he was convinced that they would lead his people into deeper liturgical prayer and when there was no existing prohibition.

Monsignor Hellriegel was also willing to sacrifice his own comfort and convenience if it meant bringing his people closer to the font of the true Christian spirit. On Good Friday he celebrated the Mass of the pre-Sanctified for his people during the hours of twelve until three, even though this meant that he had to fast from all food and even from water from midnight the previous night until after the liturgical celebration. However, he was willing to pay this price for the sake of offering to his people a greater prayer on this holy day. He felt that the previous custom of having the Mass of the Presanctified for a handful of people early in the morning and a *Tre Ore* service between twelve and three, when many more people came, was to feed the greater part of the flock with the prayer of man rather than with the prayer of Christ and thus deprived them of the opportunity of entering fully into the mystery of the day. The liturgical celebration combined learning and praying and doing. Explanations were given before each part of the service; translation of the Latin text and congregational participation were provided for by the use of the Good Friday booklet which Hellriegel had arranged while he was at O'Fallon. All present were given the opportunity to venerate the cross.[45]

The night vigil from Holy Thursday evening to Good Friday morning was also a target for the efforts of the pastor. On Holy Thursday evening he invited twelve men of the parish to the rectory for supper and himself served them. From 11:30 p.m. to 12:30 a.m. he scheduled a parish holy hour during which the priestly prayer of Christ was read and the feet of the twelve men were washed by the pastor. Four hundred people participated in the holy hour and some stayed to pray throughout the night.[46] The pastor had shown his people through his own example as well as through the word of the scripture what Christ had done and said on this night. Hellriegel did not spare himself in his work of leading his people into the meaning of the liturgy of the day.

The people of Holy Cross were encouraged to participate in the full liturgy of Holy Saturday. Monsignor Hellriegel was careful not to avoid any suggestions that the ceremonies before Mass were a sort of an optional extra that one could easily miss as long as he arrived in church by the time the Mass started. Rather he took care that his people understood the deep significance and saving power of the new fire and of the blessed water of the baptismal font. Again he took advantage of Lenten sermons and worked with his choirs to prepare for congregational participation and understanding. The school children were involved in decorating an urn for the new fire and baptismal font with greens and flowers. Twelve of the older boys were trained to read the lessons in English as the celebrant read them in Latin. An adult who had been taking instructions in preparation for converting to Catholicism was prepared for baptism during the Easter vigil liturgy. When the day came, the faithful were provided with a text for the service. They gathered around the urn to witness the blessing of the new fire and take part in the prayers. The lessons were proclaimed for all to hear and reflect upon. The blessing of the baptismal font took place in front of the church and was followed by the baptism of the new convert who was robed in a white tunic. All present participated in this baptism by praying the *Pater Noster* and the *Credo* with the newly baptized and by renewing their own baptismal promises. This renewal climaxed the word of renewal of heart which had been undertaken at the beginning of Lent; it was the final step before the experiencing of the new life of the risen Christ.[47] The faithful were invited to take some of the blessed water into their homes as a sign that the revitalization of Easter was also coming into their family lives.[48]

Monsignor Hellriegel's first Easter at Holy Cross Parish was one in which he was able to lead his congregation to an experience of the joy of the risen Christ. The day's celebration began at 6:00 a.m. on a beautiful Easter morning. The people assembled at the empty tomb, a structure built for the day for the purpose of bringing the truth being celebrated and made present to a greater aliveness in the minds of the people. A chanted service began here and continued into the church for the high Mass, the *Lux et Origo* Paschal Mass. Twenty-five children who were to make their first communion carried candles which had been lighted from the Paschal Candle. These children were grouped in a semicircle around the altar throughout the Mass. They joined in the singing of the responses and carried the altar breads in procession at the offertory of the Mass. After the Mass, the first communicants, along with their parents and godparents, were invited to the parish hall for an agape.

The Eucharistic celebration closed with the blessing of the lamb (or meat) and eggs and bread, the same blessing from the Roman Ritual which had been used in Monsignor Hellriegel's boyhood parish in Heppenheim and which he himself had used at O'Fallon.[49] The people of Holy Cross were to take their blessed food home and have an Easter agape for their own families. Their pastor gave them some helpful suggestions as to how to go about planning a family Easter agape. He recommended a large adorned candle as the symbol of the risen Christ for the centerpiece and a small candle to be lit from the large one for each person's place. The meal could open with the singing of an Easter hymn followed by the scripture reading of the account of Jesus meeting his two disciples on the road to Emmaus. After the meal of the blessed food the family could conclude with the postcommunion prayer from the Easter Sunday Mass and an Easter hymn. Again Monsignor Hellriegel was showing his people how to let the blessing from the altar flow into their homes.[50]

Monsignor Hellriegel was careful not to let Easter Week be a spiritual desert land for his people. Having led them to the wealth of the liturgy during Lent and Holy Week and Easter, he wanted them to continue to share in the full blessings of the liturgical celebrations of the whole Easter season. Therefore, a daily high Mass was celebrated in the parish, with the first communicants wearing their white garments and taking their privileged places in a semicircle around the altar.[51] The significance of full participation in the liturgy was surely brought home to these youngsters through the ceremony that surrounded the week.

When the rogation days came, the parish saw another first. Monsignor Hellriegel delved into the Roman Ritual and found for his people the prescribed service for a procession and blessing of the fields on the rogation days. The people were not only grateful for this sacramental exercised in their behalf. One woman even brought to Church a box of ground to receive the blessing; she intended to strew the blessed ground over her fields.[52]

Another "regular" begun during Monsignor Hellriegel's first year of his pastorate at Holy Cross was the Sunday evening service. The service most often consisted of Compline, chanted in English. Special seasonal services were planned for Advent and Lent and the rosary was the prayer for October. For the Sunday evening service about one-hundred fifty to two-hundred people would gather.[53]

By the end of the second year of his pastorate at Holy Cross, Monsignor Hellriegel had introduced his people to the fullness of liturgical celebration for the various feasts and seasons of the year. He made use of the whole of the Roman missal and breviary and ritual, bringing to his people many forms of prayer which were virtually unknown to the lay Catholic of the United States. He carefully prepared his people through commentary on the inner meaning of the words and gestures they part in; he drew them through his own deep conviction of the value of the prayer forms to which he invited his flock. Monsignor Hellriegel conducted each service with such beauty and faith that he evoked a wholehearted response from his congregation who were themselves never passive onlookers but full participants. Stimulation to attentiveness to the reality at hand through symbol and music and prayer were constant; the people were always involved in praying together and in singing together; they came into physical contact with the liturgical symbols by carrying candles or palms, by venerating the cross or relics, by walking in procession or gathering about a newly blessed fire. Active participation, both internal and external, let the people experience that this was their prayer, their liturgy; it was not something merely performed by another in their presence. The sense of meaning and beauty and deepened faith which the congregation experienced at any one liturgical celebration drew them back for the next one. In a matter of a few months, Monsignor Hellriegel had developed in his people very positive expectations toward any new form of prayer and liturgical participation he suggested to them. His own creativity in bringing his people to involvement with the central mysteries of the liturgy was certainly a key factor. The people came into touch with the heart of the saving realities they professed; they were touched by the presence of the redeeming Christ. The understanding and prayer and participation opened the way for grace to touch the people more deeply. Once this opening occurred, the drawing power could not be stifled. The fullness of the spirit of liturgical prayer continued to flourish.

During the second year of his pastorate, Monsignor Hellriegel added further paths for congregational participation in the many feasts of the year and introduced prayer forms drawn from liturgical sources for occasions that were not actually liturgical feasts but did seem to warrant some special congregational prayer. Monsignor Hellriegel believed in following the example of the early Christian Church and "baptizing" secular holidays and significant events.

One example from this latter category is the blessing of the school on the first day of the new school year. The pastor went in procession with the children and with servers carrying the cross, candles, and holy water. He bestowed his blessing not only on the "bricks and mortar but especially (on the) teachers and children."[54] For this occasion Monsignor Hellriegel used one of the blessings for a school contained in the Roman ritual. The blessing took place after the Mass on the first day of the school year. The custom of daily Mass begun during 1940-41 continued throughout Monsignor Hellriegel's pastorate. The children, within a short time, learned to sing ten of the chant Masses, about two hundred hyms, and eighteen different alleluias. The Mass would be suited to the feast day celebrated; it would be either a dialog Mass or a high Mass, in either case with full congregational participation and appropriate hymns sung on the days on which a dialog Mass was held.[55]

Another occasion that was nonliturgical in the strict sense but on which Monsignor Hellriegel devised liturgically based communal prayer for his parish was New Year's Eve, an occasion geared more to the adults of the parish than to the children. Here, as with the Halloween party the principle of not taking something away unless you put something in its place was followed. Hellriegel wanted to offer his parishioners an alternative to the traditional type of New Year's Eve party; he did not simply exhort his congregation to sobriety on that night; he gave them something to do. He planned a midnight celebration consisting of a holy hour and holy Mass. The holy hour took into account the occasion as the octave of the birth of Christ, the end of the old year, the beginning of the new year as the nameday of Jesus. It combined appropriate hymns with prayers drawn from the breviary and missal with announcements of and thanksgiving for all the momentous events that took place in the parish and the lives of its members during the year. Included here was a mention of all those baptized during the year, those married during the year, and finally those who were deceased during the year. At the end of the ceremony, bells rang out the old year and in the new year. Monsignor Hellriegel published his New Year's Eve ceremony in a booklet entitled *Deo Gratias* in 1950.[56] Days such as Thanksgiving and Fourth of July received similar attention.

For every major feast of the liturgical year, Monsignor Hellriegel found imaginative ways to direct his people into fuller liturgical participation. The Christmas season offered ample opportunity. One occasion to which the children of Holy Cross always looked forward was the feast of St. Nicholas, December 6. Each year St. Nicholas, dressed in his episcopal robes, would visit the parish bringing candy for the children. However, being a recipient of the candy was never a sure thing because along with St. Nicholas came his companion Rupprecht all dressed in black and carrying a switch. Had any child not been behaving he could have gotten the switch instead of candy. There's no record of Rupprecht's ever having used that switch, but his presence built up suspense and added to the excitement of receiving the candy.

Also, the real identity of both St. Nicholas and Rupprecht was always a well kept secret, so guessing who they could be also added to the fun.[57]

The feast of Christmas itself was always celebrated with great solemnity. The congregation of Holy Cross Parish began its celebration of the feast of the season with a prayer service based on the Matins of the feast and held at 11:30 p.m., before the midnight Mass. In addition to the two more traditional high Masses of the next morning, the children were invited to join in a special afternoon service centered around the crib and the adults could share in the chanting of Christmas vespers at 7:30. The latter services were for those "who wish to come."[58] No pressure was put on people to attend, but usually at least one hundred came. Had the number been considerably smaller, Monsignor Hellriegel would not have been disturbed. Prayers such as vespers were said in praise of God and are a prayer that the priests would be saying regardless of whether or not any of the people wanted to join in. He was happy that some did want to join.

The feast of St. John offered another occasion for bringing into comprehensive usage the prayer of the Roman Ritual. The text for this feast says that St. John "without detriment drank the poisoned wine proffered by his enemies." Therefore, on this feast day the people of the parish were given a drink of blessed wine after the Mass. After the blessing a brief talk was given on the symbolism of the wine in the life of Christ as as element used in his first public sign in the changing of water into wine and in his last gift to man in the changing of the wine into his precious blood.[59]

On the Sunday nearest the feast of the Holy Innocents, the blessing of the Roman Ritual is directed toward preschool chil dren. At the Holy Cross there was a special ceremony in which the young children came to church for prayers and hymns in honor of the divine Child, the telling of the story of the feast by the pastor, a procession during which each child made an offering to the Holy Childhood Association before an image of the divine Child, and finally the blessing for children from the Roman ritual. On leaving the Church each child received a bag of candy and nuts and cookies from their pastor. The children were learning at an early age to associate joyful experiences with attending Church.[60]

Great efforts were made to have the feast of the Holy Family be a joyful, positive, uplifting occasion for the families of the parish. Monsignor Hellriegel was careful to avoid using his sermon on the day to lament the ills that have befallen family life in the modern world; rather he tried to provide for his people a happy experience of family prayer on this day, both at the morning high Mass and at the special evening service. At the evening service the married couples renewed their wedding vows, the pastor blessed their wedding rings, and the children promised to their parents love, respect and obedience. The ceremony also incorporated an ecclesiastical engagement which was simply one instance of a practice that was available for couples becoming engaged at any time during the year.

Monsignor Hellriegel had devised this ceremony at the request of Archbishop Glennon in 1942 and it was available for parishes through the St. Louis Archdiocese. At Holy Cross, the couple planning an engagement would talk with the pastor about the seriousness of the step and receive a copy of the ecclesiastical engagement about a week before the actual date. After prayerfully studying the document in which the young man and woman promise marriage to one another and to preparation for that marriage by frequent reception of the sacraments, prayer, charity, mutual respect and chastity, the couple would come to the Church on the appointed day. The pastor would speak to the couple briefly. The two to be engaged would read their promises out loud and sign the document. The pastor also would sign the document and mark it with the parish seal. The pastor then would bless the ring and the young man would place it on the finger of his fiancee. After a prayer together, the pastor would invite the couple to the rectory for refreshments.[61] This last touch was not a part of the official form but was a good example of Monsignor Hellriegel's ability to combine simple natural human goods with supernatural blessings and thereby reach the whole person with both his own geniune warmth and hospitality and humanness as well as with the treasures of the graces of the sacraments and sacramentals and extra-liturgical prayers.

The Holy Family celebration also evidenced Monsignor Hellriegel's appreciation of and concern for fostering good simple enjoyment, in this case, at the level of the family group. After the prayer service, all who attended, parents and children, assembled in the parish hall for a family gathering of music, songs, and refreshments.[62]

Monsignor Hellriegel helped his parishioners get a good start in family life by giving them a real preparation, on the basis of one couple at a time, for marriage. In addition to the ecclesiastical engagement and the preparation for that ceremony, the young couple were introduced to the significance of the biblical symbols involving marriage. They were brought to see marriage as a symbolic, yet real, share in the union between Christ and the Church.[63] They were taught their role as ministers of the sacrament to one another. The significance of their deep union in marriage partaking of the union between Christ and the Church was brought out in the wedding ceremony itself. As an attempt to bring out more clearly the mystery being celebrated, the Eucharistic food for the bride and groom was consecrated at the same Mass in which the two are wed.[64]

Twice during the year mothers of newborn babies were invited to bring their infants to Church for a special blessing. The first of these occasions was Candlemas Day, February 2. On this day the blessing was combined with thanksgiving to God for the gift of the child. The day was also an occasion for celebrating the feast of light and of coming to a deeper understanding of the symbolism of the candle. The people of Holy Cross celebrated this day as the bridge between the Christmas and Paschal seasons, the connecting link between the two great feasts of light. Again complete explanation given in both school and church made the event one in which the members of the parish could intelligently and meaningfully take part. They took part in the procession with the blessed candle, and as they took the candles into their homes, they were reminded that the candles were the symbol of the light that they themselves were to be to the world. The newborn children departed with their mothers especially aware of their cause for rejoicing.[65]

A second time during the year when the babies born after February 2 could be brought for a blessing was October 11. On this day, the feast of the maternity of the Blessed Mother, all mothers and married women were encourage to unite with one another in the offering of the Mass and the receiving of holy communion. The blessing of the newborn infants was an occasion of rejoicing for all present. About 86% of the new mothers of the parish participated in the blessing their newborn.[66]

October was also seen by Monsignor Hellriegel as the ideal time to begin a parish scripture group. He was realistic, if nonetheless regretful, regarding the possibility of such an endeavor to succeed during the summer months. However, the fall of the year seemed to bring with a less strong lure of the outdoors more time for and interest in more serious subjects. The feast of St. Luke, October 18, seemed to be an ideal time to launch a group for the ensuing season. The Holy Cross groups followed a fairly informal format but did have some structure. They would open with prayer to the Holy Spirit and invocation to St. Luke. The first step in approaching scripture was a reading of the text; this was followed by explanation, discussion, and application to daily life. The Magnificat closed the session. In this way the Catholic layman for whom the Bible was unknown territory gradually came to be more familiar with the Word of God and therefore more able to hear and to respond to that Word as it continued to be addressed to him in worship.[67]

The nine days preceding the feast of Pentecost offered an opportunity for Monsignor Hellriegel to utilize with his people the prayer form of the novena. Hellriegel felt that overemphasis had been placed on the novena as a prayer of petition but that it had been neglected as a way of preparing oneself for the celebration of a great feast.[68] Monsignor Hellreigel had taken the initial step to correct the erroneous novena thinking by introducing his flock to the Christmas novena, one that asked for no special material favor, but only that the people may be made ready for the coming of their Savior. The novena in preparation for Pentecost had a similar emphasis: that the people may be made ready for the coming of the Spirit. To guide his flock in the prayer of the nine days before Pentecost Monsignor Hellriegel used the booklet *Veni Creator Spiritus*, the one that he had prepared from the prayers of the missal and breviary and select scriptural readings for the sisters at O'Fallon.

When the day of Pentecost arrived Monsignor Hellriegel led his people not merely to a commemoration of a past event but to a realization of the power and the presence of the Spirit in their own lives. He took advantage of this occasion to talk to his people about their own receiving of the Spirit, especially in the sacrament of Confirmation. The people were given an opportunity to reflect upon the meaning of the sacrament upon their own personal lives, their family lives, their life in society, especially as it affects their responsibility toward Catholic Action, and finally as it affects their own share in the priesthood of the laity. After sufficient reflection the people could renew the dedication of themselves through an act of renewal based on the rite of Confirmation.[69] Thus the feast of Pentecost became more than an historical remembrance; it was a coming of the Spirit in the here-and-now and a coming that brought with it practical effects that required notice and response. Again there can be seen Monsignor Hellriegel's masterful way of bringing the reality of what was being celebrated in the liturgy home to his people in a concrete, practical, meaningful way. He did not create artificial gimmicks but simply used the prayer and sacrament which were a part of the official prayer of the Church.

The spirit of Pentecost was carried on throughout the week. Prayer for those ordained during Pentecost week was encouraged. Pentecost Saturday was devoted especially to prayer for the sick. The gospel of this day spoke of Christ curing Peter's mother-in-law. The choice of this day for a special service for the sick brought out to those in need of healing the understanding of the presence of Christ as healer for them also on this day. The sick were brought near the sanctuary for the celebration of the Eucharist and the reception of Christ in communion. After the Mass the pastor blessed oil, using the blessing of the Roman ritual, and anointed each person who was ill or elderly. The oil was given as a sign of the Spirit and the power and the strength which he could bring to those who received him.[70]

Although the Church was definitely and intentionally the center of parish activities and the place of contact between members of the parish and between the members and their priests, there were also occasions when the priests of the parish visited parishioners in their homes. On these occasions too Monsignor Hellriegel emphasized the pastoral role which he and the other priests of the parish played for their people. The home visit was used not only to insure accurate information on the parish record but as an occasion to foster good sacred art and solid reading material for the home. In the case of one family moving out of a home or apartment and another moving in a "calling card" was left for the new resident informing him of the name and location of the parish church.[71]

The rectory office, another place of meeting between pastor and people, was also viewed by Monsignor Hellriegel as a place in which learning, directly or indirectly, could take place. An example of his fostering the latter type of learning was the display of pertinent books and magazines which he tried to arrange in an eye-catching manner. The office also was kept equipped with a number of items that could do double duty in furnishing decoration and serving as concrete examples in giving instruction in the faith, especially to converts. The plants added freshness and cheer to the room, but also came in handy when using Christ's example of the vine and the branches to explain the Mystical Body.[72] A candle was another attractive addition to the room; its usefulness was proven in illustrating the reality of Baptism. The unlighted candle could be compared to the unbaptized individual. With Baptism came that new relationship with Christ and that new light of the Spirit that made one have within himself a new inner light analogous to the lighted candle. These are typical of the concreteness with which Monsignor Hellriegel approached all attempts to communicate new understandings to his people and also of his resourcefulness in being able to utilize many different kinds of objects and occasions opportunities to convey new understandings. Yet, his people did not feel that they were constantly being preached to; his interest in each person, his knowledge of each family situation, his own ability to live and enjoy the simple things of life, his own human warmth and understanding of human nature all worked together to create an attitude of mutual love and respect between Monsignor Hellriegel and the people of his parish.

Mention has already been made of Monsignor Hellriegel's general approach to parish organizations. This general approach can be seen as eptiomized by the change he brought about in the parish sodalities. Before his assumption of the pastorate at Holy Cross parish, there were large sodalities of men and of women as well as of young men and women. Once a month each of these sodalities would have a communion Sunday followed by a short meeting. This was roughly the extent of sodality activity. Monsignor Hellriegel, however, did not find it "particularly edifying to see two hundred or more sodality members at high Mass present in body and absent in voice."[73] Monsignor Hellriegel gently and charmingly transformed the sodality meetings into occasions for the study of the missal, the chant, the church year, the sacraments and the sacramentals. The women were given suggestions as to how to use the sacramentals in their homes. As usual, he was not content to stop with intellectual learning but promptly helped his sodalities translate their new knowledge into doing. They were soon involved in making Advent wreaths and vestments and antependia as well as working to help cancer patients and orphan children.[74]

Holy Name Society meetings consisted of discussion of the encyclicals and especially of their application to current problems. The response asked of Christians to these problems in the light of their membership in the Mystical Body of Christ was a topic thoroughly aired by the two-hundred sixty-five members. The life of the Christian man in the world and his work in the lay apostolate were the focus of much attention by the men.[75]

The young men's servers' organization was another key nucleus in the parish. This group numbered about eighty-six men and boys between the ages of fourteen and thirty-six. They would assist the celebrants at designated Masses during the week and on Sunday and be a part of all special liturgical celebrations. Part of their regularly monthly meetings would be devoted to practice for liturgical celebrations conducted by the president of the group. The second part of the meeting would be a friendly discussion in the parish hall. These discussions would provide opportunity for these young men to grow in their understanding of the Christian life.[76]

Monsignor Hellriegel's talents in art and in music were also put to work in his parish ministry. When his people needed a hymn for a given occasion, Monsignor would search for one that was musically good and theologically sound. If there were no such hymn existing, he would write one. This would sometime involve writing music for a prayer or verse from the breviary or ritual; it would sometimes involve writing words to a classical melody; it would sometimes involves fresh composition of both words and music. It was in honor of the feast of Christ the King that Martin Hellriegel composed a text for the old German melody of *Ich Glaub' An Gott* of the 1870 Mainz Gesangbuch. The hymn was entitled "To Jesus Christ Our Sovereign King"; it was written in 1941 and has been widely used ever since. Eventually he had published a parish hymnal which contained both hymns he had collected for the use of his people and hymns he had written. His zeal in bringing to his people a fine quality of music for worship was also seen in his willingness to finance a good organ and a competent director of music.

His tendency was to add touches rather than to tear down and totally rebuild. Monsignor Hellriegel knew that the people of Holy Cross loved their Church and, therefore, concentrated on fostering the inner spirit of liturgical prayer, letting that spirit be expressed in the Church with its main structure as it was. One change that he did make, however, shortly after his arrival at Holy Cross was the constructing of a new entrance from the sacristy to the sanctuary. The new entrance was at the side of the Church; it enabled the celebrant and servers to enter the sanctuary with a solemn introit procession. The procession could move down the side aisle, across the back of the Church and up the center aisle on solemn occasions; the everyday procession went across the front of the church, past the Blessed Mother altar to the sanctuary. Monsignor Hellriegel was attached to the passage before the Blessed Mother altar because of Mary's "intimate connection with the mystery of Calvary."[77]

Because of the importance with which he regarded the Blessed Mother altar, it was to this site that Monsignor Hellriegel turned his first major effort in adding new beauty to the church. He commissioned Gottfried Schiller, with whom he had worked at O'Fallon, to design a new Blessed Mother altar. The carved statue would not be replaced but given a new setting. The altar is distinctive in that it is a double triptych, that is, it has two sets of "wings" that can be folded in front of the statue giving three changeable views: the statue of the madonna and child with the wings opened and with representations of the patron saints of the previous pastors of the parish; or, with the first set of wings closed and the second set opened, a series of paintings unfolding the story of Mary's divine motherhood, from the annunciation scene to her coronation; or, with both sets of wings closed, simply a large crown of thorns. The altar has its third view during passiontide when images of the saints and of the Blessed Mother are not appropriate.[78]

The new St. Joseph altar, constructed soon after the Blessed Mother altar, is also distinctive artistically and theologically. It too was designed by Gottfried Schiller as a new setting for the carved statue already in the church. The altar was designed in conjunction with a new baptismal font which was placed just in front of the St. Joseph altar. This plan was decided upon in recognition of St. Joseph as the patron of the universal Church. As new members would be received into the Church through the sacrament of Baptism, they would simultaneously be placed under the patronage of St. Joseph.[79]

The style of the altar is similar to that of the Blessed Mother altar but is a single triptych rather than a double one. The scenes along the opened wings are on the theme of Baptism. At the base of the altar is the inscription:

> I think more of the place where I was baptized than of the Cathedral of Rheims where I was crowned. For the dignity of a child of God which was bestowed at Baptism is greater than that of the Ruler of the Kingdom. The latter I shall lose at death; the other will be my passport to everlasting glory.

The inscription is a statement made by Saint King Louis.

The font itself is a distinctive structure made of marble. It is represented in one of the pictures on the wings of the St. Joseph altar. Over the font is a baldachino or crown made of wood and carved with symbols of the sacraments. The dedication of the new altar and font took place on August 15, 1945. They were financed not from general parish funds but from many small gifts from parishioners made over a period of two years.

Thus, already by 1943, within three years after becoming pastor at Holy Cross, Monsignor Hellriegel had already interested his parishioners in supporting for their church art work that was rooted in sound theology and was of a superior quality. His own knowledge of and talent for sacred art had contributed both to this appreciation on the part of his people and to the actual development of the art work. His sensitivity to the people and to their cultural roots kept him from seeking to tear down the old structure and build a new liturgically avant-garde church. Monsignor Hellriegel always brought the liturgy to the people. He never expected them to do a total about-face and enter into culturally foreign forms of expression in sacred worship. His endeavors built upon the cultural and religious roots from which the faith of his people had grown.

The result of this careful combination of continuity with the immediate culture and religious heritage of the people plus an opportunity for new understanding of and involvement in the ancient prayer of the Church was great spiritual growth for many individuals, a spirit of unity among the people of the parish, and an experience of vitality and joy in worship. After three years of active participation in the liturgy, the parishioners of Holy Cross were becoming conscious of the change that was being wrought in their lives. On one occasion a man of the parish who worked as a gardener and was somewhat of a rugged individual of few words, remarked to Monsignor Hellriegel that even though Monsignor had been pastor of the parish only a short while, the parish had undergone a complete change. He went on to say that the people had become much happier about going to church and many had definitely changed their behavior regarding such things as the kind of language they used, the kind of jokes they told, and the kind of activities they engaged in. Furthermore, he told his pastor that he had learned more about his religion in the past three years than he had in the whole of his life.[80]

The change was not something experienced only by isolated individuals. The many common experiences of active participation in the liturgy had the effect of creating among the people of the parish a close knit family spirit.[81] The families of the parish, the special parish organizations, the choirs and servers — all became an organic whole in praying together and celebrating together the feasts of the liturgical year. All worked together both to assure beauty and dignity in their praise of God and in looking after the needs of their fellow parishioners. Monsignor Hellriegel was able to weld the people of his parish into cooperative activity in both the celebration of the liturgy and in the feeding and clothing of those within the parish who were in need. Again, Monsignor Hellriegel saw borne out in practice the thesis of his first published work, *The True Basis of Christian Solidarity*. These people who prayed together the prayer of the Church did develop a sense of caring about one another and active involvement in meeting one another's needs. For the people of Holy Cross this task was not always easy as the parishioners were not wealthy; they were mostly working class people who had little left over after they met the simple needs of their own families.

The many hours that the people spent in Church (and they were many because the majority of the people of the parish attended and took part in the majority of the celebrations) were spent willingly and joyously; going to Church was not an obligation to be fulfilled but a rewarding experience, a self-validating one that drew the individual back for the next celebration. Even the children, who spent many hours practicing for the various liturgical celebrations, liked going to church. There was mutual love between the pastor and his children. He knew each of them, not only by name, but really knew them. The children considered such things as being choosen to carry the stational church banner or being the one to retrieve the buried "Alleluia" on Holy Saturday or getting to carry one of the relics in the Halloween procession as real honors. They were very conscious of the meaning of all that was done and there was no giggling or fidgeting. The children strove to do their best because of their own inner desire. Monsignor Hellriegel managed to touch their heart and motivate them from within. Monsignor emphasized for the children the idea that they were Christ-bearers and that since Christ lived within each of them, they should treat one another with respect. Not all skirmishes were avoided, but the children did get the idea of respect for one another.[82]

This deepening of Christian living, Monsignor Hellriegel often said, was inevitable once the people of a parish were led to real liturgical prayer. For Pius X had pointed out the liturgy was the primary and indispensable source of the true Christian spirit. Once people are really in contact with the source, the rest will follow. The immersion into the source came about for the people of Holy Cross because a man with great theological and liturgical knowledge, with great spiritual depth and personal holiness, with human warmth and understanding of human nature, with a feeling for people and their heritage as well as a feeling for beauty and propriety, with a strong and deep faith in the sanctifying and unifying power of the liturgy, with creative and imaginative abilities, with a dynamic and forceful personality, with stateliness and generosity, with skills in teaching and communicating mustered all of these forces and channeled them with total and single-minded dedication and untiring work into the parish to whose ministry he was assigned.

He touched the minds and hearts of his people. He took literally St. Paul's admonition to preach the Word. The homily that flowed from and was an intrinsic part of the liturgy of the day was a key means of reaching his parishioners. The gospel message — not a "bawling out" or a series of moralistic or pietistic exhortation — was what the people of Holy Cross heard from their pastor. The message of the faith was brought to them through sacrament and sacramental, through liturgical and paraliturgical and extraliturgical prayer, through visits with individuals and with families, through discussions at parish meetings. Union with Christ and with one another was key to all else. Upright Christian living flowed from the awareness of this union. The positive aspects, the joyous realities of the Christian faith were always the primary focus. Monsignor Hellriegel brought his people to a joyous experience of these realities; once experienced, there were fewer wrongdoers to scold.

Monsignor Hellriegel's efforts to involve his people at the experiential level in the joy of their faith were untiring. The liturgical celebrations that so moved his flock were the product of much hard work, careful planning, minute attention to detail, generous giving of self on the part of Monsignor Hellriegel.[83] He himself would frequently attend choir practices, not because the choir director needed help but to show the choir members the importance and dignity of their work.[84] Practices were carried out with a spirit of dedication and enthusiasm. Nothing connected with divine worship was too much trouble. Externals were regarded as significant insofar as they helped to create an atmosphere of reverence and prayer and helped to foster understanding and attentiveness. Hard work and generous self-giving with joy on the part of Monsignor Hellriegel inspired like behavior on the part of the members of the choirs and servers and the people of the parish.

Monsignor Hellriegel succeeded in cultivating a spirit of vitality in liturgical prayer and thorough penetration of the prayer of the Church in the great majority of his parishioners for the entire time of his pastorate because of his own personality and talents, his dedication to the Church and to its prayer, his love for and understanding of his people, his liturgical scholarship, and finally his daily hard work.

CHAPTER NINE

The Liturgical Conference

The year of Monsignor Hellriegel's assumption of the pastorate at Holy Cross Parish coincided with the year of the beginning of the National Liturgical Weeks. The reputation he had gained as a leader in things liturgical through his work at O'Fallon, his writings, especially in *Orate Fratres*, his lectures and his travels resulted in his being solicited as a speaker for the initial Liturgical Weeks. At these he told of the growing liturgical life of his parish. The result was a steady stream of visitors to his parish and more speaking invitations.

In addition to being a frequent speaker at the National Liturgical Weeks, Monsignor Hellriegel also served in its parent organization, the Liturgical Conference, as officer, board of directors member and advisory council member. The Liturgical Conference itself was the outgrowth of another organization, the Benedictine Liturgical Conference. This latter group was formed as a result of interest in the liturgy evidenced by the response of catechists at their 1939 National Congress in Cincinnati to a number of talks dealing with the significance of the liturgy in the teaching of religion.[1] The group was spearheaded by Father Michael Ducey, a Benedictine monk who became the secretary-treasurer of the group. The Benedictine Conference arranged to hold the first National Liturgical Week in Chicago. Local preparations were handled by Monsignor Joseph Morrison, the rector of the cathedral where the actual meetings would take place. The theme of the week was the Parish and Its Worship. The speakers' program featured seven Benedictines, twelve priests of other orders and of the diocesan clergy, and three laymen. Thus, from their beginning, the Liturgical Weeks were drawing on a somewhat broad base of Catholic leaders.

The Weeks of 1941 and 1942 proceeded fairly smoothly, but by 1943 most of the Benedictine abbots of the country were of the opinion that the Liturgical Conference should not remain under the auspices of the Benedictines. Abbot Deutsch of St. John's Abbey, for instance, felt that the Benedictine sponsorship of the Liturgical Conference made it appear that the liturgy was the Benedictine's specialty rather than an area of important and equal concern to the whole Church. Therefore, Monsignor Morrison was asked to appoint a committee to devise a new sponsoring body for the Weeks. Father Ducey, who had hoped to retain a Benedictine sponsored group, wound up being the only Benedictine on the committee.[2] The committee drew up a constitution and set of bylaws which provided for the leadership to be in the hands of an elected board of directors as well as four officers: president, vice-president, secretary, and treasurer. An advisory council, consisting of past presidents of the Liturgical Conference and past Liturgical Week Chairmen, was also set up.

The 1944 Liturgical Week was scheduled for Christmas time in New York. Previous to that, in October, a special meeting of Liturgical Conference members was called at St. Meinrad's Abbey to attend to the business of the conference and to provide an opportunity for a more scholarly study of the liturgy than the more diversified audience of the liturgical weeks would be ready for. It was at this meeting that the new constitution and bylaws were adopted and a board of directors for the coming year elected.

Monsignor Hellriegel was one of the men elected to this board; he served on the board until 1956 at which time he became a member of the advisory council. From 1946 through 1948 he held the office of vice-president; from 1949 through 1951 he was the Conference President. The major tasks for the officers and board members were the planning of the programs for the liturgical week, including theme, speakers, place, and the offering of assistance to diocesan and local groups who may be wishing to plan liturgical programs of some kind.

In 1946, the year in which Monsignor Hellriegel became the vice-president of the conference and Father Thomas Carroll of Boston became its president, a shift took place in the general orientation of the themes of the weeks. An attempt was made to bring into the treatment of the various topics and into the overall thrust of the week more emphasis on the application to normal Catholic life and problems.[3] The theme for the 1946 week, which was held in Denver, was The Family in Christ. Father H. A. Reinhold described the week as the "first tentative steps into a new kind of liturgical realism."[4] Such a pastoral orientation was typical of Monsignor Hellriegel's approach to the liturgy on the smaller scale of his own parish.

However, Father Michael Ducey, the original moving force of the weeks, was disappointed with the more active, less monastic turn of the tempo of the weeks; he resigned from the board of directors after the Denver Week.[5] The orientation of the Liturgical Weeks toward practical living for all Catholics was clearly established.

Another significant step taken by the board of directors of the Liturgical Conference during 1946 was a resolution passed in July of that year. It stated:

> Be it resolved that the Liturgical Conference will not sponsor a Liturgical Week within the confines of any diocese where it will be necessary that laws of segregation and discrimination of any racial group shall be imposed at the meeting of the Liturgical Week.[6]

This resolution was another indication of the relationship which the members of the Liturgical Conference saw between involvement with the liturgy and with social problems.

Monsignor Hellriegel's most significant contribution to the administrative sector of the Liturgical Conference was his ability to inspire his fellow board members and officers. He was able to speak with the authority of one who had succeeded in putting the ideas they discussed into practice on the pastoral level. A good number of the annual planning meetings for the Liturgical Weeks took place at Holy Cross Rectory where Monsignor Hellriegel was the gracious host and animating force.[7] Hellriegel was not eager to hold the office of president of the conference and refused to accept it the first time his name was submitted, but he was finally persuaded by his fellow conference members to accept the post.[8] His confreres were eager to confer the presidency upon him as "a token of the devotion and esteem which liturgists throughout the country entertain toward him."[9]

Because the officers and members of the board of directors were often themselves giving talks at the Liturgical Weeks and were always the ones to set the theme and topics for the weeks, they very much influenced the general tenor of the weeks. During the first several years the orientation of the weeks was the encouraging of the full understanding and appreciation of the various aspects of the liturgy and the implementing, at every level, of the existing norms for liturgical celebrations and congregational participation in those celebrations. It was only in 1948 at the ninth Liturgical Week that there came a public expression of a hope for liturgical reform.[10] This expression came from Monsignor Hellriegel as a part of his introduction to this commentary which accompanied a dramatization of the Easter Vigil. The hope which he expressed was one that he had held for a long time and had actually experienced himself during his O'Fallon days. He expressed his hope in his usual spirit of dedication to the Church:

> Realizing our Holy Father's love for the sacred liturgy and his paternal desire "that the people committed to his charge be schooled in the correct spirit and practice of the liturgy" (*Mediator Dei*), we may be permitted to express the hope — humbly, patiently, and courageously — that from his generous heart he would grant to the Christian world as a "jubilee gift in the Holy Year 1950," to celebrate the nocturnal paschal mysteries in "that night in which heavenly things are united to those of earth, and things divine to those which are human."[11]

Again the following year Monsignor Hellriegel expressed a hope for another jubilee gift in the form of a rubrical change. As a part of his introduction to his demonstration of the high Mass, which was held on the evening of August 23, 1949, he said, "...some day we may come together at an evening hour and have a 'real' Solemn High Mass! Perhaps our Holy Father — as a jubilee year gift — will grant also to us a permission which he has already given to so many other countries."[12]

Both of Monsignor Hellriegel's daring (for the time) hopes were granted, although not in the jubilee year. The permission for the night-time Easter Vigil on a limited and experimental basis came in 1951; the permission for evening Masses in the United States came in 1954. With these and other reforms, such as the revised American Ritual, coming from Rome, the Liturgical Conference began to feel more comfortable in taking the initiative in asking for further reform.

The first occasion on which the Liturgical Conference's ideas for reform were publicized outside the conference itself took place in 1956. At its annual meeting in London, Ontario, in August of that year the board of directors drew up a list of twenty resolutions which they saw as a continuation of the reforms already initiated by Rome. Their resolutions dealt with such suggestions as simplification of the rubrics, the offering of the Mass with the celebrant facing the people (a practice which took place at some of the Liturgical Weeks), having the Mass of the Catechumens in the language of the people, a three- or four-year cycle of scripture readings in the Mass, a limitation on the use of the Requiem Mass, a provision for a brief form of the prayer of the faithful within the Mass, the singing of the complete Sanctus (including the Benedictus) before the continuation of the Eucharistic Prayer, permission for concelebration on specified occasions, permission for priests in the active ministry to recite the Breviary in their mother tongue.[13]

The month after these resolutions were passed, September, 1956, was the time of the first International Liturgical Congress at Assisi, Italy. A number of the members of the board were attending this conference. Father Aloysius Wilmes, one of the members of the liturgical seminar which Hellriegel had begun back in 1938, then secretary of the Liturgical Conference, had copies of the resolutions printed and distributed informally as a matter of interest to those in attendance.[14] Monsignor Hellriegel was at Assisi as a part of the American group. On one occasion when an informal discussion was taking place on the subject of the vernacular and some of the representative from the British Isles were showing themselves to be not favorably disposed to its introduction into the liturgy, Monsignor Hellriegel "in a pointed but friendly way spoke in Latin on the subjet and thus demonstrated pretty effectively the need for the introduction of the vernacular."[15] His scholarship and creativity had done the trick again.

In spite of the significant administrative contribution Monsignor Hellriegel made to the Liturgical Conference through his ability to inspire, his insistence on concreteness, and his imaginative way of getting his points across, an even more significant contribution was the one he made on the speakers' platform. His presentations were unusually effective because he was able to speak with the authority of one who had successfully carried out his ideas in his own parish, because his "style and personality were extraordinarily charismatic,"[16] and because he could devise imaginative means of showing others how to implement better liturgical practices in their own ministry.

Some of Monsignor Hellriegel's presentations dealt with various aspects of the Church and the liturgy from a theological viewpoint. In other talks he related to his audiences experiences of his own in living the liturgy at the family or parish level. Another whole series of presentations consisted in demonstration and dramatizations, illustrating to the audience ways to bring about beauty and inspirational meaning in liturgical power.

At the first Liturgical Week in 1940, Monsignor Hellriegel was asked to speak on the subject of the parish. In this talk he developed a carefully worked out theology of the parish, showing that the parish was the Mystical Body of Christ, in miniature but in reality, and, therefore, the Eucharist is the center of the parish just as it is the center of the Mystical Body. Thus it follows that priority should be given to the celebration of the Eucharist, preparation for and participation in the Eucharist, and the physical setting for its celebration. With emphasis on the Eucharistic liturgy within the parish all other functions assume secondary roles. Duties of the pastor, the school, and the parish societies can be fitted into this hierarchy of values.[17]

Talks were given in subsequent years developing such topics as the relationship between the Mass, the sacraments, and the divine office; the sermon of the Mass as an intrinsic part of the liturgy and therefore necessarily an elucidation of the scripture readings of the day, the liturgy as it relates to the preaching of retreats and to religious vocations, and an explanation of the ritual for the consecration of virgins. In each of these talks, Monsignor Hellriegel was able to bring his impressive historical and theological knowledge to his audience in simple terms and concrete images. To explain the relationship between the Mass and the sacraments he devised the image of a sun surrouned by six planets which are not self-illuminating but are illuminated by their center. He then developed each sacrament individually to show its orientation to and fulfillment through the Eucharist. The relationship of the divine office to the Mass was also illustrated through an image; the divine office was like a garment, the Mass like the body clothed with or surrounded by that garment. The garment and body fit together and enhanced one another.[18]

In explaining the relationship of the liturgy to the preaching of retreats, Monsignor Hellriegel expanded the image he utilized in explaining the relationship of the Mass to the sacraments. This time the comparison was to five concentric circles. The first was the Eucharist, the second the other six sacraments, the third the Word of God in the scripture, the fourth the sacramentals and the fifth externals associated with the celebration of the Eucharist such as vestments, organ, etc. A liturgical retreat is simply one that takes into account this system of priorities in the structuring of retreat conferences and activities. The Eucharist rather than elaborate holy hours should be the center of the prayer of the retreatants. The conferences should have less of a moralizing and apologetic emphasis and have more of a joyful proclamation of the reality of the presence of the saving mysteries celebrated and made present throughout the Church year. Monsignor Hellriegel also stressed that the Church's own annual retreat, the season of Lent, should be taken more seriously as retreat time.[19] Monsignor Hellriegel presented these ideas regarding retreats to a national audience of retreat masters in 1961. It was the early sixties that saw, in retreats given in the Roman Catholic Church at this time, precisely the emphasis which he had recommended, and at least in part, thanks to his efforts.

The relationship between the liturgical movement and religious vocations and religious profession was also a subject on which Monsignor spoke forcefully to the audiences of the Liturgical Weeks. In a rather strong talk given in 1955, he showed how active participation in the liturgy, by drawing a young person into the core of the Church's life, could be quite effective in arousing in that person a desire to dedicate himself or herself entirely to the living and promoting of that life through a life in a religious order or in the priesthood. He also showed that if a young person, upon entering a convent or seminary, found not the active liturgical life which he or she had been expecting but a weak sentimental piety, there would arise a conflict, a disillusionment, and possibly the final decision that life in this religious group was not really life at the center of the Church and therefore lead to withdrawal from that group. Monsignor Hellriegel gave an example of a girl who had had just that kind of experience.[20]

The rite of consecration of virgins, which Monsignor Hellriegel had reworked for contemporary use while at O'Fallon, was another aspect of religious life about which he shared his ideas with the Liturgical Week participants. He explained the value of the rite of consecration in terms of its making evident the religious vocation as a call by God and by the Church. The emphasis was on divine action rather than on human action. The rite made clear that the deeper insertion into the life of the Church was the work of Christ.[21]

Monsignor Hellriegel's talks that were somewhat of an explanative, theological nature were greatly appreciated by his listeners because he could always find an imaginative and interesting way to explain even the profoundest concepts. One of his confreres said of him, "He was obviously the most skillful kind of pedagogue, able to use language and symbol most attractively to deepen the spiritual awareness of the people whom he addressed."[22] The same skills in communication which made his work at Holy Cross Parish so effective were equally fruitful in the Liturgical Conference.

Another category of presentations which were even more appreciated by the Liturgical Week participants were those in which he simply related his own experience in living the liturgy and leading others to do the same. On one occasions he simply described the liturgical practices which he had experienced in his own family in Heppenheim; he suggested to his audience the possibility of implementing some of them at the current time as extensions of the prayer of the altar into the home.[23]

An even more impressive talk of this same nature was given at the 1941 Liturgical Week, just a little over a year after Monsignor Hellriegel had become pastor of Holy Cross. He related for his listeners what had been his experience as a first-year pastor in promoting liturgical participation in his parish. He told quite simply of the congregation that had been transformed within that year from silent attendance at Mass to the singing of high Masses by the whole congregation and the full use of the *Missa Recitata*; he also cited participation in the prayer of the divine office. The response of the audience could be described by the chairman of the session only as "rapt attention."[24]

The features for which Monsignor Hellriegel was most famous in the Liturgical Weeks were his demonstrations and dramatizations. A recurring item on the program of the Liturgical Weeks was his demonstration of Holy Mass. Father Aloysius Wilmes assumed the role of celebrant and Monsignor Hellriegel gave the commentary. His words never failed to both enlighten and inspire all who took part. Monsignor Hellriegel emphasized the Christian's part in sharing in the great sacrificial offering of Christ. The offertory was presented as the time for drawing all persons and the whole of the world into the transforming power of the Sacrifice. The conscious offering of self in and with Christ was stressed as central to participation in the Mass. Communion was explained as a ". . . great 'triangle' of unity. Christ and my brethren. Christ and I. My brethren and I." The *Ite, missa est* was the sending out of apostolic men and women to "transform the world and to radiate the Christ-life."[25] The demonstration of Holy Mass was described by the editor of *Worship* as "invariably the high point of the week."[26]

A very special dramatization was the one of the Easter Vigil done in 1948, before many were even bold enough to hope for its restoration within their own life times and again in 1952 when the ceremony was being used on an experimental basis. Monsignor Hellriegel was responsible for the planning and execution of this event, as was the case with the demonstration Masses. Again he took the role of the commentator, educating and uplifting all who heard his words. He was able to explain beautifully and simply all the symbolism of the ritual. His explanations not only made understandable the words and signs but brought to life the divine realities which they embody in the real liturgical celebration. The 1948 demonstration was described by an article in the *Catholic Art Quarterly* as the "...most impressive item on the program." The author went on to described the audience as "breathless" at the time of the lighting of the Paschal candle. He also commented, "That evening we understood better our Holy Baptism, and we rejoiced in it and responded with vibrant Alleluias."[27]

Through demonstrations such as these Monsignor Hellriegel was not only verbally explaining to his fellow priests how to grow in their ability to celebrate the liturgy with beauty and meaning and so draw their congregations more deeply in to the prayer of the Church; he was giving them a positive model, one which would be a great help to many who wanted to improve the quality of their liturgical celebrations but were in doubt as to how to proceed. The many homilies which Monsignor Hellriegel was called upon to give as a part of the liturgical celebrations of the Liturgical Weeks were further concrete models of the concepts Monsignor Hellriegel had explained in his talks on the role of the sermon within the Mass. In these homilies he never failed to bring to life for his listeners even the most ordinary biblical or liturgical text.[28]

Thus, at the Liturgical Weeks as at Holy Cross, Monsignor Hellriegel drew those with whom he had contact into a greater closeness to the primary and indispensable source of the true Christian life by his leadership in action as well as through his spoken word. One writer, assessing the strains of influence in the liturgical movement in the United States said of Monsignor Hellriegel:

> Probably his greatest influence, however, has been owing to his platform manner, which compounded of dignity, earnestness, geniality, and what the old rhetoricians called pectus, is well nigh charismatic, and in hundreds of lectures, sermons, and retreats across the country he has charmed audiences and won them to sympathy with new ideas.[29]

In 1964 Monsignor Hellriegel was celebrating the golden jubilee of his ordination to the priesthood. In order to have an opportunity to express publicly the gratitude and affection which so many members of the Liturgical Conference felt toward him, the Conference decided to hold the Liturgical Week in St. Louis in that year.[30]

As a further mark of honor, it was Monsignor Hellriegel who was chosen to be the first priest to offer a High Mass in English in the Roman Rite; the Mass took place as a part of the Liturgical Week celebrations but had not yet been introduced for general use.[31] In retrospect, 1964 turned out to be the peak year of the Liturgical Weeks. It drew a record crowd of about 20,000 and the last really united endeavor to promote the liturgy. That Liturgical Week closed with a tribute to Monsignor Hellriegel given by Father Thomas Carroll, a fellow office holder and board member in the Liturgical Conference. The tribute documents Monsignor Hellriegel's work at Holy Cross and in the Liturgical Conference, telling of both his difficulties and successes. It was punctuated by many long periods of applause by the audience. It was clear that something of that warmth which the people of Holy Cross felt toward Monsignor Hellriegel was experienced on a broader scale.[32]

Many Holy Cross parishioners were a part of that audience; seeing the national recognition given to their pastor reinforced their already strong conviction that his guidance was sure and reliable. Thus his success in his parish in the promotion of liturgical prayer made him more desirable as a conference speaker; his acclaim by the conference made his parishioners even more ready to accept his leadership.

CHAPTER TEN

Lecturing and Writing — Holy Cross Years

B y 1940, the year of his inauguration as pastor of Holy Cross and the year of the beginning of the Liturgical Weeks, Monsignor Hellriegel was already receiving frequent requests to give retreats and lectures in various parts of the country as well as to continue his writing, especially for *Orate Fratres*, which, by this time, was under the editorship of Godfrey Diekmann. Local liturgical days were being planned for diocesan clergy with growing frequency and Monsignor Hellriegel was often called upon to help with the overall plans or to address those attending. Two typical examples of such days were the Priests' Liturgical Day in Atchison, Kansas, in December of 1941 and the Milwaukee Liturgical Day held the following spring. On both of these occasions Monsignor Hellriegel was asked to speak.

In both cases Monsignor Hellriegel gave an introduction to the meaning of the liturgy, explaining it as the principal means through which the divine life of Christ is made present in His acts of Redemption. When speaking to the priests at Atchison, Monsignor Hellriegel made sure his listeners knew that liturgy and rubrics were not synonymous; he compared rubrics to the fence and liturgy to the garden. Typically using a concrete image to get his point across, he helped the priests to see that although rubrics are important, they are a means rather than an end. The real emphasis should be on sharing in the life and action of Christ. Those who are more concerned when something goes wrong with the fence than with a weedy garden are missing the boat. He made his point by noting, "There lived a group of fence watchers 1,900 years ago who caused a great deal of trouble to Him 'who came to give them life that they may have it in abundance...' The liturgical movement does not stand for innovations, it stands for a 100% 'sentire cum Ecclesia' ..."[1]

Thus, in his usual interesting manner, Monsignor Hellriegel left no doubt about his main point in the minds of his listeners. He went on to give practical advice to the priests on how to develop a greater liturgical spirituality for themselves through the use of their missal and breviary as well as how to lead their congregations into an understanding of the liturgy and an active participation in it. In his talk, Monsignor Hellriegel also paid tribute to Pope Pius X who had begun the liturgical renewal with his *Motu proprio* of 1903 and expressed the idea that a "new *Quadragesimo Anno*" may be coming out in its commemoration in 1943.[2] This did prove to be the year in which Pope Pius XII issued his encyclical on *The Mystical Body of Christ*; it came twenty-one years after Martin Hellriegel began teaching it consciously and explicitly at O'Fallon.

The liturgical day in Milwaukee was geared to laity as well as to clergy. The general introduction to the meaning of the Mystical Body, the liturgy of Church, and something of the history behind how the Church got to its present stage was followed by discussion of the liturgy as a source of the power to reconstruct society on a basis of true justice and charity. He also gave practical suggestions for the intensification of the life of the liturgy through the living of a liturgical life in both parish and home.[3] Throughout his presentations and discussions he used illustrations with a blackboard and chalk. So frequently did he use this technique in lecturing that on one occasion when he was asked what initial "B" in his name stood for, he replied, "Blackboard." Here again can be seen Monsignor Hellriegel's skill in using simple tools to aid in the communication with his audiences. His illustrations helped to bring all that he said to a concrete level where it could be easily grasped by his listeners. In discussing the Mass, he used an even more vivid visual aid, a set of slides which he himself had made while he was at O'Fallon.[4] His ability to use imaginative means of presentations came largely through his own creative talent and his hard work. In the early 1940's slide lectures were a rarity.

Both days were quite successful. The Milwaukee one was described as "attended by over 800 enthusiastic listeners."[5] The Atchison day was sponsored by three cooperating bishops, one of whom was Bishop Winkelmann, Monsignor Hellriegel's former associate at St. Charles during his newly ordained days. It was described by the editor of *Orate Fratres* as the "most 'official' gathering, and easily ranking first among the Liturgical Days thus far observed."[6] Monsignor Hellriegel continued enlightening and charming audiences during these kinds of days for over twenty years.

Religious communities were also eager to plan liturgical days and institutes for their members. Again Monsignor Hellriegel ranked high on the list of those likely to be invited to lead the group through talks and discussions. The monks of Conception Abbey enlisted him to present a talk on the Mass during a liturgical institute held from August 8 to 16 in 1942. During this institute, he spoke to about seventy seminarians. Talks on occasions such as this one were given at many other places also.[7]

Monsignor Hellriegel also continued to be active in supporting the activities of the Central Bureau, the group that had published his first article back in 1925. He addressed the 1942 annual convention of the Catholic Union of Missouri and the Catholic Women's Union on the subject of sanctifying the Sunday through a deeper love for and appreciation of the Holy Sacrifice of the Mass.[8] That same year Monsignor Hellriegel was on hand to lead Compline at the closing of the annual national convention of the Catholic Central Verein of America held in St. Louis[9] as well as simply tell them about it. The most far distant place to request this presentation was his home parish of Heppenheim. He obliged and gave his talk on "the life and activities of Holy Cross Parish at St. Louis" in the parish hall in Heppenheim in October of 1949.[10]

Monsignor Hellriegel also came to be a favorite speaker for religious communities for occasions such as reception and profession and for monasteries on solemn events such as the blessing of a new abbot. One example of a talk of the former category is the one he gave to the Sisters of St. Mary in St. Louis. He typically stressed at such ceremonies the progressive stages of reception of the habit, first vows, and final vows, emphasizing that the most significant step was the last one. In it there was not only the human action of the sister making life-long vows to God, but God acting to consecrate her to His love and service in a special way. He was able to inspire the sisters to realize that what was occuring in their final profession was more than their taking of vows but was caught up in the action of Christ made present in the liturgy of the Church.[11]

When the monks of New Subiaco Abbey were installing their new abbot in 1957, Monsignor Hellriegel was invited to address the group. He beautifully unfolded for the monks the role of the abbot as the mediator of the grace of Christ. He compared the monastic family to the Mystical Body of Christ and showed that for both the well spring of life was the sacred liturgy: the Mass, the sacraments, and the divine office.[12] In talks such as this Monsignor Hellriegel demonstrated his ability to reach both those who had some initiation into liturgical studies as well as those for whom the field was foreign territory. His same sincerity and inner depth and ability to inspire were present in each situation.

Religious communities and diocesan seminaries were both highly interested in having Monsignor Hellriegel as a retreat master. During his life he gave over seventy-five retreats for groups of priests. There was no set series of conferences; each retreat was influenced by the season of the liturgical year, the feast days which occured during the retreat, and the needs of the particular group, but the themes of membership in the body of Christ and participation in the reenactment of His saving mysteries were ever present. The current teachings of the official Church in regard to liturgy would also affect the content of the retreat. When Pope Pius XII issued his *Mediator Dei* in 1947, Monsignor Hellriegel focused on its message. By 1964 the Vatican Council's *Constitution on the Sacred Liturgy* was available. It then became a basis for much of the content of the retreat conferences.[13] For Monsignor Hellriegel this involved constant study and reflection on both the liturgical texts and on the documents embodying Church teaching on the liturgy.[14]

Seminaries were often interested in Monsignor Hellriegel as a lecturer as well as a retreat master. He gave a series of lectures at Mundelein Seminary on the Holy Sacrifice of the Mass in 1941. He repeated the lectures for the Holy Cross parishioners during the following Lent. In these lectures he explained the Mass, section by section, insisting that there were not three principal parts of offertory, consecration, and communion as usually held, but two principal parts, the fore-Mass and the sacrifice-Mass. The former was explained as a dialog between man and God. Man speaks his sorrow and praise and petition. God gives His word through the scriptural readings and their explanation in the sermon. The Word of God is seen as not only instruction, but revelation. It is both God's message and God's presence.[15] The sacrifice-Mass is Christ drawing man into His self-gift to the Father; it is the objective presence of Christ's work of redemption.[16] Historical background was given in order to make certain parts of the Mass more understandable. Realizing what the offertory of the Mass originally was like can enhance the meaning for present-day participants. All of these ideas, greatly appreciated by the audience at Mundelein were the daily bread of the people of Holy Cross. They were presented in a systematic fashion during the lenten lecture series but were brought into the very life stream of all that went on in the parish. Again, the ideas that Monsignor Hellriegel clarified and worked out for his lecture enriched his congregation at Holy Cross, and, conversely, his experience of having lived out his own ideas in his own parish lent irreplaceable creditibility to his statements in his talks.

By the 1950's colleges and universities were also beginning to seek out the knowledgeable and dynamic Monsignor as speaker and lecturer. For the summer of 1950 Monsignor Hellriegel planned for Fontbonne College, St. Louis, a series of daily lectures for the summer school session. The lectures were based on *Mediator Dei* and were given by a team of priests, most of whom were members of the liturgical seminar group which had been meeting under Monsignor Hellriegel's leadership for many years. In the talk Monsignor Hellriegel himself delivered, he referred to *Mediator Dei* as the "Magna Carta" of the liturgy. He pointed to Christ as the "Mediator between God and man, the only One through whom we can come to God and through whom all life flows from God." But the divine Mediator mediates in specific ways, the primary of which is the liturgy. Monsignor Hellriegel told his audience, "If the liturgy means the primary fountains of life, then we must wholeheartedly return to these fountains in order to have life."[17] He noted that although law is important in protecting life, legalism stifles life. He encouraged his audience to be aware of the origin of this life by developing a consciousness of their Baptism and its ongoing effect. He also urged prayerful study of *Mediator Dei*, saying, "It will awaken in you a great love for our Holy Lord, will enkindle a new appreciation of holy Baptism."[18] The lecture series was then continued by the rest of the team while Monsignor Hellriegel went to New York to teach at the Pius X School of Liturgical Music.[19]

Both courses were met with such success that an encore was requested for the next summer. Again Monsignor Hellriegel organized the Fontbonne programs but let his confreres do most of the actual teaching. Simultaeously, he was giving daily lectures for three weeks at the Pius X School in New York and then departed for the Trapp music center in Vermont for two more weeks of daily conferences.[20]

During the summer of 1955 Monsignor Hellriegel found himself on the faculty of Notre Dame teaching in its liturgy summer program. During this session, he gave one special lecture entitled "How to Make the Church Year a Living Reality." This lecture was repeated in St. Louis at the National Catholic Educational Association Convention the following spring. It consisted mainly of suggestions of ways in which teachers and pastors could work with children in a school situation to bring them to a lively appreciation of and enthusiasm for participation in the liturgy. In giving this presentation he cited many examples of activities at Holy Cross School. His talk was published first in the National Catholic Education Association Bulletin and later in booklet form and is characteristic of much of the writing which Monsignor Hellriegel was doing along with his extensive lecturing and his intensive program of liturgical prayer in his own parish.[21]

From 1940 to 1956 Monsignor Hellriegel had at least thirty articles published in which he gave suggestions for practical ways of celebrating the liturgical year at the parish level. One series of eleven articles appeared in volume fifteen of *Orate Fratres* during

1940 and 1941. Entitled "Merely Suggesting," it was regarded by many as the single most influential series of articles to appear in that journal.[22] It drew heavily on practices which Monsignor Hellriegel was initiating during his own first year as pastor at Holy Cross. For pastors who were interested in implementing litugical participation but searching for the "how," these articles constituted a most valuable guide. Fifteen years later, Monsignor Hellriegel did another similar series for the same journal, by then called *Worship*. Many of his same suggestions remained but they were tried and proven by fifteen years of pastoral experience. Monsignor Hellriegel had decided to do a sequel to his earlier series because he was still receiving by mail and in person many requests for help and suggestions in implementing liturgical participation at the parish level. He finally found it impossible to answer "by typewriter or pen all these requests." The series proved fruitful and provoked a different kind of mail, namely letters expressing appreciation for the articles and the help they were giving.[23] In the interim between series occasional articles on the same themes appeared both in *Orate Fratres* and *Living Parish*.[24]

Monsignor Hellriegel's writings have come to the public in book form on only two occasions. Both of these books originated as the spoken word in lectures and homilies. The same material then appeared in series of articles, and the final step was the collection into book form. The first of his two books to be published was the one which grew out of the lecture series on the holy sacrifice of the Mass at Mundelein Seminary and again at his parish. The *Living Parish* Vol. III and IV, 1942-1943, carried the series of articles. The book, the *Holy Sacrifice of the Mass*, came out in 1944. The publication in book form did result in the material having a wider circulation. It was praised by reviewers and recommended for those interested in Catholic Action. Comments of reviewers include this excerpt from *Orate Fratres*: "[The *Holy Sacrifice of the Mass*] is distinguished above most of its predecessors by the warmth of its language, the directness of it personal applications, and its simple manner of stating profound spiritual truths. In a word, it makes the Mass live in mind and heart."[25] The same warmth, simplicity, and practicality which had so readily enabled Monsignor to reach the people of his own parish also enabled him to reach a wider audience.

The other book authored by Monsignor Hellriegel is a collection of meditations on the various feasts and Sundays and weekdays of Lent and Advent. The evolution of this volume was similar to that of the first one. The meditation originated in the thoughts which he shared with his congregation at the homily of the Eucharistic celebration. They were the product of Monsignor Hellriegel's own study and reflection and prayer. They were spoken with his usual simple yet forceful style. The next step was the transferring of the spoken word to the printed page. In the transition nothing was lost either of the simplicity and directiveness nor of the profundity and inspirational value. The first printed form was a series of twelve articles in volume eighteen of *Orate Fratres* during 1943 and 1944. Favorable responses from readers prompted Monsignor Hellriegel to commit his work to a more permanent form.[26] In 1948 *Vine and Branches*, containing his series of articles and some additional material, was published.

Praise from reviewers of this second volume even exceeded that for the first. Father Thomas Carroll, writing in *Orate Fratres*, characterizes the book as having not only "his simplicity and his depth" but also "his love for the living Church." He goes on to predict that the reader will be left with "a deep realization of the warmth and the life of the Church's year."[27] Father Carroll seems to pinpoint here significant characteristics not only of this one work by Monsignor Hellriegel but of all his work. His ability to communicate not only information about the Church and her liturgy but a love for that Church and liturgy, his ability to combine depth with simplicity, his ability to leave his listener or reader not only greater intellectual understanding but with a warmer heart and a sense of life — these seem to be traits which account for his unusual success in bringing a life of vibrant liturgical prayer to those whom he touched, and most especially to those he touched so regularly for so long, namely the people of his own parish.

In addition to these major undertakings in writing, Monsignor Hellriegel also wrote regular articles and short pamphlets on a variety of topics related to the liturgy. These included general explanations of the liturgy and the liturgical movement, treatments of the sacraments, pleas for the sanctification of the Sunday, commentaries on the teachings of *Mediator Dei*, biographical sketches on Pius X, and many more.[28] In all of these writings his usual practicality and simplicity were evident. His eye was always on the reader; nothing was ever lost by big words or abstract contexts; all related to the life situation of the reader, taking him where he was and moving him closer to an identification with Christ and with His Church.

Yet, Monsignor Hellreigel knew that the printed word was not always the most effective medium of communication. Therefore, he tried to reach out in other ways. During the 1950's, when audiovisual materials were not yet commonplace, Monsignor Hellriegel was making records and movies to try to spread understanding of the liturgy and to facilitate participation in the liturgy. For the 1949 Liturgical Week, Monsignor Hellriegel had arranged a booklet for congregational participation in the high Mass. His booklet was entitled simply *Our Sung Mass*; it consisted of selections from different Masses from the *Liber*, chosen for ease in being learned by a group. These selections were *Kyrie* III, *Gloria* X, *Sanctus* XII, *Agnus Dei* IV, *Credo* III. The boys' choir of Holy Cross recorded this Mass; their singing was described as "fresh, vigorous, yet reverent; and rhythmically alive."[29] The record came to be an effective means of promoting congregational participation in the high Mass. The widespread success of this record encouraged a second, a recording of the "Novena for Christmas," including hymns, prayers, and Gregorian chant selections again by the choristers of Holy Cross. This record, which came out in December 1951, was another great asset in enabling other groups to learn to pray together in song appropriate to the season of the liturgical year.[30] These were followed by further recordings of selected parts of the propers of various feasts.[31]

An even further reaching audiovisual aid to liturgical education was Monsignor Hellriegel's 16mm film, "We Give Thanks," presenting an explanation of the Holy Sacrifice of the Mass as a commentary to the actions of the priest at the altar. This film had the effect of making Monsignor Hellriegel's demonstration of Holy Mass, which had become a prominent part of the Liturgical Weeks, available to a much wider audience. The film was available for rental by the late 1950's.[32]

The outstanding work of Monsignor Hellriegel in the Liturgical Apostolate did not go unrecognized. In 1949 the rank of Domestic Prelate was bestowed upon him in "explicit recognition of his liturgical activities."[33] Tribute came from the official Church again in 1964 when Monsignor Hellriegel was made Protonotary Apostolic. On this occasion Cardinal Ritter said of him, "If there is anything that marks him..., it is his zeal, that fire that consumes him for the glory of God, for the honor of His Church, His Altar and His sanctuary."[34] These words were addressed to the parishioners of Holy Cross in whose presence and church the ceremony took place. Monsignor Hellriegel chose to celebrate this rare honor with the people to whom the greatest of his efforts were directed and in whom the greatest of his fruits could be seen. It was they who had benefited from that zeal for Church and altar and sanctuary, and that extraordinary zeal was a significant factor in the great spirit of liturgical prayer found among the people of Holy Cross.

The academic and literary worlds within the Church also showed an awareness and appreciation of the great work Monsignor Hellriegel had done and was continuing to do. In 1955 St. Benedict's College of Atchison, Kansas, awarded him the honorary degree of Doctor of Humane Letters.[35] *Orate Fratres* acknowledged that "his articles, his friendship and his advice have been a determining factor in *Orate Fratres'* history."[36] That same periodical awarded to him the Blessed Pius X Medal "given in grateful recognition of twenty-five years of generous collaboration as Associate Editor."[37] By 1957, that same magazine now called *Worship* reported that in thirty-one years Monsignor Hellriegel had written for its pages a total of sixty-two articles. On the occasion of his fiftieth jubilee of his ordination to the priesthood, the editor of *Worship* Godfrey Diekmann devoted two full pages to the praise of Monsignor Hellriegel. His closing words summarize a widespread feeling, "We are grateful to God for Monsignor Hellriegel's vision and priestly example.[38]

His "nickname" as the "American Pius Parsch" dated back to his pioneer days at O'Fallon. By 1952 his reputation as a pastoral liturgist had spread to the extent that an effective way to describe the English Father Clifford Howell to American readers proved to be "an English Hellriegel."[39] Perhaps this recognition of Monsignor

Hellriegel's work is less direct than those previously cited, but it nonetheless conveys common knowledge of Monsignor Hellriegel's great work.

Monsignor Hellriegel was not only the recipient of tribute from others; he was also quite ready to give recognition and praise to his fellow workers in the liturgical apostolate. He often made it a point to write articles of tribute upon the death of one of his fellow workers. His homilies and articles were cherished for their sensitivity and positiveness, and a number of them wound up in print.[40] The choice of Monsignor Hellriegel as celebrant and/or homilist at the funeral Masses of many of the other "greats" of the liturgical apostolate is also an indication of the close personal ties which Monsignor Hellriegel developed with those with whom he worked. This trait of building close personal relationships is another quality that contributed both to his work as a national leader in the liturgical apostolate and to his work at Holy Cross Parish. The senses of warmth and personal concern which continually radiated from him were powerful forces in drawing others to him personally and to the message which he spoke.

Monsignor Hellriegel kept up an extraordinary schedule of work, combining a usual participation in parish activities with a staggering amount of writing and lecturing. During this time he also retained the customs begun at O'Fallon of extensive correspondence directed to all parts of the United States as well as to many places in Europe and even as far away as Australia combined with playing host to a steady stream of visitors, again from all over the United States, Europe, and beyond, who came to Holy Cross to learn more about participation in the liturgy and how to foster that participation on their own turf. Many went away profoundly influenced by their visit to Holy Cross. It is this influence on individuals and on specific groups that will be the focus of the next chapter.

CHAPTER ELEVEN

The Influence
of Monsignor Hellriegel

For more than fifty years of his priestly life, Monsignor Martin Hellriegel was a national and international leader of the liturgical apostolate. His most outstanding work was on the pastoral level; the people to whom he directly ministered at O'Fallon and at Holy Cross were the foremost beneficiaries of his labors. Yet, his range of influence went far beyond these centers. The thousands of people who heard him speak during his many retreats, lectures, liturgical conference presentations, and courses were without exception moved to a deeper understanding of and love for liturgical prayer. His writings brought spiritual enrichment to many. Yet, Monsignor Hellriegel not only carried out a liturgical apostolate himself, he prepared others to do the same.

One of the first men, himself to become prominent as a liturgist, influenced profoundly by Hellriegel, was Alphonse Westhoff, a boy server at O'Fallon when Hellriegel first went there as chaplain. Alphonse finished the two-year parish high school and was tutored by Fathers Hellriegel and Jasper during the next two years in preparation for entering the seminary. Hellriegel concentrated especially on lessons in Greek for his young friend; however, the young Westhoff learned more than Greek. He also imbibed something of his tutor's zeal for the liturgy. When Westhoff was a student at Kenrick seminary in the 1920's, he found his background in the liturgy almost unique. Therefore, he organized an unofficial study group for a group of seminarians. They began to read and study and discuss articles on the liturgy supplied by Hellriegel via Westhoff. The priests at Kenrick looked upon the group as a bit eccentric but harmless, so they were allowed to continue. This study club served as an introduction to the liturgy for two other men who would in time prove to be ones who took initiative in things liturgical: Mark Ebner and Victor Suren. All three of these men were active in the Liturgical Conference as speakers at Liturgical Weeks and as directors. Westhoff held the office of vice-president of the conference in 1957. Westhoff and Ebner both came to be pastors of parishes in the St. Louis area during the 1940's and to implement to a significant degree the liturgical participation pioneered at O'Fallon and Holy Cross. Westhoff also contributed articles to *Orate Fratres*. He was represented in its first volume as coauthor, with Hellriegel, of an article on the history of the liturgical movement; at that time he was still a seminarian. He authored a number of articles by himself in later years. Most of the articles centered on themes which were also often the subject of addresses and articles by Monsignor Hellriegel.[1]

Hellriegel's influence on the early visitors to O'Fallon has already been mentioned. Gerald Ellard was certainly the most outstanding of those early visitors. His work is too vast and well known to be discussed here.[2] A Jesuit who had accompanied Gerald Ellard to O'Fallon in those early days was William Puetter. He came often both to O'Fallon and later to Holy Cross and came to take an active part in the Liturgical Conference as a speaker and participant in the Liturgical Weeks. He contributed his creative talents to such family helps as the *Christian Life Calendar*.[3]

By 1938 Archbishop Glennon had become active in promoting understanding of the liturgy in the St. Louis Archdiocese and had enlisted Martin Hellriegel to begin a priests' study group in order to have a core of priests in the archdiocese who would be knowledgeable in regard to the liturgy and able to take leadership.

The study group came to include some of the members of Father Westhoff's seminary group; Westhoff himself, Ebner, Suren, as well as a number of other priests who took leadership locally in the liturgy and Father Aloysius Wilmes who became a leader of the Liturgical Conference. Work on a local level included the giving of impetus to liturgical participation in various parishes as well as exerting leadership in promoting liturgical understanding through courses and sermons. It was from this group of priests that Monsignor Hellriegel drew the lecturers for the summer courses at Fontbonne College during the early 1950's. Through this study group liturgical renewal in the St. Louis area was put on firm theological ground and the St. Louis Archdiocese came to be in the "forefront of dioceses in terms of liturgically active pastors and parishes."[4]

In addition to a contribution in the St. Louis area, Father Wilmes was outstanding in his work in the Liturgical Conference. It was he who was Monsignor Hellriegel's partner in the many demonstration Masses given at the Liturgical Weeks; he held the office of secretary for about ten years and the office of vice-president one year. He was responsible for editing the proceedings of the Liturgical Weeks, thereby bringing the talks in printed form to many throughout the country. He was also a frequent speaker at the Liturgical Weeks.[5] It was Father Wilmes who submitted regular write-ups on the Liturgical Weeks to *Worship*, thus performing a valuable service in giving publicity to the Liturgical Weeks.[6]

Although there were many who responded favorably to the work of Monsignor in the liturgy, this favorable response was far from universal. Some suspicion toward his work in the liturgy existed already during his O'Fallon days. When he managed to implement the same liturgical practices and instill the same spirit at Holy Cross, in a parish setting, his critics who had said, "It can't be done," were not silenced. Snide remarks and insinuations about all the "goings on" at Holy Cross were not infrequent, especially among other priests who lacked a deep understanding of and appreciation of the liturgy. One example of the false stories that made the rounds was that on Palm Sunday Monsignor Hellriegel rode a donkey down the main aisle of the Church. Less sensational criticisms tended to take the form of:

"Everyone knows that Martin Hellriegel is a wonderful priest...
But why does he have to do this, or why does he have to do that?
...It is these things that upset the clergy..."[7] His suggestions for
evening Masses and relaxed Eucharistic fast, made in 1942,
merited the accusation of being "Not quite Catholics." His
advocating of the use of the vernacular in the liturgy caused
some to allude to the Robber Synod of Pistoia; his use of the
dialog Mass brought another crop of condemnations. When in
1948 he made his historic statement expressing hope for a restored Paschal Vigil liturgy in the near future, accusations ranged
from affronting the Holy See to being an unrealistic dreamer who
should realize that such changes were at least a century away.[8]

Problems also came to Monsignor Hellriegel from official
channels in the Church. By the early 1950's there was developing
some active resistance to the progress that had been made in
bringing the people to active participation in the liturgy. There
was also at this time a prevailing feeling that the spirit of the
Church was to be found in canon law and that anything that was
not explicitly provided for by canon law was not to be practiced.
Some of the officials at the St. Louis Chancery Office were of this
mind and wrote to Rome regarding the offertory processions that
were held at Holy Cross Parish. In 1945 a reply was received from
Rome and the response was that the practice of offertory processions should not be continued. Archbishop Glennon notified
Monsignor Hellriegel to this effect but included a personal statement of commendation for his work in the liturgical movement.[9]
Hellriegel promptly stopped the processions with a complete
willingness to follow the explicit direction of Rome. He was
noticeably free of the reformer-martyr complex.

In spite of the problems and the opposition, the reputation of
Holy Cross Parish continued to grow and to attract more and
more visitors. Many came to spend several days in order to drink
in the spirit of the parish, converse with its pastor, and thus prepare themselves to go home and try to communicate its spirit in
their own ministry. To accomodate these visitors, the unused
third floor of the rectory was converted into guest rooms and the
rectory itself was enlarged by building on a section which con-
nects with the Church. The number of visitors was so great that
during one typical three-month interval the housekeeper at Holy

Cross served four hundred and twelve extra meals.[10] All who came found in their host a genuinely congenial hospitality. Many long hours were spent by Monsignor Hellriegel sharing ideas with those who had come to learn. The number of guest participants in the liturgy of Holy Cross between 1940 and 1965 is estimated by Monsignor Hellriegel to be approximately 25,000. Some came with initial skepticism; nearly all left with the joyous realization that here they experienced very vividly and very beautifully the Mystical Body at prayer. The guests included priests, religious, lay Catholics from all parts of the United States and from Europe. Bishops and abbots were also among those who came to pray with the people of Holy Cross. A sampling of the Holy Cross guest book shows entries from as far north as Minnesota, as far south as Louisiana, as well as from both coasts. France and Germany are the most frequently represented foreign countries, but visitors also came from Canada, England, and Australia. The Trapp Family are probably the most widely known of the visitors; most of the national leaders of the liturgical movement are represented. The Archabbot of Beuron wrote on May 10, 1950: "A second time received as a pilgrim in this house of Christian clarity, I have only one dream, and one desire, that from this 'Resurrection' church of Holy Cross the true apostolic form of parish life may penetrate all over through America and the whole world."[11]

Another figure prominent in the liturgical apostolate who was impressed by a visit to Holy Cross was Father Clifford Howell of England. On August 14, 1949, he participated with Father Gerald Ellard and Monsignor Martin Hellriegel in the usual Sunday 9:30 high Mass. The experiences made such an impact on him that he went home and wrote a detailed account of "A High Mass in St. Louis" for London's *Catholic Herald*.[12] He was especially struck by the realization that the extraordinary spirit and beauty of this occasion was not at all extraordinary for the people of Holy Cross but was their usual Sunday experience.

Two visitors to Holy Cross during this same time became involved, partly as a result of their experience at Holy Cross, in an unusual sequence of events. These two visitors were Irvin Arkin and Ernest Beck, both students at Concordia Seminary preparing for the Lutheran ministry. Both of them were very impressed by and drawn to the liturgy as they experienced it at Holy Cross. After ordination as Lutheran ministers, each of them had a parish in the East, but stayed in some contact with Hellreigel. By 1954 Arkin and Beck and both of their families had decided to come into the Catholic Church. They moved back to St. Louis and were baptized by Hellriegel at Holy Cross during the Easter Vigil of that year and confirmed there the following Eastertide. For the next two years, Irvin Arkin worked as the organist at Holy Cross and later took a teaching position at St. Louis University. He went on to become a noted theological lecturer in the area. Ernest Beck also remained in close association with Holy Cross for a few years; he assumed the responsibility for conducting the parish Inquiry Forum. However, Beck desired to be ordained as a Roman Catholic priest. Pope Pius XII had granted a dispensation to Lutheran clergy in Germany who converted to Catholicism, allowing them to be ordained even if they were already married. Monsignor Hellriegel tried unsuccessfully to obtain from the American hierarachy a petition for a similar dispensation. When his efforts here proved futile, Hellriegel helped Ernest Beck to move to Germany where he was able to be ordained and to work as a priest of the Mainz diocese.[13]

The contributions to the parish of outstanding men such as Arkin and Beck, plus the steady stream of prominent and devoted visitors to Holy Cross, gave added vitality to the already vital parish spirit. The guests put their whole hearts into praying the liturgy and participating in the prayers and hymns. The people of the parish were made more aware of and appreciative of the uniqueness of the treasure which they possessed in the spirit of their parish by the many who came to witness and experience that spirit. There was little chance for routine to set in when there were always new people coming; there was little chance for a taking-for-granted attitude to develop when the freshness of someone's new experience of liturgical participation developed in the parish by Monsignor Hellriegel attracted visitors and the steady stream of visitors nourished that spirit.

Monsignor Hellriegel's influence on religious communities and on the religious education in which they were engaged was also significant. Of course, the order to receive the greatest of his influence was the Precious Blood order. Paul Marx, Virgil Michel's

biographer, says of them in 1957, "There is today perhaps no better liturgically trained sisterhood in the United States than the
Sisters of O'Fallon, thanks to Father Hellriegel's twenty-two years
(1918-1940) of pioneer work as chaplain." The sisters themselves
did retain a solid tradition of liturgical prayer long after Monsignor Hellriegel had left O'Fallon. They also spread this tradition to the schools and parishes in which they worked and were
active in sharing with others through discussion and through
writing ideas for religious education centered in the liturgy.

By the 1930's the sisters who were trained by Hellriegel were
making an impact on the religious education programs in the
schools in which they worked. Hellriegel's pamphlet *The Holy
Sacrifice of the Mass* was being used to introduce children to the
dialog Mass. The sisters were using drawings, posters, construc-
tive work of the children to teach the message of the gospel of the
various Sundays and feast days. Holy Week was given special
attention. The children were brought to understand the three
parts of the Good Friday liturgy, the significance of the blessing
of the fire and water of Holy Saturday, and Holy Thursday as the
special day both for the Eucharist and for the reconciliation of
the public penitents.[14]

Advent was another special focus of attention in religion
classes. The children were taught to look to the three great models of this season: Isaias, John the Baptist, and Mary. They used
an Advent wreath in the classroom and were taught the meaning
of the O Antiphons. Thus their preparation for Christmas was
grounded solidly in the prayer of the Church.[15]

The liturgical value of the time after Christmas was not
neglected in the sisters' religion classes. The children were led
into full participation in the liturgies of such days as the
Epiphany and Candlemas. They were taught the relationship between the feast of the Epiphany and the final epiphany of the
parousia of Christ. They became familiar with the symbolic value
of the candle for the Christian. The children thereby grew in both
their understanding of the Christian faith and in their ability to
enter intelligently and prayerfully into the liturgy.[16]

Consciousness of Baptism and Confirmation in their lives were
further goals which the sisters set for the children. Feasts such as
Pentecost were used not only for instruction on the scriptural and

liturgical background of the feast but also on the here and now impact of the reception of the Spirit through Baptism and Confirmation on the lives of the children.[17] Of course, the occasion of the actual reception of Confirmation in a parish afforded another occasion for renewing this sacramental consciousness. Preparation for Confirmation took the form of a study of both the meaning and the rite of the sacrament. The children were prepared to enter actively into the ritual for the sacrament. Every effort was made to insure an understanding of what was going on by those who were actually receiving the sacrament. The day was memorialized by giving each newly confirmed child a card with a symbol of the Holy Spirit, his name, and the words of the sacrament.[18]

The sisters soon came to be known as assets to a parish. Monsignor Mark Ebner, pastor of St. George Parish, St. Louis, found a great help in leading his parish to liturgical participation in the work of the Precious Blood Sisters. Archbishop Glennon once said of them, "Every parish priest in Missouri who has the Precious Blood Sisters wants them to stay, and those who have new parishes want them also."[19]

The Precious Blood community also came to be known for its leadership in the promotion of liturgically appropriate Church art and of Gregorian chant. Their artistic efforts were channeled into the making of vestments and later into designing liturgically fitting cards for such occasions as Baptisms, Confirmations, weddings, birth announcements, condolence cards. Each contained a text taken from the liturgy and "chosen with intelligent care."[20] It is no wonder that the Precious Blood community merited an article of appreciation in *Orate Fratres* on the occasion of the centenary of their foundation. In it the author expressed gratitude to them for the work they have done "for the restoration of the true Christian spirit."[21] He also points to the inspiration and direction of Father Martin Hellriegel as the guiding force behind the direction taken by the community.[22]

The clergy and religious were not the only groups inspired by Hellriegel to become themselves apostles of the liturgy. The laity were also stimulated by his leadership to contribute to the growth of the liturgical apostolate. One Hellriegel-inspired nucleus of lay liturgical activity centered around Pio Decimo Press. Its founders,

Mignon McMenamy and David Dunn, first came into contact with Hellriegel through the Catholic Worker. They were active in its St. Louis branch and had gone with Peter Maurin to visit at O'Fallon in the late 1930's. The seed was planted and interest in the liturgy grew. Finally, in 1940 came the decision to begin a press dedicated to "the spread of the sacramental apostolate, for the purpose of furthering a deeper appreciation of Christ's Mystical Body."[23] It was Monsignor Hellriegel who suggested the name after the pope who had given the first impetus to liturgical renewal in the Church. The press chose, as its final location, a site in Baden so as to be close to the source of its inspiration, the liturgy as prayed at Holy Cross. However, the actual work of the press was done completely by the laity. A monthly magazine *The Living Parish*, was an outgoing project from 1940 until about 1956. It proved a valuable source for information on and education in the liturgy. Pio Decimo also published many books and pamphlets on the liturgy, thus aiding both understanding of the liturgy and making available prayer pamphlets which could facilitate participation in the liturgy. The shop headquarters also served as a neighborhood center for praying the divine office. It was open to visitors every afternoon, and the office was prayed either in English or in Latin, either in shortened form or in full length, depending on the background and interests of those who happened to be present on any given day.[24]

The people of Holy Cross Parish were also numbered among those who themselves became leaders in promoting the liturgy. Although few of them had the educational background to begin a liturgical press or to even contribute an article to a liturgical journal, many of them had learned from their pastor and the opportunity he provided them from their early years to assume leadership on the parish and community levels. Thus many of the children whom Monsignor formed in the liturgy in the 1940's and 1950's have gone on to raise their own families in other parishes and to be catalysts for education and family prayer life centered in the liturgy. The origin of the annual Badenfest, a community event aimed at preserving the culture of the neighborhood, was the direct outgrowth of the efforts of Holy Cross parishioners, again illustrating the social consequences of involvement with the liturgy.[25]

Perhaps one of the most recent liturgical leaders to feel the influence of Monsignor Hellriegel is Father Nicholas Schneider who was Hellriegel's associate at Holy Cross from 1958 to 1971. Schneider had become acquainted with Hellriegel during his own seminary days through the liturgical weeks, especially the 1949 week which was held in St. Louis. He began attending services at Holy Cross for the feast days of the liturgical year. After his ordination he requested an assignment at Holy Cross, and after spending his first two years in the priesthood in the home missions in southeast Missouri, he was sent to Holy Cross. Here he shared fully in the pastoral work of the parish and worked closely with Monsignor Hellriegel in the carrying out of the prayer of the Church. He developed his own competence and creativity and while at Holy Cross contributed to liturgical educational resources by putting together a "little dictionary" of the common of the Mass. The dictionary contained all the words found in the ordinary of the Mass and gave their Latin form and the English translation. The book was primarily for the children of Holy Cross but was made available in limited supply to others also. It proved a help in 1960 when the ordinary of the Mass was still in Latin and teachers were seeking to make the Latin prayer intelligible to the children.[26] Schneider's talents were also directed into writing a biography of John Cardinal Glennon, the Archbishop who had given so much encouragement to Monsignor Hellriegel during the early trying days of liturgical renewal. After leaving Holy Cross Parish, Father Schneider was made a pastor and the executive secretary of the Archdiocesan Liturgical Commission. He has been able, through these two positions, to transfer some of what he learned from Monsignor Hellriegel to his own parish community and to the diocese as a whole.

It was the same charism which enabled Monsignor Hellriegel to successfully bring the people of his own parish into an active liturgical life that enabled him to inspire others to follow in his footsteps. He led by doing; anything he advocated, he was practicing. His work in inspiring liturgical leadership among others can aptly be summarized by an image suggested by Mignon McMenamy. Monsignor Hellriegel was like a pebble thrown into a pool of water. Ripples went out in all directions from the center that he himself constituted.[27]

CHAPTER TWELVE

His Last Years

M artin Hellriegel was outstanding in regard to both the quality and the quantity of the contributions he made to the liturgical movement. He literally devoted all his energy to his work in the liturgy and his priestly ministry throughout the sixty-six years of his priestly life from his ordination in December 1914 to his death in April 1981. He was extraordinary in the really insightful and far-reaching ideas he was putting into practice while still a young priest in his 20's and in the national leadership he had assumed by age 35. On the other end of the age spectrum Martin Hellriegel was equally extraordinary. He was 74 years old in 1964 when he was the celebrant at the first Roman Rite high Mass in English held in St. Louis during the largest liturgical week in history. It was here that he inspired thousands of people with his love for the liturgy and the beauty he brought to its celebration. He continued full pastoral and administrative duties at Holy Cross until 1973 when, at age 83, he needed to be relieved of some of his duties because of a heart problem that had developed two years previously. At this time Rev. Paul Zipfel (who became Bishop Zipfel in 1989) became the administrator of the parish and Monsignor Hellriegel continued as pastor until 1976 when, at age 86, he became pastor emeritus. He continued to live at Holy Cross and take an active part in parish functions up to a few months before his death in 1981.

Even his failing eyesight and total blindness by 1979 did not stop his parish involvement.

During the last five years of his life, while Martin Hellriegel was pastor emeritus at Holy Cross, he really had no formal responsibilities. Yet, even though he was in his upper 80's, he continued to contribute to the lives of his parishioners and to his friends and disciples throughout the United States and Europe. He continued his practice of nuturing in prayer his own relationship with Christ in the Scriptures and in the Eucharist.

During these years, and including the time during which Mosignor Hellriegel was totally blind, he continued hearing confessions each day for twenty to thirty minutes prior to the 8:00 a.m. Mass. Many people came to him for confession and he often continued to be the confessor for people who had moved out of the parish. He celebrated the daily children's Mass, continuing even after he was blind as he had the Eucharist prayer memorized. He gave a daily homily, always carefully prepared the night before and, as long as he was able, with notes to guide his comments. Communion calls to the sick of the parish were another of the activities that occupied his "retirement" years.

The special celebrations of the liturgical year which Monsignor Hellriegel had begun in the 1940's were still being carried out during his final years at Holy Cross. He continued to take an active part in these celebrations and was able to provide background to the various celebrations to the priests who were carrying them out during the 1970's. He retained a lively interest in the parish and its various problems and policies but did not try to impose his ideas on what practical decisions should be made.

The school children remained close to Monsignor Hellriegel's heart. He visited their classrooms as long as he was able and even conducted an annual retreat for the eighth grade. The children looked forward to a visit from the renowned Monsignor and regarded these occasions as privileges.

During these years, Monsignor Hellriegel continued, even after his blindness with the help of his life-long friend Felix Tuger, to carry out an extensive correspondence. These letters continued to inspire and encourage and to reveal the inner person of Martin Hellriegel. On July 11, 1980, he wrote to a young man about to be ordained: "...the liturgy is and ever will be the life of the Church, the divine arteries and the veins which supply our heart and our whole being with the immortal life of the Risen Lord Jesus. ...To discover the liturgy is like an acorn, which only in time with the sunshine and the dew from above will become the mighty oak tree, and once you have caught its spirit, it will, God be thanked, remain with you and achieve it perfection and complete maturity."[1] Surely this comment can be seen as an autobiographical one. Martin Hellriegel was himself that person in whom the discovery of the liturgy had achieved perfection and maturity, supplying with the life of the Risen Lord Jesus.

His famous Christmas letters reached nearly 1,400 persons each year. His Christmas letter of 1978 reflects something of his own personal spirituality:

> From the nose to the toes I am feeling well, but above the nose not so well since my right eye is completely blind and the left eye is weekly worsening. I am able to see in the distance even though it is "cloudy," but nearby very little. Reading and writing are almost zero. Two faithful helpers read my mail to me, one the German and the other the English. Won't that be a joy when the eternal light surrounds us. Then we will not need any drops four times a day, nor eyeglasses, nor magnifying glass.
>
> Keep me in your prayers, please, that Our Lord will spare me from the two insects of self-pity and sympathy-seeking. Both are worthless. My motto is: 'Pro Deo' (for God), not 'pro ego' (for me). The first (with its three letters) bears fruit, the second (with its three letters) is like 'that fig tree' in the Gospel.[2]

These comments clearly show Martin Hellriegel's God-centeredness and hopefulness in spite of his own declining physical health.

Limited physical capacity did not limit the sphere of Monsignor Hellriegel's interests. Even after he became totally blind, he continued to be interested in both local and world events. During the final years of his life, one of the associate pastors at Holy Cross, Fr. James Rutkowski, read to him from the daily local newspaper as well as from theological journals and from the missal for Monsignor Hellriegel's daily preparation of the Scripture readings for the next day's liturgy.

His continued broad range of interests extended to a love for those European centers that had nutured his own love for liturgy. In 1977 Martin Hellriegel made his last of many trips to Europe. At this time he paid his final visit to the Abbey of Maria Laach that had contributed so much to Martin Hellriegel's theological appreciation of the liturgy. He was able to concelebrate Mass with the prior of the abbey on the feast of the Assumption of Mary, the patronal feast of the abbey. This occasion brought much joy to Monsignor Hellriegel and was the highlight of his final trip to Europe.

Creative contributions to liturgical celebrations were another part of Monsignor's Hellriegel's work that he continued into the last years of his life. He wrote a complete set of musical compositions for all the responsorial psalms for all the Sundays of the liturgical year as well as a book of bidding prayers for various occasions. He was in contact with the World Library of Sacred Music regarding publication of these works but they were never published.

Monsignor Hellriegel lived the final years of his life in the same way he had lived the rest of his life. His energies were totally focused on the praise of the Lord. He was not one to waste time or to pursue activities unrelated to the central purpose of his life. He was described by Bishop Zipfel, who lived with him at Holy Cross for the last ten years of his life, as a man who was "in love with the Lord from head to toe."[3]

Even though Monsignor Hellriegel was a man with a single strong focus in his life, he also had a heart that reached out to all. He was a person of great sensitivity and gentleness and graciousness. He had a geniune interest in each person and an ability to communicate to each person that he or she was instantly accepted and loved. As one person commented, "Once you met him, you felt as if you had known him all your life.'[4] Even to the end of his life Martin Hellriegel radiated that same personal warmth that Dorothy Day had experienced when she visited Holy Cross in 1952. She commented at that time that she came to Holy Cross, as many others do, "to warm themselves at Monsignor

Hellriegel."[5] He retained a healthy sense of humor and a common sense approach to life. He lived by one of his favorite sayings, "Keep your feet on the ground, your heart on the cross, and your head in heaven."

The final two years of Monsignor Hellriegel's life, when he was totally blind were difficult for him. Although he was able to continue some of his priestly functions, he did need help with the little things of daily life and with personal tasks. He accepted help graciously and gratefully and was never cross or critical. He was able to face blindness with a joyful resignation and to continue living with a spirit of prayer.[6] He spent his days calmly, centered in the Lord, as he had been during his more active years. Ann Kosciolek, who lived at Holy Cross during Monsignor Hellriegel's latter years and served as parish cook, gave much personal assistance to Monsignor Hellriegel. She described him as humble during his time of sickness and incapacity and appreciative and kind toward all who assisted him.[7]

During his final years, Monsignor Hellriegel continued to enjoy recognition for his work in the liturgical movement. In 1976 he received the Kendrick Seminary Distinguished Alumnus Award in recognition for "an exemplary life of priestly service."[8] In 1980 he received the Mathis Award for exceptional contributions to pastoral liturgy.[9]

It was only in January of 1981 at age 90 that the illness began which finally prevented Monsignor Hellriegel's continued functioning at Holy Cross. He was hospitalized in February and in March returned to the Motherhouse of the Precious Blood Sisters at O'Fallon, the place of his original work in liturgical renewal and the place that he himself had described as the "cradle of the Liturgical Movement." Monsignor Hellriegel, at this point, needed more care than could be provided at Holy Cross, and it was the sisters whom he had nurtured during their novitiate who cared for him at the end of his life.

Monsignor Hellriegel lived at O'Fallon from March 16, 1981, until the day of his death on April 10, 1981. During these weeks, he was described by the sisters who cared for him as a "model of patience and humility." He remained cheerful, never complaining, never depressed. He spent his final days praying and meditating as well as receiving visitors. On most days he was able to celebrate the Eucharist which he called "the Sunshine of my life."[10].

During this time he retained both his sense of humor and his concern for others. On one occasion one of the sisters commented that he was getting so thin that he should be called "Father Bones." Monsignor Hellriegel retorted, "When one is travelling upward, he should not have too much in the bag."[11] He was heard talking and laughing with some of the young aides at O'Fallon less than two hours before his death.

On the afternoon of his death, he phoned his friend from Holy Cross, Ann Kosciolek, who was ill and hospitalized at the time. Ann told Monsignor Hellriegel that she was going home soon. Monsignor Hellriegel replied that he too was going home. It was only later that evening, when she received word of Monsignor Hellriegel's death that the earlier remark made its full impact.[12]

Martin Hellriegel suffered his final heart attack about 8:00 p.m. on April 10, 1981, in his room at O'Fallon. He was given emergency medical care as well as spiritual care from both Monsignor Charles Schmitt, who was also in retirement at O'Fallon and had taken Monsignor Hellriegel's place as chaplain in 1940, and Monsignor Aloysius Wilmes, Monsignor Hellriegel's long time associate in the National Liturgical conference and partner in the demonstration Masses at the National Liturgical Weeks and the current chaplain at O'Fallon. Monsignor Hellriegel was taken to St. Peter's Hospital in St. Peter's Missouri and was pronounced dead of cardiac arrest. The time of his death was 9:00 p.m.

He was honored at his death by a wake and Mass at Holy Cross followed by a memorial Mass at the St. Louis Cathedral the next day and finally a funeral Mass and burial at O'Fallon on April 15, 1981. Monsignor Hellriegel had left a request that there be no eulogy at his funeral but that his good friend and colleague, Monsignor Alphonse Westhoff read a spiritual testament which he had written in 1960. The testament reads as follows:

1. With profound gratitude I bow down before our heavenly Father, His only begotten Son, our Redeemer, and before

the most Holy Spirit for the grace of membership in the **One, Holy, Catholic** and **Apostolic Church**, which I embrace with my whole heart and mind, in which I desire to live all the days of my life and in whose bosom I desire to close my earthly life.

2. I am deeply thankful to the most Holy Trinity for the call to the priesthood of Christ. I have thanked God daily for this holy and unmerited gift. If I had to become a priest again, I would, with all the strength of my soul, once more embrace and receive it, only more humbly, more readily, more gracefully. May the Divine High Priest in His unspeakable mercy pardon my many shortcomings and repair with His Precious Blood whatever weaknesses have occurred in others through lack of faith, generosity and thoughtfulness on my part.

3. I herewith renew my loyalty to our Holy Father, the Pope, to my Archbishop and to all who, as representatives of Christ the Lord, have been set over me as superiors and leaders.

4. I pardon wholeheartedly anyone who has caused me grief and ask all whom I have offended, willingly or unwillingly, to forgive me in the Charity of God.

5. In heaven I shall pray for all, particularly for those who bore with my shortcomings. I shall thank the eternal God for the love and inspiration which the good people of St. Peter's Parish in St. Charles, the noble and devoted Sisters of the Precious Blood Community of O'Fallon and my beloved flock of Holy Cross Parish have given me.

6. From all my heart I bid all **Farewell**. I wish to assure the children of the parish of an unending love with which my heart was always filled toward them. May all of them grow up to full maturity in Christ, faithful to Mother Church, devoted to their parish, an honor to Holy Cross, to their parents and to their shepherd who will never forget them.

7. Last, but not least, may the faithful Sisters of the O'Fallon Community who during 22 years of my chaplaincy have given me an abundance of inspiration and encouragement, and my dear flock of Holy Cross who

since 1940 have so loyally stood behind my priestly efforts, continue to **Love more and more** the most **Holy Sacrifice of the Mass**, the source of all holiness, the bond of true Christian fellowship and the foremost token of our glorious immortality and never-ending joy. And when gathered around the altar with their priests may they in their charity remember their shepherd and father in Christ.

Monsignor Westhoff did read this testament and also addressed a short eulogy to a crowd that packed the cathedral. He drew a comparison between Monsignor Hellriegel and the prophet Elijah and suggested that just as Elisha had prayed for something of Elijah's spirit to remain with him, so too the congregation may pray that something of Martin Hellriegel's spirit may be left with them.[13]

Monsignor Hellriegel had also left a request regarding an inscription for his tombstone. He asked that it read simply, "He loved the Church." This is indeed inscribed on his tombstone in the cemetery at O'Fallon along with the dates of his birth, baptism, ordination, and death.

The death of Monsignor Hellriegel took place on the Friday before Holy Week. In his sermon at the Chrism Mass on Holy Thursday, Archbishop John May recognized Monsignor Hellriegel's commitment to liturgical prayer up through the end of his life with the comment in his homily, "Monsignor Hellriegel arranged to celebrate Holy Week in heaven. And, of course, he would never have interferred with the Triduum."[14]

Immediately following Martin Hellriegel's death, there were a number of articles in contemporary journals paying tribute to him. Fred Moleck wrote in the *Pastoral Music* issue of June 1981:

It was his life that propelled the liturgical movement of the 20th century. He was the architect whose unearthing and whose scaffolding provided much of the design of today's liturgy. If there was ever a heroic life with struggle and frustration and triumph delayed, his life was one of them.

Armed with his *Liber Usualis*, Msgr. Hellriegel excited and cultivated vocal participation in the liturgy. Sidestepping ecclesiastical reprimand, he dodged forward and championed sung prayer at sung liturgy. This was years before the emergence of the statement that "musical liturgy is normative." His pioneer work with the Liturgical Conference inspired new respect for the flow and beauty of ritual well done. The demonstration Masses' and his presiding style were models for the American Church. And of course, his hymn "*To Jesus Christ Our Sovereign King.*" was a harbinger of what spirited hymn writing and singing were to be.

Viewed as a giant from the safe distance of time, his work is work of prophecy — not in the rattling words of a Haggai or an Amos, but in the style of a prophet who plants himself in the front waters of a current that was to move his Church into a period of ferment and fruit. This fruit we all have enjoyed as we now find ourselves in the second decade of post-Conciliar liturgy....

The truimph of Msgr. Hellriegel is now part of the liturgical life of the Church. We celebrate a liturgy that is "simple, clear and dignified." If the liturgy falls short of this, it is because *we* are not "simple, clear and dignified." We sing in our language. If the language is less than heroic, it is because our own heroism sags. The personal truimph of Msgr. Hellriegel is one that is sung in the last phrases of his hymn — "To you and to your Church, great King / We pledge our hearts' oblation: /Until before your throne we sing / In endless jubilation." May his heroism continue to ring and inspire. May he continue to sing in endless jubilation.[15]

In the May 8, 1981 issue of *National Catholic Reporter*, Godfrey Diekmann, OSB, himself a giant of the liturgical movement, gave the following praise to Monsignor Hellriegel:

Hellriegel was already an old man when Vatican II occurred. More important, perhaps, the council sanctioned far more than he and other pioneers had ever dared hope for. We now had a "new deal."

But Hellriegel *did* lay the necessary foundations even for the newer developments. He loved the church. And he always remained young enough to appreciate the need of flexibility according to ever-new pastoral exigencies. Such openness and boundless dedication in the service to God's people are "liturgical" lessons every generation can profit from.[16]

Throughout his life Martin Hellriegel's talks and writings were always generously sprinkled with images and symbols. Among his favorite was his comparison of the liturgy to a garden. He saw the ceremonies that made up the tangible, external part of the liturgy as the fence that surrounded the garden. The fence was important so that the garden could flourish, but it was not the garden itself. Liturgy itself, the garden, was seen as the union of the heart and mind with Jesus Christ in giving praise and thanks to the Father. Martin Hellriegel, referred to on occasion as the "liturgical gardner,"[17] now has no more need of the fence; he is caught up for eternity in the enjoyment of the fruit of the garden.

CHAPTER THIRTEEN

Conclusion

A t Holy Cross Parish in St. Louis, liturgical renewal reached those for whom it was intended, according to the first issue of *Orate Fratres*. In the words of its editor, liturgical renewal came to affect "both the individual spiritual life of the Catholic and the corporate life of the ...parish."[1] At Holy Cross Parish the liturgy was lived outside a specialized center. Has this achievement been a unique event, dependent upon the personality of Martin Hellriegel and impossible without his charismatic leadership? Is his work repeatable? Can those interested in liturgical renewal today learn something from the Holy Cross experience that would be applicable to their own situations?

It is clear that Monsignor Hellriegel's personality included many of the most significant reasons for his success. He was a strong person who held firm to his convictions and prudently acted on his beliefs in spite of oppositions or lack of appreciation. He was a charming person, one who immediately evoked a positive response. He radiated a warmth and a concern for each person; he was thoughtful and sensitive and generous. He was able to convey to the other a sense of being valued and significant. he had a gentle sense of humor and was able to captivate those around him with his interesting anecdotes. In his presence one sensed a personal depth of knowledge and spirituality; one perceived an individual of dignity and responded with respect.

Martin Hellriegel had the ability to carry out a number of tasks at once, doing each carefully and thoroughly and all with a sense of calm and unhurriedness. He genuinely liked people and had the ability to bring people together and to let everyone feel included in and a necessary part of whatever was going on. He had a sense of propriety which flowed from a deep respect for all persons as well as for history and for culture. He was talented in and had an appreciation of both good art and good music. He was able to create beauty and appreciation for that beauty. He was able to devise imaginative ways of communicating with people on their level. He inspired and motivated those he contacted by his own sincerity and genuiness.

Clearly Martin Hellriegel was an unusually gifted human being, and as a person was certainly unique and unrepeatable. Still, each person is unique and unrepeatable. All will not have the depth and breadth of his gifts, yet any person working in the area of liturgical renewal can do what Monsignor Hellriegel did in the sense of mobilizing the talents he has and bringing them to bear on the task at hand. Although it is rare that such a combination of assets will be found in one person, a team approach to ministry would bring together several individuals who, working together, could bring a comparable collection of talents to the work of liturgical renewal. Perhaps an approach to ministry in which the starting point is the question of what abilities are needed in the particular situation and the follow-up is finding a group of people who collectively possess those abilities can come close to simulating the talents which, in this unusual case, were found in one man. Repetition of the personal characteristics is, therefore, possible, probably not by one person but by a team. That such a combination of personal attributes would be a great aid to effective work in the liturgical renewal at the parish level today seems obvious.

Monsignor Hellriegel's method of working with his people can be briefly stated by saying that he proceeded from the inside out. This movement took place first of all within himself. His work in liturgical renewal began with his own study and prayer. He prepared himself by years of study of scripture, the fathers of the Church, the history of the development of the liturgy; he daily meditated upon the Word of God proclaimed in the liturgy of the day. His own mind and heart were centered on the liturgy. His growth in understanding continued as he assiduously read the new publications of the leading theologians and liturgists of Europe and of the United States. Time was spent in planning how to transfer this knowledge gleaned from theological study into a form understandable to the people; thus the daily homily was a carefully thought-out work. Further planning went into the what and the how of bringing about active participation in the liturgy. The liturgy and its celebration were given a high priority both in terms of time and parish finances. A good organ and organist were provided. Good music was collected or, when none was available, written by Monsignor Hellriegel himself. The people were always well prepared for any new step in liturgical participation. In devising creative ways to lead his people to more active involvement with the liturgy, Monsignor Hellriegel always kept in touch with the cultural roots of the people; he built upon nature; he worked with a sense of poetry and with imagination. Everyone was actively involved in all that went on; there was no room for a spectator; the people were led to see that taking special roles in liturgical celebrations, such as serving, or reading, or being in the choir were privileges; Monsignor bestowed special honor on these roles. He moved forward with prudence, combining determination with gentleness. He worked hard and gave generously of his time and energy; he led by doing.

An analysis of Hellriegel's approach to the liturgy reveals the theology of the liturgy which emerged through the living experience of his parish. Liturgy was lived at Holy Cross as the worship of the people. It was first and foremost *worship*. Its function was always clearly the praise of God and the bringing of the people into the presence of their Lord. Monsignor Hellriegel himself radiated a God-centered focus in all liturgical celebrations. The sense of contact with a great mystery was always evident; liturgy was more divine than human. The experience of involvement with the sacred was intrinsic to the worship. Liturgical celebrations were carried out in a spirit of reverence; folksiness had no part in them.

Secondly, the liturgy at Holy Cross was the prayer of the *people*. They were never made to feel that their previous prayer experiences were "wrong" or inferior. Monsignor Hellriegel genuinely respected the spirit of prayer that he found among the people when he came to be their new pastor. He had nothing but praise for his predecessors and for the work they had done in the parish. Hellriegel never suggested that the people drop the prayer forms to which they had been accustomed. Rather, he built on the spirituality that was there and worked to nourish it and help it grow.

The wisdom and sensitivity of Monsignor Hellriegel are made apparent by a look at the contrasting situation often found in the introduction of the post-Vatican II liturgical changes into the parish situation. People were often made to feel that their previous prayer lives had been backward or second rate. Something precious seemed to be under attack and the reaction was defensiveness.

In introducing new forms of liturgical prayer, Hellriegel never forced participation from without; he showed the people the significance of the prayer form and emphasized that taking special roles in liturgical celebrations was a privilege. Persons who had proven themselves to be outstanding in some way were the ones asked to be in processions or to do readings. Participation in the liturgy was seen as an honor and people felt complimented to be asked to participate, either in a specialized role or communally. Participation flowed from the inside out.

Again a contrast can be seen with the manner in which the post-Vatican II liturgical reforms were often introduced. Many of them were imposed on people from without. The new liturgical practices were seen by many as a nuisance. Actually the requirements of participation were in fact often a distraction from prayer rather than a form of prayer. Getting the prayers and handshakes right often did, in the experience of many people, get in the way of their focus on the presence of the Lord. This was especially the case when planning and preparation had been poor. At Holy Cross planning and preparation were always so thorough that the mechanics of the liturgical action could be carried out without themselves becoming the main focus of attention. The minds and hearts of the people could be occupied in the worship of their God.

Another important element in the process of liturgical change is timing. Monsignor Hellriegel introduced most of the new forms of liturgical prayer into his parish during the first year or so of his pastorate. In contrast the liturgical reforms following the Vatican Council were introduced gradually over a period of seven years. The gradualism prescribed for the post-Vatican II era was supposed to provide time for pastors and people to understand and assimilate one thing at a time. However, the result during the interim years was often a liturgical hodgepodge and a very unsettled feeling among the people. They knew that more changes were coming but didn't know exactly what to expect. The acceptance of change is always something of an ordeal; the post-Vatican II liturgical changes touched a sensitive area and prolonged the experience. Hellriegel led his people immediately and directly into the ways he saw as best and then let things be.

Once Monsignor Hellriegel had acquainted his parishioners with the full riches of the liturgical year, he did little to vary the format from year to year. Thus the people developed a sense of at-homeness with the special prayer forms for the various feasts and seasons of the year. These prayers became truly their prayers. They did not have to live with the "what next?" feeling for very long. There was diversity in the various celebrations for the various feasts, but any one feast was celebrated very much in the same way year to year. Thus the people could develop a sense of rhythm in their prayer lives and a sense of identity with their celebrations of worship. Perhaps the emphasis on diversity in the post-Vatican II liturgy has been too strong to allow the sense of familiarity and identity to develop for most people.

The streamlining toward simplicity and brevity of the new *Ordo* is also at variance with the practices of Hellriegel. He wanted to bring to his people the fullness of the prayer of the Church. He knew that to involve heart as well as head he had to use ceremony and action and repetition. He did so freely with little regard for the length of the ceremony. Holy Cross had the reputation for having the longest Masses anywhere in the city. The Vatican II changes advocated streamlining in order to meet the needs of the people; yet people flocked to Holy Cross from all parts of the metropolitan city and far beyond. Perhaps it was Hellriegel who was really in tune with the needs of the people and perhaps that is why his program of liturgical renewal went so much smoother than that of the post-Vatican II Church.

To a large extent his method can be duplicated. Certainly the preparation for liturgical activity through study is more accessible today than it was during the seminary and early priestly years of Martin Hellriegel; also keeping up with reading is within the grasp of anyone who makes the effort. The daily prayerful reflection on the word of the gospel is open to all. The awareness of the religious and cultural sensitivities of the people is a bit more difficult to come by but not impossible if one genuinely tries to discern where people are before presenting a new program. Conveying to others the specialness and the dignity of taking active roles in liturgical celebrations will probably have to be approached differently today because of the familiarity with active participation; it will probably be mostly through personal relationship with the leaders of the liturgy that people today will come to sense the significance of their participation in that liturgy. Another avenue is a depth of theological understanding, but that is probably more difficult to convey at the parish level. Even here more could be done by using Monsignor Hellriegel's techniques of letting the Sunday homily be an occasion for liturgical instruction and by working through parish organizations to prepare the leaders of the parish to exert their leadership also in this area of liturgical renewal. Working with determination and prudence, with gentleness and generosity is a high ideal but one toward which progress can be made with effort. Again, it is hard to see that an initiating of Monsignor Hellriegel's methods would be anything other than effective at a parish level. One individual may not be able, for example, to follow his lead in both theological expertise and creativity, but certainly two individuals, each having one or other ability, could effectivity work together.

In regard to the specific liturgical activities to which Monsignor Hellriegel led his people, many would not seem to be effective today, even if it were theoretically possible to repeat them. One big reason for this is the changes brought about by the 1970 *Ordo*. For example, the change of the gospel for the Wednesday of the third week of Advent from the account of the angel Gabriel appearing to Mary to the story of the disciples of John the Baptist seeking the identity of Jesus would involve a different emphasis in the liturgical celebration of the feast. Some of the parish customs, such as the Schnitzelbank, were too specifically German in their origin to have the same community-building effectiveness elsewhere. Yet, the general thrust of celebrations such as this one is appropriate for today. To find kinds of festivities in touch with the cultural roots of the people and to utilize them to build spirit and unity within the parish and at the same time relate them to the liturgical season, as the Schnitzelbank was the final celebration before the season of Lent, is certainly worth imitating and feasible. Also planning of ways for the people of the parish to enter more actively into the liturgy of the day, whatever the new theme and form of that liturgy, can be effective in the pursuit of liturgical renewal.

The development of liturgical prayer and song in common is both possible and desirable today. The level of musical selections in many parishes today is fairly low. Gregorian chant cannot be a universal answer today, but the philosophy behind Gregorian chant, namely putting into song the actual text of the liturgical prayer is still possible and desirable. Thus, even though the specifics of the liturgical celebrations in many cases belonged to the time and place of Holy Cross Parish in the pre-Vatican II liturgy, what Monsignor Hellriegel did, namely, build upon the liturgy of the day and the culture of the people, can be done today with the new forms of the liturgy and the differing cultural heritage.

ENDNOTES

Chapter 1: MARTIN HELLRIEGEL'S BOYHOOD

1. Prosper Guéranger (1805-1875) was a priest in the diocese of Le Mans, France. In 1833 he and five other priests moved into the deserted monastery at Solesmes and began living according to the Rule of St. Benedict. In 1837 the monastery was incorporated into the order of St. Benedict and Guéranger became its first abbot. The monastery soon became the center of the liturgical revival in France. The most well-known and influential of Guéranger's works, in addition to his *L'Année liturgigue*, is his *Institutions liturgigues* in three volumes (Paris, 1840-1850). This latter work offers a criticism of the great variation in liturgical practice in France.

2. A fuller commentary on Guéranger's accomplishments can be found in Joseph Jungmann, *The Mass of the Roman Rite*, trans, Francis A. Brunner (New York: Benziger, 1951) 119.

3. A critique of Guéranger's work is presented in Louis Bouyer, *Liturgical Piety* (Notre Dame: University of Notre Dame Press, 1955) 53-55.

4. Oliver Rousseau, "The Liturgical Movement from Dom Guéranger to Pius XII," in *The Church at Prayer:* Introduction to the Liturgy, ed., Aimé G. Martimont (Shannon: Irish University Press, 1968) 52.

5. Johann Adam Möhler (1796-1838) taught church history at Tubingen in Munich. He is especially known for his work in ecclesiology. Among his principal works are: *Die Einheit in der Kirche*

(1825), *Athanasius der Grosse* (1827), *Symbolik* (1822), *Neue Untersuchungen der Lehrgegensätze Zwischen Katholiken und Protestanten* (1834).

Joseph Matthias Scheeben (1835-1888) taught at the seminary in Cologne. He is especially known for his work in speculative theology. Among his important works are: *Handbuch der Katholischen Dogmatik*, 3 volumes (1873-82) and *Die Mysterien des Christentums* (1865). He was in the process of revising this latter work when he died. Editions published after his death either failed to utilize his notes for revision or used them inadequately until Josef Hofer, in 1941, produced an edition which was faithful to Scheeben's notes or revision. Hofers version was translated into English by Cyril Vollert and published under an English title *The Mystery of Christianity* in 1951.

6. For a complete discussion of the controversies surrounding earlier translations of parts of the missal, see Bussard, Paul, *The Vernacular Missal in Religious Education* (Washington, D.C.: Catholic University, 1937) 1-36. Also, an English translation of the missal antedates the French, but its significance for the liturgy in Germany and France was minimal as there was much less interaction with England than between France and Germany.

7. This was not the first complete translation of the German missal, but it was the first to enjoy such widespread usage. For a discussion of earlier editions, see Bussard 29-35.

8. Foreword to *Das Kirchenjaht* (Mainz, 1888) as translated by and quoted by Martin Hellriegel, "Sixty-Six Years Ago," *OF* (2 July 1940) 406.

9. Martin B. Hellriegel, interview held at Holy Cross Rectory, St. Louis, Missouri, 24 January 1975.

10. Phea Felknor, "Meet Msgr. Hellriegel," *St. Louis Review* (21 August 1964) 13.

11. Even though the old church was torn down in 1900, the famous entrance and tower have remained and been incorporated into the new church.

12. Martin B. Hellriegel, interview held at Holy Cross Rectory, St. Louis, Missouri, 24 May 1974.

13. Martin B. Hellriegel, interview held at Holy Cross Rectory, St. Louis, Missouri, 12 June 1975.

14. *The Centennial of Holy Cross Parish* (St. Louis; Holy Cross Parish, 1964) 30.

15. The work of Pius X in liturgical renewal will be considered in Chapter Four rather than at this time because his work was still so new during Martin Hellriegel's final years in Germany as to not yet have widespread influence.

16. Felknor 13.

17. Martin B. Hellriegel, interview held at Holy Cross Rectory, St. Louis, Missouri, 24 May 1974.

18. *The Centennial of Holy Cross Parish* 29.

19. Martin B. Hellriegel, interview held at Holy Cross Rectory, St. Louis, Missouri, 24 January 1975.

20. Martin B. Hellriegel, "Family Life, the Liturgical Year, and the Sacramentals," *The Family in Christ*, Proceedings of the National Liturgical Week, vol. 7 (Highland Park, Illinois: The Liturgical Conference, 1947) 98.

21. *Ibid* 99.

22. Felknor 13.

23. Martin B. Hellriegel, "Family Life, the Liturgical Year, and the Sacramentals" 101.

24. Felknor 13.

25. Martin B. Hellriegel, "Family Life, the Liturgical Year, and the Sacramentals" 103.

26. *The Centennial of Holy Cross Parish* 30.

27. Martin B. Hellriegel, interview held at Holy Cross Rectory, St. Louis, Missouri, 24 January 1975.

28. *Ibid*.

29. *Ibid*.

30. Felknor 13.

31. Martin B. Hellriegel, interview held at Holy Cross Rectory, St. Louis, Missouri, 28 February 1975.

Chapter 2: LITURGICAL RENEWAL IN THE U.S.

1. Baltimore, Archives of the Archdiocese of Baltimore, Special Section C, C-1.

2. Peter Guilday, *The Life and Times of John Carroll, Archbishop of Baltimore*, 2 vols. (New York: Encyclopedia Press, 1922) 1:131.

3. Baltimore, Archives of the Archdiocese of Baltimore, Special Section C, C-1.

4. *Ibid.*

5. Guilday 1:131.

6. John Tracy Ellis, "Archbishop Carroll and the Liturgy in the Vernacular," *Perspectives in American Catholicism* (Baltimore: Helicon, 1963) 131.

7. The statement is dated November 19, 1810. It is in the Baltimore Cathedral Archives, Case 2 J 1.

8. John England, ed., *The Roman Missal Translated into the English Language for the Use of the Laity* (New York: William H. Creagh, 1822) iii.

9. *Ibid.* xxiii-xxv.

10. Peter Guilday, *The Life and Times of John England*, 2 vols. (New York: Encyclopedia Press, 1927) 1:330.

11. John K. Ryan, "Bishop England and the Missal in English," *American Ecclesiastical Review* 95 (July 1936) 35.

12. Sebastian Messmer, ed., *The Works of the Right Reverend John England*, 7 vols. (Cleveland: Arthur Clark Co., 1908) 5:312, 338, 370-378, 366, 388.

13. *Acta et Decreta Concilii Plenarii Baltimorensis Tertii*, pp. 120-121, quoted in William Busch, "Voices of a Plenary Council," *OF* 21 (September 1947) 456-457.

14. *Ibid.*

15. *Ibid.* 454.

16. *Ibid.* 455.

17. *Ibid.* 456.

18. *Ibid.* 454.

19. Paul Marx, *Virgil Michel and the Liturgical Movement* (Collegeville, Minnesota: The Liturgical Press, 1957) 79.

20. Alfred Young, "Church Music," *Catholic World* 10 (December 1869) 408.

21. *Ibid.* 404.

22. *Ibid*. 409.

23. *Ibid*. 403.

24. *Ibid*. 404-412; 598-610;743-754.

25. *Ibid*. 604.

26. Thomas O'Gorman, "Worship and Grace," *OF* 20 (October 1946) 495-502.

27. *Ibid*. 495.

28. Marx 88.

29. *Ibid*. 88-89.

30. W. F. P. Stockley, "The Pope and the Reform in Church Music," *Ecclesiastical Review* 30 (March 1904) 279-281.

31. *Ibid*. 292.

32. *Ibid*. 279.

33. The one article is J. McSorley, "The Mystical Body," *Catholic World* 81 (June 1905): 307-314. See John Bluett, "The Mystical Body of Christ: 1890-1940, A Bibliography," *Theological Studies* 3 (May 1942) 261-289.

34. Marx 85.

35. *Ibid*. 86-87.

Chapter 3: EARLY YEARS OF MARTIN HELLRIEGEL
IN THE U.S.

1. *The Centennial of Holy Cross Parish* (St. Louis; Holy Cross Parish, 1964) 31.

2. Martin B. Hellriegel, interview held at Holy Cross Rectory, St. Louis, Missouri, 24 January 1975.

3. *Ibid*.

4. Felknor 13.

5. *Ibid.*

6. *The Centennial of Holy Cross Parish* 31.

7. Hellriegel, interview of 24 January 1975.

8. *Ibid.*

9. *The Centennial of Holy Cross Parish* 31.

10. Hellriegel, interview of 24 January 1975.

11. *Ibid.*

12. *Ibid.*

13. Felknor 13.

14. Hellriegel, interview of 24 January 1975.

15. The exact date of the following incident was September 5, 1917. This was right after Martin Hellriegel had left St. Charles.

16. Martin B. Hellriegel, interview held at Holy Cross Rectory, St. Louis, Missouri, 24 May 1974.

17. Martin B. Hellriegel, "Vom Aufbau Des Leibes Christi, in *Universities*, ed: Ludwig Lenhart (Mainz: Matthias Bruenwald, 1960) 457.

18. The missal by Father Lasance was available at this time and was the one used by the sisters. Dom Gaspar Lefebvre's *St. Andrew's Missal* was not available until 1924. See William O'Shea "Liturgy in the United States, 1889-1964," *Americna Ecclesiastical Review* 150 (January-June 1964) 176-196.

19. Martin B. Hellriegel, interview held at Holy Cross Rectory, St. Louis, Missouri, 25 May 1974.

20. *Ibid.*

21. *Ibid.*

22. John Rothensteiner, *History of the Archdiocese of St. Louis*, 2 vols. (St. Louis: Blackwell Wielandy, 1928) 2:430.

23. Hellriegel, interview of 28 February 1975.

24. Hellriegel, interview of 24 May 1974.

25. *The Family in Christ*, Proceedings of the National Liturgical Week, vol. 7 (Highland Park, Illinois: The Liturgical Conference, 1947) 94.

Chapter 4: LITURGICAL DEVELOPMENTS IN EUROPE

1. For original Latin text see "Inter Pastoralis Offices," *Acta Sanctae Sedis* 36 (1903-1904) 387-395.

2. Kevin R. Seasoltz, ed., *The New Liturgy: A Documentation*, 1903-1965 (New York: Herder and Herder, 1966) 4.

3. *Ibid.*

4. Theodor Klauser, *The Western Liturgy and Its History*, trans. F. L. Cross (New York: Morehouse-Gorham, 1952) 57.

5. Dom Beauduin had begun his priestly life as diocesan priest in the diocese of Liege. For eight years he had worked as a specially appointed "Chaplain of Workmen." He was one of a group whose special function was to implement the practical application of the principles enunciated by Pope Leo XIII in his *Rerum Novarum*. Dom Beauduin felt the need for a more profound spirituality in order to carry out this work and turned to the abbey of Mont Cesar. He entered the abbey in 1906 at the age of 33 and became a Benedictine monk. Here Dom Beauduin pursued the work of developing a profound spirituality and *taking that spirituality to the lay Catholic*. Dom Beauduin saw that Pius X had given the answer to the question of wherein lies the source of the true Christian spirit, namely, in the liturgy and in active participation in that liturgy. Therefore, in order to bring spiritual depth to the people, Dom Beauduin saw the necessity of bringing them to active participation in the liturgy. See Seasoltz xxvii.

6. Bouyer, Louis, *Liturgical Piety* (Indiana: University of Notre Dame Press, 1955) 60-61.

7. Koenker Ernest, *The Liturgical Renaissance in the Roman Catholic Church* (Chicago: University of Chicago, 1954) 14.

8. The abbey itself dates back to 1093. It was suppressed by Napoleon in 1803. It was in 1892 that the abbey came into the possession of the monks of Beuron. See Damascus Winzen, "Progress and Tradition at Maria Laach," Liturgical Arts 10 (November 1941) 19.

9. H. A. Reinhold, *The Dynamics of the Liturgy* (New York: Macmillan, 1961) 1-2.

10. Winzen 20.

11. Michael Ducey, "Maria Laach and the Liturgy," *OF* 9 (January 1935) 109-111.

12. Dom Odo Casel (1886-1948) became a Benedictine in 1905. Dom Casel's liturgical writings emphasized the liturgical actions of the Church as making present the saving actions of Christ. The specific feasts of the liturgical year were seen as celebrations of the mysteries of Christ.

Casel's principal works include: *Das Gedächtnis des Herrn in der altchristlichen Liturgie* (Freiburg, 1918); *Die Liturgie als Mysterienfeier* (Freiburg, 1922); *The Mystery of Christian Worship (Westminster, Md., 1962); La Fête de Paugues dans l'Eglise des Pères* (Paris, 1963); *Das Mysterium des Kommenden* (Paderborn, 1952); *Das Mysterium des Kreuzes* (Paderborn, 1954).

13. Ducey 112.

14. *Ibid.* 111.

15. Reinhold 4-5.

16. Felknor 13.

17. Jungmann, Joseph, *The Mass of the Roman Rite.* Translated by Francis Brunner. (New York: Benziger, 1951) 122.

18. Lancelot Sheppard, ed., *The People Worship: A History of the Liturgical Movement* (New York: Hawthorn, 1967) 45.

19. Bouyer 65-66.

20. Sheppard 44.

21. Seasoltz xxx.

22. Hellriegel, interview of 28 February 1975.

Chapter 5: A FULL LITURGICAL LIFE AT O'FALLON

1. Martin B. Hellriegel to Virgil Michel, 23 September 1925, Michel Papers, St. John's Abbey, Collegeville, Minnesota.

2. Christophers Rengers, "Headstarter in Liturgical Revival," *The Priest* 24 (November 1968) 867-868.

3. Martin B. Hellriegel, interview held at Holy Cross Rectory, St. Louis, Missouri, 28 December 1964.

4. *Ibid.*

5. Hellriegel, interview of 28 February 1975.

6. Hellriegel, interview of 28 December 1964.

7. Felknor 13.

8. Precious Blood Motherhouse, interviews held with Precious Blood Sisters who personally participated in the liturgical activities discussed above, 17 February 1975.

9. Gerald Ellard, "A Pilgrimage and a Vision," *America* 34 (12 December 1925) 203; Martin B. Hellriegel to Virgil Michel, 23 September 1925, Michel Papers; William Leonard, "The Liturgical Movement in the United States," in *The Liturgy of Vatican II*, 2 vols., ed: William Barauna (Chicago: Franciscan Herald Press, 1966) 2:296.

10. The Novitiate, O'Fallon, Missouri, "Advent in a Convent," *OF* 1 (28 November 1926) 26-27.

11. The Novitiate, O'Fallon, Missouri, "A Convent Christmas," *OF* 1 (26 December 1926) 56-58.

12. Martin B. Hellriegel to Virgil Michel, 18 March 1929, Michel Papers.

13. [Felix Tuger,] "Lent in a Convent," *OF* 9 (23 March 1935) 215.

14. Martin B. Hellriegel to Virgil Michel, 18 March 1929, Michel Papers.

15. "Liturgical Briefs," *OF* 12 (20 March 1938) 230.

16. Precious Blood Sisters, interview of 17 February 1975.

17. *Ibid.*

18. Ellard 202.

19. *Ibid.*

20. Martin B. Hellriegel to Virgil Michel, 23 September 1925, Michel Papers.

21. Ellard 202.

22. Precious Blood Sisters, interview of 17 February 1975.

23. *Ibid.*

24. Hellriegel, interview of 25 May 1974.

25. Precious Blood Sisters, interview of 2 February 1975.

26. Martin B. Hellriegel, "Conferences on the Sacred Psalms," lectures given at the Precious Blood Motherhouse, O'Fallon, Missouri, 1936-1937.

27. Hellriegel to Virgil Michel, 23 September 1925. The article was later translated by William Busch and published as a separate pamphlet by the Central Bureau, St. Louis, Missouri.

28. Martin B. Hellriegel and A. J. Jasper, *The True Basis of Christian Solidarity*, trans. William Busch, (St. Louis: Central Bureau of the Central Verein, 1947).

29. Marx 113, 180.

30. Lawrence Madden, "The Liturgical Conference of the USA: It Origin and Development: 1940-1968" (Ph. D. Dissertation, Theological Faculty of Trier, 1969) 274.

31. Frederick Kenkel, Director of the Central Bureau of the Central Verein to Virgil Michel, 30 June 1928, Michel Papers.

32. *Ibid.*

33. Virgil Michel, *The Liturgy of the Church* (New York: Macmillan, 1938) 61-83.

34. Hellriegel to Michel, 23 September 1925, Michel Papers.

35. *The Centennial of Holy Cross Parish* 34.

36. *Ibid.*

Chapter 6: THE LITURGICAL MOVEMENT IN THE U.S.

1. Marx 106.

2. Hellriegel to Michel, 23 September 1925, Michel Papers.

3. Martin B. Hellriegel to Virgil Michel, undated prospectus, Michel Papers, St. John's Abbey, Collegeville, Minnesota.

4. Marx 131.

5. *America* 34 (25 April 1925) 37.

6. Martin B. Hellriegel, interviewed held at Holy Cross Rectory, St. Louis, Missouri, 1 September 1969, quoted in John Leo Klein,

"The Role of Gerald Ellard (1894-1963) in the Development of the Contemporary Catholic Liturgical Movement" (Ph. D. dissertation, Fordham University, 1971).

7. *Ibid.* 70.

8. 34:201.

9. *Ibid.* 70.

10. *America* 34 (19 December 1925) 241.

11. The Pilgrim [psued.] "With Scrip and Staff," *America* 45 (19 September 1931) 570.

12. Rengers 873.

13. Klein 72.

14. *Ibid.* 78-79.

15. Martin B. Hellriegel to Virgil Michel, 22 August 1926, Michel Papers, St. John's Abbey, Collegeville, Minnesota.

16. Martin B. Hellriegel to Virgil Michel, 11 December 1926, Michel Papers, St. John's Abbey, Collegeville, Minnesota.

17. "The Editor's Corner, *OF* 1 (26 December 1926) 60.

18. The Novitiate, O'Fallon, Missouri, "Advent in a Convent," *OF* 1 (28 November 1926) 26-27; The Novitiate, O'Fallon, Missouri, "A Convent Christmas," *OF* 1 (26 December 1926) 26-27.

19. Martin B. Hellriegel to Virgil Michel, 20 September 1926, Michel Papers, St. John's Abbey, Collegeville, Minnesota.

20. (19 February 1928) 113-115; (18 March 1928) 151-153.

21. Martin B. Hellriegel to Virgil Michel, 27 March 1926, Michel Papers, St. John's Abbey, Collegeville, Minnesota.

22. Martin B. Hellriegel and Alphonse Westhoff, "The Liturgical Year," *OF* 1 (12 October 1927) 360-361.

23. *Ibid.* 362-363.

24. For specific articles see: Martin B. Hellriegel and Alphonse Westhoff, "The Liturgical Year," *OF* 2 (13 May 1928) 205-210; Martin Hellriegel, "The Lord Our Coming King, Hasten to Adore Him," *OF* 2 (25 December 1927) 33-44; Martin Hellriegel, "The Purification," *OF* 2 (22 January 1928) 65-70; Martin Hellriegel, "Viriliter Agite," *OF* 3 (24 February 1929) 97-102; Martin Hellriegel, "A.D. 37-1937," *OF* 11 (13 June 1937) 346-351; Martin Hellriegel, "Liturgical and 'Liturgical' Retreats," *OF* 14 (9 June 1940) 342-352; Martin Hellriegel, "Outline of a First Mass Sermon," *OF* 4 (18 May 1930) 295-300.

25. Martin B. Hellriegel, "The Liturgical Movements and the Sacraments," *OF* 10 (31 October 1936) 503-510.

26. *Ibid*. 504-505.

27. *Ibid*. 506.

28. *Ibid*. 508-510.
29. *OF* 14 (24 December 1939) 63-65.

30. *Ibid*. 63.

31. *Ibid*. 64-65.

32. Martin B. Hellriegel to Virgil Michel, 2 May 1927, Michel Papers, St. John's Abbey, Collegeville, Minnesota.

33. For a discussion of the subject see the following letters: Martin Hellriegel to Virgil Michel, 21 September 1928; Virgil Michel to Martin Hellriegel, 27 September 1928; Virgil Michel to Martin Hellriegel, 21 August 1929, Michel Papers, St. John's Abbey, Collegeville, Minnesota.

Chapter 7: PROMOTION OF THE LITURGICAL APOSTOLATE

1. Martin B. Hellriegel, interview held at Holy Cross Rectory, St. Louis, Missouri, 26 May 1974.

2. Klein 78.

3. Martin B. Hellriegel to Virgil Michel, 29 January 1929, Michel Papers, St. John's Abbey, Collegeville, Minnesota.

4. "Liturgical Briefs," *OF* 5 (1 November 1931) 576.

5. Martin B. Hellriegel to Virgil Michel, 22 August 1926, Michel Papers, St. John's Abbey, Collegeville, Minnesota.

6. *Ibid*. 16 October 1926.

7. *Ibid*. 13 September 1927.

8. Martin B. Hellriegel to Virgil Michel, 13 January 1928, Michel Papers, St. John's Abbey, Collegeville, Minnesota.

9. *Ibid*.

10. Quoted by Hellriegel in Felknor 20.

11. Martin B. Hellriegel to Virgil Michel, 18 June 1928, Michel Papers, St. John's Abbey, Collegeville, Minnesota.

12. *Ibid.* 2 May 1927.

13. *Ibid.* 18 June 1928.

14. *Ibid.* 6 February 1926.

15. *Ibid.* 11 December 1926 and 2 May 1927.

16. "Liturgical Briefs," *OF* 1 (17 April 1927) 192.

17. "Liturgical Briefs," *OF* 2 (5 August 1928) 318.

18. *OF* 3 (24 February 1929) 121.

19. "Liturgical Briefs," *OF* 14 (12 May 1940) 328.

20. Martin B. Hellriegel to Virgil Michel, 2 May 1927, 12 June 1927, 12 June 1927, 18 June 1927, 22 November 1927, Michel Papers, St. John's Abbey, Collegeville, Minnesota.

21. "The Program," *OF* 3 (8 September 1929) 322.

22. "Liturgical Briefs," *OF* 1 (15 May 1927) 223.

23. John Glennon, "Christmas Pastoral Letter on Church Music," 17 December 1932, Archives of the Archdiocese of St. Louis, St. Louis, Missouri.

24. "Liturgical Briefs," *OF* 7 (15 May 1933) 280.

25. The secretary of the commission met with over 200 organists at their October meeting and addressed them on these points. See "Liturgical Briefs," *OF* 8 (2 December 1933) 37.

26. "Liturgical Briefs," *OF* 8 (30 December 1933) 87.

27. "Liturgical Briefs," *OF* 8 (19 May 1935) 330.

28. Martin B. Hellriegel to Virgil Michel, 2 May 1927, 12 June 1927, 12 June 1927, 18 June 1927, 22 November 1927, Michel Papers, St. John's Abbey, Collegeville, Minnesota.

29. "Liturgical Briefs," *OF* 13 (19 February 1939) 183.

30. "Liturgical Briefs," *OF* 8 (8 September 1934) 520.

31. "The Apostolate: The Peoria Liturgical Institute," *OF* 9 (1 December 1934) 34.

32. "The Apostolate: The Peoria," *OF* 9 (2 November 1935) 467.

33. Hellriegel, interview of 24 May 1974.

34. "The Apostolate: The Peoria," 567.

35. The address is reprinted as "The Spread of the Liturgical Movement," *Journal of Religious Instruction* 7 (November 1936) 208-214.

36. A detailed outline of the talk is in *National Catholic Education Associations Bulletin* 34 (August 1937) 550-556.

37. *Ibid.* 547.

38. "The Liturgical Movement," *Acolyte* 5 (August 1929) 6.

39. *Ibid.* 547.

40. Martin B. Hellriegel to Virgil Michel, 21 August 1929, Michel Papers, St. John's Abbey, Collegeville, Minnesota.

41. Collegeville, Minnesota, 1930.

42. "Liturgical Briefs," *OF* 3 (24 March 1929) 125.

43. *Ibid. OF* 12 (20 March 1931) 230.

44. Martin B. Hellriegel to Virgil Michel, 13 September 1927, Michel Papers, St. John's Abbey, Collegeville, Minnesota.

45. *Ibid.* 22 June 1935.

46. Precious Blood Sisters, interview of 12 February 1975.

47. Rengers 870.

48. Martin B. Hellriegel, interview held at Holy Cross Rectory, St. Louis, Missouri, 25 May 1975.

49. Martin B. Hellriegel, "The Ritual for the Consecration of Virgins," *Education and Liturgy*, Proceeding of the North American Liturgical Week, vol. 18 (Elsberry, Missouri: The Liturgical Conference, 1958) 177.

50. Sister Anne Catherine [McDonald], "The Profession Ceremonies of Some Congregations of Women," People's Participation and Holy Week, Proceedings of the North American Liturgical Week, vol. 17 (Elsberry, Missouri: The Liturgical Conference, 1957) 112.

51. Martin B. Hellriegel to Virgil Michel, 16 October 1926, Michel Papers, St. John's Abbey, Collegeville, Minnesota.

52. Martin B. Hellriegel to Virgil Michel, 5 January 1938, Michel Papers, St. John's Abbey, Collegeville, Minnesota.

53. Mignon McMenamy, telephone interview, St. Louis, Missouri, 10 July 1975.

54. Martin B. Hellriegel, Farewell speech, 2 July 1940, Precious Blood Motherhouse, O'Fallon, Missouri, personal papers of Sister Angelita Dittmaier, O'Fallon, Missouri.

55. "Liturgical Briefs," *OF* 14 (1 September 1940) 472.

Chapter 8: A LITURGICAL LIFE AT HOLY CROSS

1. Seasoltz v, vi, vii.

2. *The Centennial Holy Cross Parish* 21, 23.

3. Martin B. Hellriegel, "A Pastor's Description of Liturgical Participation in his Parish, *The Living Parish*, National Liturgical Week Proceedings, vol. 2 (Newark: Benedictine Liturgical Conference, 1942) 82.

4. *The Centennial Holy Cross Parish* 23.

5. Hellriegel, "A Pastor's Description" 86-87.

6. Martin B. Hellriegel, "The Parish in Practice, *The Living Parish*, National Liturgical Week Proceedings, vol. 1 (Newark: Benedictine Liturgical Conference, 1941) 31-32.

7. *The Centennial Holy Cross Parish* Hellriegel, "The Parish" 36, 32.

8. *The Centennial Holy Cross Parish* 36.

9. Hellriegel, "The Parish" 34-35.

10. *The Centennial Holy Cross Parish* 37.

11. Hellriegel, "A Pastor's Description" 84.

12. Martin B. Hellriegel, "Toward a Living Parish," *Worship* 30 (December 1955) 17.

13. Felknor 20.

14. *Ibid.* 20.

15. Hellriegel, "A Pastor's Description" 84-85.

16. *The Family in Christ*, National Liturgical Week Proceedings, vol. 7 (Highland Park, Illinois, 1947) 104.

17. Martin B. Hellriegel, "Merely Suggesting," *OF* 15 (7 September 1941) 445.

18. *Ibid.* 467-468.

19. *Ibid.* 447.

20. Martin B. Hellriegel, "Toward a Living Parish," 22-23.

21. *Ibid.* 21.

22. Hellriegel, "A Pastor's Description" 87.

23. Burke, Sister Mary Gabriel, *Liturgy at Holy Cross in Church and School* (St. Louis: Pio Decimo, 1952) 46-47. That participation in the

liturgy at Holy Cross was no passing fad but a means of real spiritual growth can be seen from the results of questionnaires circulated in the parish about ten years later. The following tabulations were printed on the pages indicated above:

Table 2

**Showing the per cent participating in the
dialogue and the sung mass**

	Dialogue Mass	Sung Mass
Use daily missal	70.5	68.5
Use leaflet missal	26.5	29.3
Use no missal	3.9	3.0
Use Kyriale or Chant Book	—	61.4
Actively participate in prayers or singing	97.5	83.6
Do not take an active part in prayers or singing	2.5	16.4

Table 3

**Attitudes Developed From Active Participation
Expressed in Percents**

	Dialogue Mass Yes	Dialogue Mass No	Sung Mass Yes	Sung Mass No
Has the use of the missal:				
1. Helped you to a greater understanding of the Diving Sacrifice?	96.9	3.1	92.8	7.2
2. Increased your knowledge of Christ and His life?	94.6	.2	94.3	5.6
3. Increased your knowledge of the Church?	94.4	2.0	96.8	2.1
4. Influenced your prayer and daily life?	92.1	7.9	93.1	.3

24. Hellriegel, "A Pastor's Description" 86.

25. Martin B. Hellriegel, "Merely Suggesting," *OF* 15 (2 November 1941) 534-536.

26. Martin B. Hellriegel, *How to Make the Church Year a Living Reality* 14. This was confirmed by an interview held with former parishioners Robert and Clara LaRose, St. Louis, 22 July 1975.

27. Hellriegel, "A Pastor's Description" 86.

28. *Ibid*. 87.

29. Hellriegel, *The Church Year A Reality* 17.

30. Hellriegel, "A Pastor's Description" 87.

31. Martin B. Hellriegel, "The Apostolate: Christmas to Epiphany," *Worship* 30 (January 1956) 153.

32. *Ibid*.

33. Martin B. Hellriegel, "Merely Suggesting," *OF* 15 (23 February 1941) 151-157.

34. *Ibid*. 158.

35. "Liturgical Briefs" *OF* 22 (25 January 1948) 139.

36. Martin B. Hellriegel, "Towards A Living Parish," *Worship* 30 (February 1956) 215.

37. Hellriegel, "The Church Year A Reality" 21-22.

38. *The Centennial of Holy Cross Parish* 61.

39. Hellriegel, "The Church Year A Reality" 22-23.

40. Martin B. Hellriegel, "Merely Suggesting," *OF* 15 (23 March 1941) 206-207.

41. Hellriegel, "A Pastor's Description" 88.

42. Hellriegel, "Merely Suggesting," 208.

43. Martin B. Hellriegel, "The Apostolate: Holy Week," *Worship* 24 (April 1950) 217.

44. Hellriegel, "A Pastor's Description" 88.

45. Martin B. Hellriegel, "Merely Suggesting," *OF* 15 (23 March 1941) 210-211.

46. Hellriegel, "A Pastor's Description" 89.

47. *Ibid*.

48. Martin B. Hellriegel, "Merely Suggesting," *OF* 16 (20 April 1941) 253.

49. Hellriegel, "A Pastor's Description" 89.

50. Martin B. Hellriegel, "Merely Suggesting," *OF* 16 (20 April 1941) 254.

51. Hellriegel, "A Pastor's Description" 89.

52. *Ibid*. 90.

53. Martin B. Hellriegel, "Towards A Living Parish," *Worship* 39 (September 1956) 518.

54. Martin B. Hellriegel, "Merely Suggesting," (7 September 1941) 445.

55. Hellriegel, *The Church Year A Reality* 6.

56. Martin B. Hellriegel, "The Apostolate: Christmas to Epiphany," *Worship* 30 (January 1956) 149.

57. Robert and Clara LaRose, interview held in St. Louis, Missouri, 22 July 1975.

58. Hellriegel, "Christmas to Epiphany," 145.

59. *Ibid*. 146-147.

60. *Ibid*. 148.

61. Martin B. Hellriegel, "Towards A Living Parish," (December 1956) 100.

62. "Liturgical Briefs" *OF* 18 (20 February 1944) 186.

63. *The Family in Christ*, National Liturgical Week Proceedings, vol. 7 (Highland Park, Illinois: The Liturgical Conference, 1974) 44, 33.

64. *Christ's Sacrifice and Ours*, National Liturgical Week Proceedings, Boston, The Liturgical Conference, 1948) 8, 91.

65. Martin B. Hellriegel, "Merely Suggesting," (26 January 1941) 103-105.

66. Martin B. Hellriegel, "Towards A Living Parish," *Worship* 30 (October 1956) 572; Martin B. Hellriegel, "Vom Aufbau Des Leibes Christi," in *Universitas*, ed: Ludwig Lenharr (Mainz: Matthias-Gruenwald, 1960) 464.

67. Martin B. Hellriegel, "Merely Suggesting," *OF* 15 (5 October 1941) 488-489.

68. Martin B. Hellriegel, "Towards A Living Parish," (December 1956) 102.

69. Martin B. Hellriegel, "The Apostolate: Seasonal Suggestions," *Worship* 30 (May 1956) 381.

70. *Ibid*. 383.

71. Martin B. Hellriegel, "Merely Suggesting," (5 October 1941) 490-491.

72. Martin B. Hellriegel, "Merely Suggesting," *OF* 15 (2 November 1941) 540.

73. Albert Sutter, former Holy Cross parishioner, interview held in St. Louis, 18 July 1975; Martin B. Hellriegel, "Merely Suggesting," *OF* 15 (2 November 1941) 540.

74. *Ibid*. 538-540.

75. Hellriegel, "Vom Aufbau," 463.

76. *Ibid*.

77. *Mary in the Liturgy*, National Liturgical Week Proceedings, vol. 15 (Elsberry, Missouri: The Liturgical Conference, 1954) 89.

78. *The Centennial of Holy Cross Parish* 37-39.

79. *Ibid*. 41.

80. Hellriegel, "Vom Aufbau," 460.

81. "Liturgical Briefs" *OF* 18 (23 January 1944) 138.

82. Robert and Clara LaRose, interview of 22 July 1975.

83. Irvin Arkin, interview held in St. Louis, 7 July 1975.

84. Martin B. Hellriegel, "Towards A Living Parish," (December 1955) 24.

Chapter 9: THE LITURGICAL CONFERENCE

1. Madden 20-21.

2. *Ibid*. 39, 40.

3. *Ibid*. 50.

4. "Denver and Maria Laach," *Commonweal* 45 (8 November 1946) 87.

5. Madden 51-52.

6. Archives of the Liturgical Conference, Washington, D. C., Minutes of the Meeting of the Board of Directors, quoted in Madden 61.

7. Fredrick McManus to Noel Barrett, 19 June 1975, St. Louis University Library, St. Louis, Missouri.

8. Martin B. Hellriegel, "Remarks of the New President of the Liturgical Conference, *Sanctification of the Sunday*, National Liturgical Week Proceedings, vol. 10 (Conception, Missouri: The Liturgical Conference, 1949) 189.

9. "Foreword," *Worship* 26 (December 1951) 4.

10. Madden 84.

11. Martin B. Hellriegel, "The Mother of All Vigils, *The New Man in Christ*, National Liturgical Week Proceedings, vol. 9 (Conception, Missouri: The Liturgical Conference, 1949) 120.

12. Martin B. Hellriegel, "Demonstration of High Mass, *Sanctification of the Sunday*, National Liturgical Week Proceedings, vol. 10 (Conception, Missouri: The Liturgical Conference, 1949) 94.

13. London, Ontario, Resolutions of Meeting of the Meeting of the Board of Directors, Meeting of 20-23 August 1956, reproduced in Madden 291-295, Appendix B.

14. Madden 87.

15. Mcmanus to Barrett, 19 June 1975.

16. *Ibid.*

17. Martin B. Hellriegel, "The Parish in Practice, *The Living Parish*, National Liturgical Week Proceedings, vol. 1 (Newark: The Benedictine Liturgical Conference, 1941) 30-38.

18. Martin B. Hellriegel, "Holy Mass, the Center of the Sacraments and the Divine Office," *Christ's Sanctification and Ours*, National Liturgical Week Proceedings, vol. 8 (Boston: The Liturgical Conference, 1948) 125-129.

19. Martin B. Hellriegel, "The Liturgical Movement and the Preaching of Retreats," *Bible, Life and Worship*, North American Liturgical Week Proceedings, vol. 22 (Washington, D. C.: Liturgical Conference, 1961) 205-208.

20. Martin B. Hellriegel, "Where Lies the Deepest Source for the Recruitment of Vocations? How to Handle Candidates Who Have Had Some Liturgical Formation?" *The New Ritual: Liturgy and Social Order*, National Liturgical Week Proceedings, vol. 16 (Elsberry, Missouri: The Liturgical Conference, 1956) 70-73.

21. Martin B. Hellriegel, "The Ritual for the Consecration of Virgins," *Education and Liturgy*, National Liturgical Week Proceedings, vol. 18 (Elsberry, Missouri: The Liturgical Conference, 1958) 176-178.

22. Mcmanus to Barrett, 19 June 1975.

23. Hellriegel, "Family Life, The Liturgical Year, and the Sacramentals" 95-104.

24. Hellriegel, "A Pastor's Description" 82-90.

25. Martin B. Hellriegel, "Demonstration of Low Mass, *Sanctification of the Sunday*, National Liturgical Week Proceedings, vol. 10 (Conception, Missouri: The Liturgical Conference, 1949) 22, 24.

26. "Liturgical Briefs," *Worship* 33 (April 1959) 322.

27. *Catholic Art Quarterly* 11 (1948) 208, as quoted in editor's note, *The New Man in Christ*, National Liturgical Week Proceedings, vol. 9 (Conception, Missouri: The Liturgical Conference, 1958) 119.

28. McManus to Barrett, 19 June 1975.

29. Leonard, "The Liturgical Movement in the United States" 296-297.

30. Godfrey Diekmann, "Monsignor Martin B. Hellriegel," *Worship* 38 (August/September 1964) 497-498.

31. Felknor 20.

32. Thomas Carroll, "Tribute to Rt. Rev. Msgr. Martin B. Hellriegel," *Challenge of the Council: Person, Parish, World*, National Liturgical Week Proceedings, vol. 25 (Washington D. C.,: The Liturgical Conference, 1964) 273-278.

Chapter 10: LECTURING AND WRITING — HOLY CROSS YEARS

1. Martin B. Hellriegel, "To My Fellow Priests," *OF* 16 (22 February) 149, reprint of the lecture of 10 December 1941.

2. *Ibid*. 146-152.

3. "Liturgical Briefs," *OF* 16 (17 May 1942) 322-323.

4. Liturgical Day Committee, "Milwaukee Sends Forth Light," *Living Parish* 2 (June 1942) 7.

5. *Ibid*.

6. "Liturgical Briefs," *OF* 16 (28 December 1941) 90.

7. "Liturgical Briefs," *OF* 16 (14 June 1942) 377 and (6 September 1942) 470.

8. *Ibid*. (14 June 1942) 377.

9. *Ibid*. (6 September 1942) 472.

10. "Letters from Our Pastor in Europe," *Living Parish* 10 (December 1949) 8.

11. "Religious Profession: Reception, First Vows, and Final Profession," *OF* 19 (20 May 1945) 304-309.

12. "The Office of Abbot," *American Benedictine Review* 8 (Winter 1957) 355-356.

13. Martin B. Hellriegel to Godfrey Diekmann, undated, Archives of St. John's Abbey, Collegeville, Minnesota.

14. A sample of one of those seventy-five retreats given for priests can be seen from the one given at Conception Abbey in Janaury of 1958. Several talks from that retreat have been reprinted as: "Circles of the Liturgy," *Altar and Home Pocket Missal* 1 (April, 1961) 55-59; "The Church is Epiphany" *Altar and Home Pocket Missal* 1 (January, 1961) 46-48; "Bethlehem and Baptism," *Altar and Home Pocket Missal* 1 (December, 1960) 52-54.

15. Martin B. Hellriegel, *The Holy Sacrifice of the Mass* (St. Louis: Pio Decimo Press, 1944) 34.

16. *Ibid*. 54-55.

17. "The *Mediator Dei* Apostolate," *Living Parish* 11 (December 1951) 7.

18. *Ibid*.

19. "Liturgical Briefs," *Worship* 24 (August 1950) 420.

20. "Liturgical Briefs," *Worship* 25 (July 1951) 377.

21. "How to Make the Church Year a Living Reality," *National Catholic Education Association Bulletin* 53 (August 1956) 248-265.

22. Nicholas Schneider, interview held in St. Louis, 13 July 1975.

23. Martin B. Hellriegel to Godfrey Diekmann, 18 October 1955 and 16 January 1956, Archives of St. John's Abbey, Collegeville, Minnesota.

24. For a discussion of the origin of *Living Parish* see Chapter Eleven below.

25. "Liturgical Briefs," *Worship* 19 (31 December 1944) 88.

26. "Liturgical Briefs," *Worship* 23 (28 November 1948) 38.

27. *Ibid.*, (20 February 1949) 192.

28. A few samples are: *Sacred Liturgy* (St. Louis: Pio Decimo Press, 1951); "The Lord's Day," *Living Parish* 8 (September 1947) 3-6; "The Holy Sacraments," *Living Parish* 6 (December 1945) 1-2, (January 1946) 1-3, (February 1946) 3-6; "Pius X," *Living Parish* 5 (November 1944) 3-7, (December 1944) 5-7, (February 1945) 7-9; "1947 Mediator Dei 1957," *Worship* 32 (December 1957) 2-7. See bibliography for a complete list.

29. "Liturgical Briefs," *OF* 25 (June 1951) 327.

30. "Liturgical Briefs," *Worship* 26 (January 1953) 99.

31. Below is a list of the recordings made by the Holy Cross choristers and schola and distributed by the Gregorian Institute of America, Toledo, Ohio.

Records of Gregorian Chants
Made by the Choristers and Schola of the
Holy Cross Parish, St. Louis, Missouri

The Bless Virgin

1-A Introit: Gaudeamus
   Ave Maria
   Anthem: Regina Coeli

1-B Kyrie, Mass IX
   Agnus Dei, Mass IX

2-A Sanctus: Mass IX
   Introit: Salve Sancta
      Parens

Easter — Ascension

2-B Introit: Resurrexit
   Introit: Viri Galilaei

3-A Sequence: Victimae
      Paschali
   Introit: Quasimodo
   Alleluia of Ascendit Deus

Pentecost — Corpus Christi

3-B Alleluia: Veni Sancte
      Spiritus
   Introit: Cibavit eos

4-A Alleluia — Caro mea
   Antiphon: Ubi
      Caritas

Confessors:

4-B Os Justi
   Sanctus: Mass IV

5-A Introit: Statuit
   Requiem Mass

5-B Sequence: Dies Irae
   Communion: Lux
      aeterna
   Antiphon: In Paradisum

Occasional Gregorian Chants

Advent

1-A Introit: Ad te Levavi
1-B Hymn: Benedictus es
    Introit: Rorate Coeli

2-A Hymn: Creator Alme
    Siderum
    Antiphon: O Sapientia
    Communion: Dominus dabit

Christmas

2-B Introit: Puer natus est

3-A Communion: Vidmus
    Stellam

Epiphany

3-A Introit: Ecce advenit
    Alleluia of Dies Sanctificatus

3-B Offertory: Jubilate Deo

Lent

4-A Antiphon: Hosanna
    Filio David
    Antiphon: Pueri
    Haebraeorum
    Antiphon: Gloria Laus

4-B Versicle: Adjuva nos
    Sanctus XVII

5-A Gradual: Christus
    Factus Est

5-B Anthem: Ave Regina
    Coelorum
    Anthem: Alma Redemptoris
    Hymn: Stabat Mater

The above lists appeared in Sister Mary Gabriel Burke, *The Liturgy at Holy Cross in Church and School* (St. Louis: Pio Decimo, 1953) 54-55.

32. "Liturgical Briefs," *Worship* 32 (April 1959) 321-322.

33. "Foreword," *Worship* 26 (December 1951) 4.

34. *The Centennial of Holy Cross Parish* 54.

35. Martin B. Hellriegel to Godfrey Diekmann, 10 May 1955, Archives of St. John's Abbey, Collegeville, Minnesota.

36. "Liturgical Briefs," *OF* 25 (April 1951) 234.

37. *Worship* 26 (December 1951) 24a.

38. "Monsignor Martin B. Hellriegel" 497-498.

39. "Liturgical Briefs," *Worship* 26 (August 1952) 442.

40. "A Good Samaritan," *Living Parish* 9 (December 1948) 21-22, delivered at the funeral of Father Hubert Seiferle; "Father Bernard Laukemper in Pace Christi," *Living Parish* 9 (June 1949) 13-14;

"Archbishop Joseph Schlarman," *Worship* 26 (January 1952) 82-83; "Funeral Sermon for Rev. Msgr. Victor T. Suren," *Social Justice Review* 64 (July-August 1971) 142-143.

Chapter 11: THE INFLUENCE OF MSGR. HELLRIEGEL

1. Alphonse Westhoff, "Homily: Feast of St. Margaret Mary Alacoque," *The Family in Christ*, National Liturgical Week Proceedings 7 (Highland Park, Illinois: The Liturgical Conference, 1947) 137-140; "The Sundays of the Temporal Cycle," *OF* 2 (10 June 1928) 225-233; "The Liturgy and the Seminarians," *OF* 4 (18 May 1930) 306-310; "Notes on the Good Friday Liturgy," *OF* 10 (25 January 1936) 119-120; "The Parish Holy Week," *OF* 33 (March 1959) 232-241; "Parish Lenten Program" *OF* 33 (February 1959) 177-183; "Preparation for Easter," *OF* 33 (June 1959) 104-109.

2. See Klein.

3. "Liturgical Briefs," *OF* 17 (29 November 1942) 44-45.

4. Diekmann, "Monsignor Martin B. Hellriegel" 498.

5. "Remarks on Congregational Singing," *Santification of the Sunday*, National Liturgical Week Proceedings, vol. 10 (Conception, Missouri; The Liturgical Conference, 1949) 156-158; "Feast of the Immaculate Heart of Mary," *Thy Kingdom Come*, National Liturgical Week Proceedings, vol. 43 (Washington, D. C.: The Liturgical Conference, 1963) 113-115.

6. "Conference Tidings," *Worship* 30 (May 1956) 418-423 is a sample.

7. Carroll, "Tribute to Monsignor Hellriegel" 275-276.

8. *Ibid* 277.

9. Nicholas Schneider, *The Life of John Cardinal Glennon* (Liguori, Missouri: Liguori Press, 1971) 170-171.

10. Martin B. Hellriegel to Godfrey Diekmann, 15 March 1961, Archives of St. John's Abbey, Collegeville, Minnesota.

11. Raphael Walger, *Guest Book*.

12. 26 August 1949, reprinted in *OF* 23 (6 November 1949) 552-555.

13. Arkin, interview of 7 July 1975.

14. A Sister of the Precious Blood, "Liturgy in the Classroom," *OF* 11 (21 February 1937) 150, 151, 153, 154.

15. A Sister of the Most Precious Blood, "Advent in the Classroom," *OF* 14 (26 November 1939) 8-13.

16. A Sister of the Most Precious Blood, "Christmas and Epiphany Season in the Classroom," *OF* 14 (14 December 1939) 52, 55, 56.

17. A Sister of the Most Precious Blood, "Pentecost in the Classroom," *OF* 14 (12 May 1940) 309.

18. "Liturgy in the Classroom," 155.

19. O'Fallon: An Appreciation," *OF* 19 (9 September 1945) 521.

20. "Liturgical Briefs," *OF* 15 (26 January 1941) 137.

21. O'Fallon: An Appreciation," 522.

22. *Ibid* 519.

23. The Staff, *Living Parish* 7 (December 1946) 2.

24. "Liturgical Briefs," *OF* 25 (February 1951) 138.

25. Robert and Clara LaRose, interview of 22 July 1975.

26. "Liturgical Briefs," *OF* 34 (March 1960) 225-226.

27. Interview by telephone, St. Louis, 20 March 1975.

Chapter 12: HIS LAST YEARS

1. Letter of July 11, 1980, addressed to Keith. (Personal file of Felix Tuger).

2. Champlin, Joseph M., "From Liturgy's Shell to its Kernel," *Time and Eternity* (July 16 1978) 14.

3. Interview with Bishop Paul Zipfel, St. Charles, Missouri, August 8, 1989.

4. *Ibid*.

5. *Living Parish*, editoral notes (November 1952).

6. Interview with Fr. James Rutkowski, Florissant, Missouri, August 7, 1989.

7. Interview with Ann Kosciolek, Florissant, Missouri, August 7, 1989.

8. *St. Louis Review* (September 24, 1976).

9. *St. Louis Review* (June 13, 1989).

10. Letter of May 31, 1981, written by Sr. Mildred Boehmer, CPPS, O'Fallon, Missouri (Personal file of Felix Tuger).

11. *Ibid.*

12. Interview with Ann Kosciolek, Florissant, Missouri, August 7, 1989.

13. Talk given by Msgr. Alphonse Westhoff, April 14, 1989 (Personal file of Felix Tuger).

14. Quoted by Hughes, John Jay, "Martin B. Hellriegel: A Priestly Man, a Manly Priest," *The Priest* (September 1981) 15.

15. Moleck, Fred, "Ein Heldenleben," *Pastoral Music* (June 1981) 44.

16. Diekmann, Godfrey, "Pioneer Liturgist Dies," *National Catholic Reporter*, (May 8, 1981).

17. *St. Louis Review* (November 7, 1980).

Chapter 13: CONCLUSION

1. Virgil Michel, "Foreword," *OF* (28 November 1926) 1-2.

BIBLIOGRAPHY

Primary Sources

Books and Pamphlets:

Christmas Service in the Home. Conception, Missouri: Altar and Home Press. No date available, but work was in use and well known during the 1950's.

Condensed Tenebrae Service. St. Louis: Pio Decimo, 1942.

Deo Gratias: A New Year's Eve Service for Parish Participation. St. Louis: Pio Decimo. No date available but in use during the 1950's.

The Ecclesiastical Engagement. St. Louis: Pio Decimo, 1942.

The Holy Sacrifice of the Mass. St. Louis: Pio Decimo, 1944.

Music in the House of God. St. Louis: Pio Decimo, 1951.

Our High Mass. St. Louis: Queen's Work, 1930.

Parce Domine. St. Louis: Pio Decimo, 1947.

Sacred Liturgy. St. Louis: Pio Decimo, 1951.

Veni Creator Spiritus. O'Fallon, Missouri: Pax Press, 1938.

Vine and Branches. St. Louis: Pio Decimo, 1948.

Ed. *The Centennial of Holy Cross Parish.* St. Louis: By Holy Cross Parish, 1964.

With Virgil Michel. *The Liturgical Movement*. Collegeville, Minnesota: The Liturgical Press, 1930.

With A. A. Jasper. *The True Basis of Christian Solidarity* 2d ed. St. Louis: Central Bureau of the Central Verein, 1947.

Articles and Reprints of Lectures

"A. D. 37-1937," *Orate Fratres* 11 (13 June 1937) 346-351.

"Advent in the Parish," *Worship* 30 (December 1955) 59-68.

"Alleluia, Farewell!" *Orate Fratres* 19 (28 January 1945) 97-98.

"The Apostolate: Holy Week: Some Reflections and Pastoral Suggestions," *Orate Fratres* 24 (April 1950) 216-223.

"Archbishop Joseph H. Schlarman, D.D.," *Worship* 26 (January 1952) 82-83.

"A Birthday Marks the Beginning of School," *Living Parish* 1 (Time after Pentecost 1941) 11.

"Brief Meditations on the Church Year," *Orate Fratres* 18 (28 November 1943) 1-14; (26 December 1943) 49-59; (23 January 1944) 97-106; (20 February 1944) 145-158; (19 March 1944) 193-204; (16 April 1944) 241-247; (14 May 1944) 291-308; (11 June 1944) 337-348; (23 July 1944) 385-397; (3 September 1944) 433-445; (8 October 1944) 481-498; (5 November 1944) 529-538.

"Christmas" *Orate Fratres* 19 (31 December 1944) 49-54.

"Christmas to Epiphany," *Worship* 30 (January 1956) 142-154.

"Church and Parish" *Orate Fratres* 25 (October-November 1951) 489-499.

"Demonstration of High Mass," *Santification of the Sunday*, pp. 92-106. National Liturgical Week Proceedings, vol. 10. Conception, Missouri: The Liturgical Conference, 1949.

"Demonstration of Holy Mass," *St. Pius X and Social Worship*, pp. 3-25. National Liturgical Week Proceedings, vol. 14. Elsberry, Missouri: The Liturgical Conference, 1953.

"A Demonstration of Low Mass," *Santification of the Sunday*, pp. 6-25. National Liturgical Week Proceedings, vol. 10. Conception, Missouri: The Liturgical Conference, 1949.

"Demonstration of Low Mass," *The Priesthood of Christ*, pp. 3-13. National Liturgical Week Proceedings, vol. 12. Conception, Missouri: The Liturgical Conference, 1951.

"Easter Week in the Parish," *Worship* 30 (April 1956) 332-341.

"Family Life, the Liturgical Year, and the Sacramentals," *The Family in Christ*. 95-104. National Liturgical Week Proceedings, vol. 7. Highland Park, Illinois: The Liturgical Conference, 1947.

"Feast of St. Joseph Calasanctius, Confessor, August 27," *The Challenge of the Council: Person, Parish, World* 270-273. National Liturgical Week Proceedings, vol. 25. Washington D. C.: The Liturgical Conference, 1964.

"Fire from Heaven," *Living Parish* 8 (April 1947) 4-5.

"Funeral Sermon for Reverend Monsignor Victor T. Suren," *Social Justice Review* 64 (July-August 1971) 142-143.

"He Loved the Church," *Living Parish* 1 (Advent 1940) 1-2.

"Holy Mass, the Center of the Sacraments and the Divine Office," *Christ's Sacrifice and Ours* 125-129. National Liturgical Week Proceedings, vol. 8. Boston: The Liturgical Conference, 1948.

"The Holy Sacraments," *Living Parish* 6 (December 1945) 2-3; (February 1946) 3-6; (June 1946) 1-3.

"Holy Week in the Parish," *Worship* 30 (March 1956) 234-257.

"Homily on the Feast of St. Louis, King and Confessor," *Participation in the Mass* 66-70. North American Liturgical Week Proceedings, vol. 20. Washington, D.C.: The Liturgical Conference, 1960.

"Homily: Why Song Surpasses Silence at Mass," *St. Pius and Social Worship*, pp. 26-29. National Liturgical Week Proceedings, vol. 14. Elsberry, Missouri: The Liturgical Conference, 1953.

"How to Make the Church Year a Living Reality," *National Catholic Education Association Bulletin* 53 (August 1956) 248-265.

"It Behooves Us!" *Orate Fratres* 3 (21 April 1929) 161-164.

"Liturgical and 'Liturgical' Retreats," *Orate Fratres* 14 (9 June 1940) 342-352.

"Liturgical Movement and the Preaching of Retreats," *Bible, Life, and Worship* 205-210. North American Liturgical Week

Proceedings, vol. 22. Washington, D.C.: The Liturgical Conference, 1961.

"The Liturgical Movement and the Sacraments," *Orate Fratres* 10 (31 October 1940) 503-510.

"Liturgy and the Minor Seminaries," *National Cathoic Education Association Bulletin* 33 (August 1937) 550-556.

"Lord Our Coming King, Hasten to Adore Him," *Orate Fratres* 2 (27 November 1927) 33-44.

"The Lord's Day," *Living Parish* 7 (September 1947) 3-6.

"Lumen Christi! Deo Gratias! A Dramatization of the Most Holy Paschal Night," *The Easter Vigil* 141-152. National Liturgical Week Proceedings, vol. 13. Elsberry, Missouri: The Liturgical Conference, 1953.

"The *Mediator Dei* Apostolate," *Living Parish* 11 (December 1950) 7-11.

"*Mediator Dei* 1947-1957," *Worship* 32 (December 1957) 2-7.

"Merely Suggesting," *Orate Fratres* 15 (29 December 1940) 58-63; (26 January 1941) 102-105; (23 February 1941) 151-158; (23 March 1941) 204-214; (20 April 1941) 249-257; (18 May 1941) 298-306; (15 June 1941) 344-351; (27 July 1941) 390-397; (7 September 1941) 442-448; (5 October 1941) 485-491.

"The Mother of All Vigils," *The New Man in Christ* 120-130.National Liturgical Week Proceedings, vol. 9. Conception, Missouri: The Liturgical Conference, 1949.

"New Year's Eve," *Orate Fratres* 25 (December 1950) 34-36.

"The Night of Resurrection: The New Papal Permission," *Orate Fratres* 25 (April 1951) 225-229.

"1903 November 1947," *Living Parish* 8 (April 1948) 3.

"Office of Abbot," *American Benedictine Review* 8 (Winter 1957) 355-356.

"Opening Address of the National Liturgical Week," *For Pastors and People* 3-5. National Liturgical Week Proceedings, vol. 11. Conception, Missouri: The Liturgical Conference, 1950.

"Other Kinds of Retreat," *Orate Fratres* 17 (October 1943) 494-501.

"Outline for a First Mass Sermon," *Orate Fratres* (18 May 1930) 295-300.

"Pageant: The Priesthood of Jesus Christ," *The Priesthood of Christ* 174-183. National Liturgical Week Proceedings, vol. 12. Conception, Missouri: The Liturgical Conference, 1951.

"The Parish in Practice," *The Living Parish* 30-38. National Liturgical Week Proceedings, vol. 1. Newark: The Benedictine Liturgical Conference, 1941.

"A Pastor's Description of Liturgical Participation in His Parish," *The Living Parish* 82-90. National Liturgical Week Proceedings, vol. 2. Newark: The Benedictine Liturgical Conference, 1942.

"Pius X," *The Living Parish* 5 (November 1944) 3-5; (December 1944): 5-7; (February 1945) 7-9.

"Pontifical Mass Homily," *St. Pius X and Social Worship* 192-194. National Liturgical Week Proceedings, vol. 14. Elsberry, Missouri: The Liturgical Conference, 1953.

"The Purification," *Orate Fratres* 2 (22 January 1928) 65-70.

"Reception, First Vows, and Final Profession," *Orate Fratres* 19 (20 May 1945) 304-309.

"Ritual for the Consecration of Virgins," *Education and Liturgy* 176-178. North American Liturgical Week Proceedings, vol. 18. Elsberry, Missouri: The Liturgical Conference, 1958.

"The Sacred Heart of Our Redeemer," *Living Parish* 5 (June 1945) 1-2.

"St. Evaristus Decreed," *Orate Fratres* 14 (24 December 1939) 63-65.

"Seasonal Suggestions," *Worship* 30 (May 1956) 374-390.

"The Sermon Embodied in the Mass," *For Pastors and People* 103-108. National Liturgical Week Proceedings, vol. 11. Conception, Missouri: The Liturgical Conference, 1950.

"Singers and Servers," *Worship* 29 (January 1955) 83-89.

"Sixty-Six Years Ago," *Orate Fratres* 14 (21 July 1941) 406-408.

"Spread of the Liturgical Movement," *Journal of Religious Instruction* 7 (November 1936) 208-214.

"Surrexit, Alleluia," *Living Parish* 2 (April 1942) 1-2.

"A Survey of the Liturgical Movement," *Orate Fratres* 3 (8 September 1929) 333-340.

"To My Fellow Priests," *Orate Fratres* 16 (22 February 1929) 146-152.

"Toward a Living Parish," *Worship* 30 (December 1955) 14-25; (February 1956) 205-216; (August 1956) 458-470; (September 1956) 513-523; (October 1956) 569-580; (November 1957) 648-655; 31 (January 1957) 95-104.

"Viriliter Agite!" *Orate Fratres* 3 (24 February 1929) 97-10.

"Vom Aufbau Des Leibes Christi," *Universitas* 451-465. Edited by Ludwig Lenhart. Mainz: Matthias-Gruenwald, 1960.

"Where Lies the Deepest Source for the Recruitment of Vocations? How to Handle Candidates Who Have Had Some Liturgical Formation?" *The New Ritual: Liturgy and Social Order* 70-75. National Liturgical Week Proceedings, vol. 16. Elsberry, Missouri: The Liturgical Conference, 1965.

"The Year of the Shepherd and Flock," In *Liturgy for All the People* 179-190. Edited by William Leonard. Milwaukee: Bruce, 1963.

With Alphonse Westhoff. "The Liturgical Year," *Orate Fratres* 1 (2 October 1927) 359-364; 2 (13 May 1928) 205-210

Unpublished Material:

"Conferences on the Sacred Psalms." Bound volume of lectures given at the Precious Blood Motherhouse, O'Fallon, Missouri, 1936-1937. (Typewritten).

Retreat and Sermon Notes. Looseleaf volume of notes from talks given at the Precious Blood Motherhouse, O'Fallon, Missouri, 1918-1940. (Typewritten and handwritten).

Secondary Sources:

Books:

Bouyer, Louis, *Liturgical Piety*. Notre Dame, Indiana: University of Notre Dame Press, 1955.

Burke, Mary Gabriel, Sister. *Liturgy at Holy Cross in Church and School*. St. Louis: Pio Decimo, 1952.

Bussard, Paul. *The Vernacular Missal in Religious Education*. Washington, D.C.: Catholic University Press, 1937.

Ellis, John Tracy. *Perspectives in American Catholicism*. Baltimore: Helicon, 1963.

England, John, ed. *The Roman Missal Translated into the English Language for the Use of the Laity*. New York: William H. Creagh, 1822.

Guardini, Romano. *Sacred Signs*. Translated by Grace Branham. St. Louis: Pio Decimo, 1956.

Guéranger, Prosper. *The Liturgical Year*, 15 vols. Translated by Lancelot Shephard. Westminster, Maryland: Newman, 1948-1950.

Guilday, Peter. *The Life and Times of John Carroll, Archbishop of Baltimore, 1735-1815*, 2 vols. New York: Encyclopedia Press, 1922.

_____. *The Life and Times of John England*, 2 vols. New York: America Press, 1927.

Jungman, Joseph. *The Mass of the Roman Rite*. Translated by Francis Brunner. New York: Benziger, 1951.

Klauser, Theodor. *The Western Liturgy and Its History*. Translated by F. L. Cross. New York: Morehouse-Gorham, 1952.

Koenker, Ernest, *The Liturgical Renaissance in the Roman Catholic Church*. Chicago: University of Chicago Press, 1954.

Martimont, Aimé Georges, ed. *The Church at Prayer: Introduction to the Liturgy*. Shannon, Ireland: Irish University Press, 1968.

Marx, Paul. *Virgil Michel and the Liturgical Movement*. Collegeville, Minnesota: The Liturgical Press, 1957.

McAvoy, Thomas. *History of the Catholic Church in the United States*. Notre Dame, Indiane: University of Notre Dame Press, 1969.

Messmer, John, ed. *The Works of the Rt. Rev. John England*, 7 vols. Cleveland: Arthur Clark, 1908.

Michel, Virgil. *The Liturgy of the Church*. New York: Macmillan, 1938.

Reinhold, Hans A. *The Dynamics of the Liturgy*. New York: Macmillan, 1961.

206 I Martin B. Hellriegel: Pastoral Liturgist

Rothsteiner, John. *History of the Archdiocese of St. Louis*, 2 vols. St. Louis: Blackwell Wielandy, 1928.

Schalk, Adolp. *Holy Cross: The Story of a Parish and Its Pastor*. St. Louis: Pio Decimo, 1955.

Schneider, Nicholas. *The Life of John Cardinal Glennon*. Ligouri, Missouri: Ligouri, 1971.

Seasoltz, R. Kevin, ed. *The New Liturgy: A Documentation, 1903-1965*. New York: Herder and Herder, 1966.

Sheppard, Lancelot, ed. *The People Worship: A History of the Liturgical Movement*. New York: Hawthorne, 1967.

_____. ed. *True Worship*. Baltimore: Helicon, 1963.

Articles and Reprints of Lectures:

Anne Catherine, Sister. "The Profession Ceremonies of Some Con gregations of Women," *People's Participation and Holy Week* 111-117. National Liturgical Week Proceedings, vol. 17. Elsberry, Missouri: The Liturgical Conference, 1957.

Bluett, John. "The Mystical Body of Christ: 1890-1940, A Bibliography," *Theological Studies* 2 (May 1942): 261-289.

Busch, William. "The Voice of a Plenary Council," *Orate Fratres* 21 (7 September 1947) 452-458.

Carroll, Thomas. "Tribute to Rt. Rev. Msgr. Martin B. Hellriegel," *Challenge of the Council: Person, Parish, World* 273-278. National Liturgical Week Proceedings, vol. 25. Washington, D. C.: The Liturgical Conference, 1964.

Champlin, Joseph. "From Liturgy's Shell to its Kernel," *Time and Eternity* (July 16 1978) 14.

Diekmann, Godfrey. "Monsignor Martin B. Hellriegel: Holy Cross Church, St. Louis," *Worship* 38 (August-September 1964) 497-498.

Ducey, Michael. "Maria Laach and Liturgy," *Orate Fratres* 9 (January 1935) 108-113.

_____. "The New Liturgy of Holy Week," *Jubilee* 3 (April 1956) 10-19.

Ellard, Gerald. "The American Scene 1926-1951," *Orate Fratres* 25 (October-November 1951) 500-508.

_____. "The Church in Kansas Confers," *Commonweal* 35 (26 December 1941) :253-254.

_____. "A Pilgrimage and A Vision," *America* 34 (12 December 1925) 201-203.

Felknor, Rhea. "Meet Monsignor Hellriegel," *St. Louis Review* 23 (21 August 1964) 13, 20.

Fleming, David. "Dom Guéranger and the Beginning of the Liturgical Movement," *American Ecclesiastical Review* 150 (March 1964) 197-203.

Giesselmann, Mary. "A School for Christian Living," *Worship* 26 (September 1952) 476-479.

Howell, Clifford. "High Mass in St. Louis," *Orate Fratres* 23 (6 November 1949) 552-555.

Hughes, John Jay, "Martin Hellriegel: A Priestly Man, A Manly Priest," *The Priest* (September 1981) 15.

_____. "It Can Be Done," *Orate Fratres* 27 (January 1953) 100-101.

Möleck, Fred, "Ein Heldenlebon," *Pastoral Music* (June 1981) 44.

The Novitiate, O'Fallon, Missouri. "Advent in a Convent," *Orate Fratres* 1 (28 November 1926) 26-27.

_____. "A Convent Christmas," *Orate Fratres* 1 (26 December 1925) 56-58.

_____. "Palm Sunday in a Convent," *Orate Fratres* 2 (18 March 1928) 151-153.

_____. "Quadragesima in a Convent," *Orate Fratres* 2 (19 February 1928) 113-115.

O'Fallon: An Appreciation," *Orate Fratres* 19 (9 September 1945) 519-522.

O'Gorman, Thomas. "Worship and Grace," Paper presented at the Parliament of Religion, Chicago, 1893; reprinted in *Orate Fratres* 20 (October 1946) 495-502.

O'Shea, William. "Liturgy in the United States, 1889-1964," *American Ecclesiastical Review* 150 (March 1964) 176-196.

The Pilgrim. "With Scrip and Staff," *America* 45 (19 September 1931) 570-571.

Reinhold, Hans A. "Denver and Maria Laach," *Commonweal* 45 (8 November 1946) 86-88.

Renger, Christopher. "Headstarted in the Liturgical Revival," *The Priest* 24 (November 1968) 866-874.

Ryan, John K. "Bishop England and the Missal in English," *American Ecclesiastical Review* 95 (July 1936) 28-36.

A Sister of the Most Precious Blood. "Advent in the Classroom," *Orate Fratres* 14 (November 1939) 8-13.

_____. "Christmas and Epiphany Season in the Classroom," *Orate Fratres* 14 (24 December 1939) 51-56.

_____. "Holy Week in the Classroom," *Orate Fratres* 19 (24 March 1945) 228-233.

_____. "Liturgy in the Classroom," *Orate Fratres* 11 (21 February 1937) 150-156.

_____. "Pentecost in the Classroom," *Orate Fratres* 14 (12 May 1940) 309-311.

Stockley, W. F. "The Pope and the Reform of Church Music," *American Ecclesiastical Review* 30 (March 1904) 279-292; (April 1904) 383-401.

Tucker, Dunstan. "The Council of Trent, Guéranger, and Pius X," *Orate Fratres* 10 (October 1936) 538-544.

Tuger, Felix [F.T.]. "Lent in a Convent," *Orate Fratres* 9 (23 March 1935) 215-217.

Winzen, Damasus. "Guéranger and the Liturgical Movement," *American Benedictine Review* 6 (Winter 1955-1956) 419-426.

_____. "Maria Laach: Fifty Years," *Orate Fratres* 17 (24 January 1943) 111-118.

_____. "Progress and Tradition in Maria Laach Art," *Liturgical Arts* 10 (November 1941) 19-20.

Young, Alfred. "Church Music," *Catholic World* 10 (December 1969) 402-413; (February 1970) 598-610; (March 1870) 743-754.

_____. "On Congregational Singing," *Northwestern Chronicle* (17 April 1891); reprinted *Orate Fratres* 21 (15 June 1947) 356-362.

Unpublished Material:

Klein, John Leo. *The Role of Gerald Ellard (1894-1963) in the Development of the Contemporary American Catholic Liturgical Movement.* Fordam University, 1971.

Madden, Lawrence. *The Liturgical Conference of the USA: Its Origins and Development: 1940-1968.* Theological Faculty of Trier, 1969.

Virgil Michel Papers. Manuscript Collection, Collegeville, Minnesota. St. John's Abbey.